Bangladesh

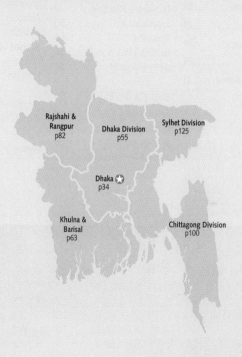

Rajshahi &
Rangpur
p82

Dhaka Division
p55

Sylhet Division
p125

Dhaka ⭐
p34

Khulna &
Barisal
p63

Chittagong Division
p100

THIS EDITION WRITTEN AND RESEARCHED BY

Paul Clammer, Anirban Mahapatra

Contents

KAMRUL HASAN 2010 / GETTY IMAGES ©

KUAKATA, P81

Contents

PAINAM NAGAR, P57

TIM GERARD BARKER / GETTY IMAGES ©

Welcome to Bangladesh

Bangladesh is south Asia's greenest jewel – a country braided with rivers, with a rich culture waiting to be explored by pioneering travellers.

A Land of Rivers

Welcome to river country. Bangladesh is braided together by more than 700 rivers, producing a deliciously lush landscape with more shades of green than you ever imagined. Travelling by boat is a way of life here, and provides a fabulous opportunity to see the country from a more unusual angle. This is one of the world's most densely populated countries, but once you're slowly floating downriver on a small wooden rowboat, it's easy to imagine you have it all to yourself. Whether you're travelling to hectic Dhaka or to the Sundarbans mangrove forests, boats will help you explore Bangladesh's riches.

Hidden Riches

The mangrove forests and tigers of the Sundarbans National Park are Bangladesh's most famous attraction, but the country has a host of lesser-known attractions that are waiting to be discovered. Highlights include the Buddhist remains at Paharpur and the 15th-century mosques and mausoleums of Bagerhat, both of which are Unesco World Heritage Sites. While modern Bangladesh is majority Muslim, its hill tracts are still home to Buddhist and Christian Adivasi tribal peoples, while temples in Dhaka and beyond attest to the influence of Hindu culture on the country.

Warm & Welcoming

Getting off the beaten track is something of a travel cliché, but Bangladesh is somewhere that tourism remains in its infancy. It's easy to get the sensation that you're breaking ground here, even if your pioneering spirit is frequently attended to by being the centre of attention. Bangla culture is famously welcoming – rarely will you have cause to suspect the ulterior motives that can sometimes bedevil travel in other parts of south Asia. If you enjoy making friends, mixing with locals and travelling without bumping into too many other tourists, then this is probably just the country to explore.

Slow Down

Be prepared to embrace Bangladesh in all its possibilities and quirks. This isn't a destination to be rushed. Poor infrastructure and an undeveloped tourist industry means that you'll be left frustrated if you're trying to travel in too much of a hurry. So slow down; don't try to pack too much into your itinerary. Bangladesh isn't a tick-the-sights-off-the-list type of country. It's a place to relax, meet people and discover new ideas and ways of life. Taking your time will allow the country to reveal the best of itself at its own pace, as sure and steady as the rivers that flow through its veins.

Why I Love Bangladesh

By Paul Clammer, Writer

It's the cycle-rickshaws that do it for me in Bangladesh. They're works of art, from their brightly decorated handlebars and the struts of their canopies to their painted backs, displaying anything from mosques to Bangla film stars. To a soundtrack of bicycle bells, they weave their way through roads as if the words 'traffic jam' were unknown. It doesn't matter if you're in the smallest village trying to find some ancient mosque or in an upscale neighbourhood of Dhaka looking for a swanky restaurant – if you want to get anywhere, then a cycle-rickshaw is the quintessential Bangladeshi way to arrive.

For more about our writers, see page 192

Above: Decorations on a cycle-rickshaw

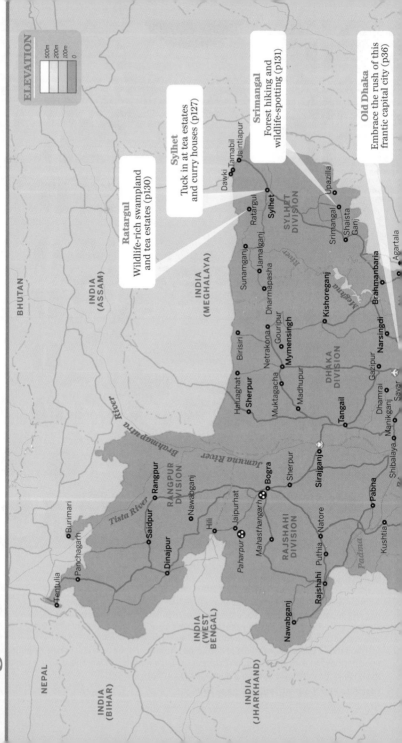

Bangladesh

Ⓝ 0 km 80 km
0 miles 40 miles

ELEVATION
500m
200m
100m
0

Ratargul
Wildlife-rich swampland and tea estates (p130)

Sylhet
Tuck in at tea estates and curry houses (p127)

Srimangal
Forest hiking and wildlife-spotting (p131)

Old Dhaka
Embrace the rush of this frantic capital city (p36)

NEPAL

INDIA (BIHAR)

INDIA (WEST BENGAL)

INDIA (JHARKHAND)

BHUTAN

INDIA (ASSAM)

INDIA (MEGHALAYA)

Tista River

Brahmaputra River

Jamuna River

Padma

Tentulia
Panchagarh
Burimari
Saidpur
Rangpur
RANGPUR DIVISION
Dinajpur
Nawabganj
Hili
Jaipurhat
Paharpur
Mahasthangarh
Bogra
Sherpur
Sirajganj
Natore
Pabna
RAJSHAHI DIVISION
Puthia
Rajshahi
Nawabganj
Kushtia
Haluaghat
Birisiri
Netrakona
Gouripur
Dharmapasha
Sunamganj
Jamalganj
Ratargul
Dawki
Tamabil
Jaintiapur
Sylhet
SYLHET DIVISION
Srimangal
Shaista Ganj
Upazilla
Sherpur
Mymensingh
Muktagacha
Madhupur
Kishoreganj
Meghna River
Brahmanbaria
Agartala
Tangail
Gazipur
Dhamrai
Manikganj
Savar
Shibalaya
Narsingdi
DHAKA DIVISION

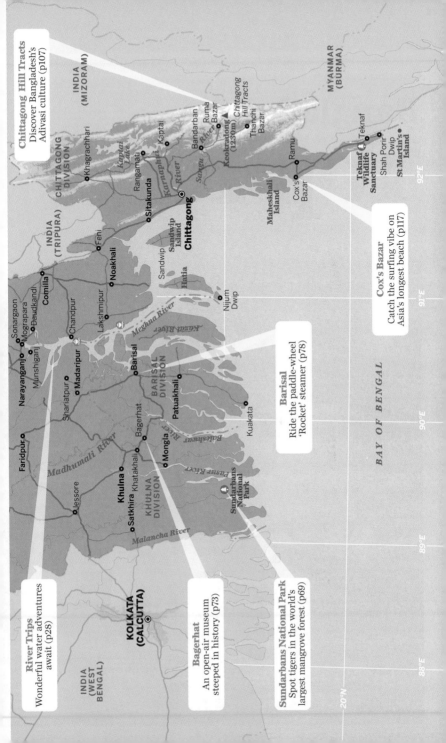

Chittagong Hill Tracts
Discover Bangladesh's Adivasi culture (p107)

Cox's Bazar
Catch the surfing vibe on Asia's longest beach (p117)

Barisal
Ride the paddle-wheel 'Rocket' steamer (p78)

River Trips
Wonderful water adventures await (p28)

Bagerhat
An open-air museum steeped in history (p73)

Sundarbans National Park
Spot tigers in the world's largest mangrove forest (p69)

INDIA (MIZORAM)

MYANMAR (BURMA)

CHITTAGONG DIVISION

Khagrachhari
Rangamati
Kaptai
Kaptai Lake
Sitakunda
Karnaphuli River
Bandarban
Ruma Bazar
Keokradong (1230m)
Sangu River
Thanchi Bazar
Chittagong Hill Tracts

INDIA (TRIPURA)

Feni
Noakhali
Comilla
Daudkandi
Munshiganj
Narayanganj
Mograpara
Sonargaon
Chandpur
Lakshmipur
Hatia
Sandwip Island
Sandwip
Chittagong
Ramu
Maheshkhali Island
Cox's Bazar
Teknaf Wildlife Sanctuary
Teknaf
Shah Porir Dwip
St Martin's Island

Nijum Dwip

Meghna River
Kirtal River

BARISAL DIVISION

Barisal
Madaripur
Shariatpur
Patuakhali
Kuakata

Madhumati River

Faridpur
Jessore

KHULNA DIVISION

Khulna
Satkhira
Khatakhali
Bagerhat
Mongla
Bhola River
Pusur River
Sundarbans National Park

Malancha River

BAY OF BENGAL

KOLKATA (CALCUTTA)

INDIA (WEST BENGAL)

92°E
91°E
90°E
89°E
88°E
20°N

Bangladesh's
Top 10

River Trips

1 Rivers are the lifeblood of Bangladesh. More than 700 of them crisscross the country, and travelling along them is an experience not to be missed. From cross-river car ferries or creaking old paddle-wheel steamers to the humble rowboat or traditional wooden yachts, it is said that there are more types of boats (p28) in Bangladesh than in any other country. So whether you fancy a multi-day adventure deep into the countryside or just a quick jaunt around a city dock, get yourself down to a river ghat, and climb aboard. Below left: Boats in Dhaka

Tracking Tigers in the Sundarbans

2 The mangrove forests of the Sundarbans National Park (p69) are home to the legendary Royal Bengal tiger and boarding a boat in search of them is an undisputed highlight of a trip to Bangladesh. For a true adventure, and to increase your admittedly slim chances of seeing a tiger, book yourself onto a four-day boat tour from Khulna. Even if you don't see a tiger, the birdlife and scenery are real Bangladeshi highlights.

DANITA DELIMONT / GETTY IMAGES ©

RUDRA NARAYAN MITRA / SHUTTERSTOCK ©

Surfing in Cox's Bazar

3 Every Bangladeshi will proudly tell you that Cox's Bazar has the longest natural beach in the world. What they might not reveal is that it's home to the country's nascent surfing (p117) scene. The waves that roll in from the Bay of Bengal are suitable for beginners all the way to those looking to catch livelier breaks. At the end of a day at the beach, chill in the evening with a plate of fresh seafood that the area is celebrated for.

Chittagong Hill Tracts

4 With most of the country being flat as a paddy field, the forested mountains of the Chittagong Hill Tracts (p107) dominate the landscape. It's an undoubtedly stunning region, but it also offers a cultural diversity found nowhere else in the country. Around a dozen Adivasi (tribal) groups live here, and more than half the population is Adivasi. Many have closer ties to the people of Myanmar (Burma) than to Bengalis, and visiting their villages to learn about their ways of life makes a trip here more than just a chance to gawp at spectacular scenery.

Old Dhaka

5 For some, the assault on the senses is too much to handle, but for others, the unrivalled chaos that is squeezed into the narrow streets of Old Dhaka (p36) is the main attraction of a stay in the capital. No matter where you've come from, or what big cities you've visited before, Old Dhaka will knock you for six with its manic streets, its crazy traffic and its nonstop noise and commotion. But the food is fabulous, the historical narrative fascinating and the sheer weight of humanity absolutely unforgettable.

Riding the Rocket

6 Steeped in almost 100 years of history, Bangladesh's famous paddle-wheel steamer (pictured above; p28) may not be the fastest thing on the waterways these days, but it gets more and more romantic each passing year. There are four remaining Rockets – all built in the early part of the 20th century – and although you can no longer ride them all the way from Dhaka to Khulna, you can still take long overnight trips on them. Book yourself a cabin to Barisal (p78), put your feet up and watch Bangladesh float by.

Swamp Safaris in Ratargul

7 Hidden under the canopies of an ever-green tropical forest, the swampy bayous of Ratargul (p130) form an enchanting landscape of silent water channels that you can explore by a wooden dinghy boat. Known to be Bangladesh's largest freshwater swampland, these outlying marshes are a perfect day trip out of Sylhet and can be accessed by a village road that cuts through some amazing tea plantations and forests.

Touring Ancient Mosques in Bagerhat

8 With the largest concentration of medieval mosques and mausoleums in all of Bangladesh, sleepy Bagerhat (p73) is a splendid open-air museum that documents the heydays of the region's Islamic history. Peppered with graceful domed mosques, this Unesco-protected town with a friendly population is a delight to explore on foot. There's even a crocodile-infested pond here to capture your imagination!

Right: Shait Gumbad Mosque

BELINDA MEGGITT / THE MULTIMEDIA TRAVELLERS / GETTY IMAGES ©

KEVIN SCHAFER / GETTY IMAGES ©

Rickshaws

9 There are cycle-rickshaws (p41) all over Asia, but in Bangladesh they're arguably more colourful, more prevalent and more integral to everyday life than anywhere else. Designs are an art form in their own right and riders take great pride in making theirs look best. Almost every town and city has a huge fleet and it's pretty much impossible to avoid travelling on one at some stage. And why would you want to avoid it? They're cheap, fun, environmentally friendly and are often the quickest way to get through the busy streets.

Hiking Off the Beaten Track

10 The country's eastern regions of Sylhet and Chittagong contain forested hills and small, rugged mountains. This is no Himalaya, but the landscape offers plenty of opportunity to stretch your legs with a number of worthwhile hikes on offer. There are relatively simple day hikes you can take from places such as Srimangal (p131), visiting tea estates, the Hum Hum waterfalls, and even spotting gibbons in the forests of Lowacherra National Park (p133). Above: Hoolock gibbon

Need to Know

For more information, see Survival Guide (p159)

Currency
Taka (Tk)

Language
Bengali (Bangla)

Visas
Almost everyone needs one: 30-day visa on arrival available for many nationalities, but check well in advance of travelling.

Money
Foreign-friendly ATMs in most big towns and cities, but not all. Take some US dollars for emergencies.

Mobile Phones
Bring an unlocked phone to use a local SIM. 3G internet widely available (4G in cities).

Time
Bangladesh Time Zone (GMT/UTC plus six hours).

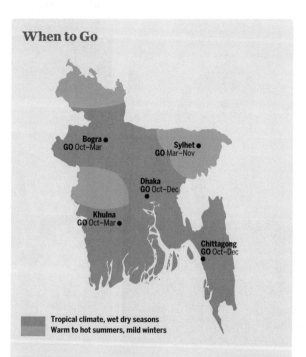

When to Go

Bogra
GO Oct–Mar

Sylhet
GO Mar–Nov

Dhaka
GO Oct–Dec

Khulna
GO Oct–Mar

Chittagong
GO Oct–Dec

Tropical climate, wet dry seasons
Warm to hot summers, mild winters

High Season
(Oct–Mar)

➡ Cooler temperatures; almost chilly in January and February.

➡ Dry; the worst of the monsoon has gone; some late rains in October.

➡ Prices in Cox's Bazar may be inflated.

Shoulder
(Apr & May)

➡ Almost unbearably hot temperatures, without the cooling monsoon rains.

➡ Join honey-harvesters for the honey-collecting season in the Sundarbans.

➡ Mangoes start ripening in May.

Low Season
(Jun–Sep)

➡ Monsoon season disrupts plans and sees much of Bangladesh under water.

➡ Hot, but the rains cool the air.

➡ Tea-picking season in full swing in Sylhet.

Useful Websites

Bangladesh Railway (www.railway.gov.bd) Timetables, train fares.

Bangla Trek (www.banglatrek.org) Guide to walking and hiking in Bangladesh.

Daily Star (www.thedailystar.net) Bangladesh's biggest English-language daily.

Dhaka Tribune (www.dhakatribune.com) Bangladesh's second English-language newspaper.

Lonely Planet (www.lonelyplanet.com/bangladesh) Destination information, hotel bookings, traveller forum and more.

Thorn Tree (www.lonelyplanet.com/thorntree) The Bangladesh branch has up-to-the-minute info.

Important Numbers

To call from outside Bangladesh, dial the country code, the city code (minus the leading zero) then the number.

Country Code	✆00880
Police	✆100
Fire	✆199
Apollo Hospital (Dhaka)	✆02-843 1661

Exchange Rates

Australia	A$1	Tk 58
Canada	C$1	Tk 58
Europe	€1	Tk 85
India	Rs 100	Tk 115
Japan	¥100	Tk 69
New Zealand	NZ$1	Tk 52
UK	£1	Tk 111
USA	US$1	Tk 78

For current exchange rates see www.xe.com.

Daily Costs

Budget: Less than Tk 1500

➡ Basic accommodation (no air-con, no hot water): Tk 500–750

➡ Meal in local Bangladeshi restaurant: Tk 80–150

➡ Regional bus ticket: Tk 80–200

Midrange: Tk 1500–4000

➡ Decent room with air-con and hot-water shower: Tk 2000

➡ Meal at air-con restaurants serving Chinese, Indian and Bangladeshi food: Tk 300

➡ Travel by non-air-con coach: Tk 200

Top End: More than Tk 4000

➡ Room in the best hotel in town, or any half-decent place in Dhaka: Tk 4000

➡ Meal in-house or at restaurants with international cuisine: TK 1800

➡ Travel by air-con coach or hire car: Tk 600

Opening Hours

Opening hours vary throughout the year. We've provided high-season opening hours; hours will generally decrease in the shoulder and low seasons. Note that Friday is the official weekly holiday in Bangladesh. Depending on the type of office or business, Saturday may either be a holiday (in full or part) or a full working day.

Banks 10am to 4pm Sunday to Thursday

Corporate Offices 9am to 5pm Saturday to Thursday

Government Offices 10am to 4pm Sunday to Thursday (sometimes 12pm to 4pm Saturday)

Restaurants 7am to 11pm (sometimes noon to 3pm and 7pm to 11pm)

Shops & Markets 10am to 8pm Sunday to Thursday

Arriving in Bangladesh

Hazrat Shahjalal International Airport (Dhaka) It takes about 30 minutes to reach the centre of Dhaka, but may take longer in traffic. Expect to pay Tk 600 to Tk 750 by taxi, Tk 300 by CNG (auto-rickshaw) or Tk 20 on a local bus.

Getting Around

Travelling around Bangladesh is extremely cheap, although in some cases it can be quite uncomfortable. Road safety is a real issue in Bangladesh. The country has some of the worst road-accident figures in the world, and the Dhaka–Chittagong Hwy is notoriously bad.

Boat In Barisal and Khulna divisions, the riverboat is the king of travel. Joining locals on a long ferry ride is one of the undisputed highlights of your Bangladesh trip.

Buses Dirt cheap if you don't mind squashing into the local ones; more comfortable, more expensive coaches are usually available, too.

Plane Domestic flights to divisional towns from Dhaka are worth considering if your time is limited.

Rickshaws (cycle-rickshaws) or **CNGs** (auto-rickshaws) Best way to get between sights in cities and between villages.

Trains Safer option than road travel, although the network and tickets are limited.

For much more on **getting around**, see p168

If You Like...

Beaches

Not the first thing you imagine when you think of Bangladesh, but this surprisingly diverse country boasts a handful of decent beaches along its Bay of Bengal coastline, including the world's longest.

St Martin's Island Soak up the beach-holiday vibe circumnavigating Bangladesh's only coral island without stepping off the sand. (p120)

Kuakata Wooden fishing boats and washed-up coconuts give Kuakata a natural feel. (p81)

Cox's Bazar The world's longest unbroken natural sand beach (125km) pulls in punters by the beach-bucket load. (p117)

Ruins

Kingdoms and religions have come and gone throughout Bengal's long and chequered past, leaving ruins scattered across the country, particularly in the northwest.

Paharpur Bangladesh's standout archaeological relic, this Unesco-protected site was once the largest Buddhist monastery south of the Himalaya. (p93)

Puthia Ancient Hindu temples and crumbling rajbaris (Raj-era mansions) dotted around friendly, tree-shaded villages. (p87)

Sona Masjid Discover half the scattered ruins of the lost city of Gaud (the other half is in India; p88).

Old Dhaka The narrow streets just north of the Buriganga River contain fascinating vestiges of the city's colonial past. (p36)

Painam Nagar A charmingly decaying street of dilapidated hundred-year-old mansions in the former ancient capital city of Sonargaon. (p57)

Markets & Bazaars

Markets come in all shapes and sizes in Bangladesh, from the huge city-centre clothes bazaars of Dhaka to small riverside markets found in pretty much every town.

New Market Dhaka's largest market sells absolutely everything. If it's not here, it's not in Bangladesh. (p51)

Banga Bazar Dhaka's bargain-bucket clothes market. Don't expect high quality, but do expect some haggling marathons. (p50)

Bangshal Rd Old Dhaka lane where the capital's multitude of bikes and rickshaws are made, decorated and repaired. (p51)

Rajbari Island Stalls Just a row of stalls where you can buy textiles woven by the Chakma people of the Rangamati region. (p115)

Boat Rides

Taking a boat trip is a quintessential Bangladesh experience, but with more than 700 rivers and around 150 different types of boats, where do you begin? Here are some ideas:

The Rocket Climb aboard this early 20th-century paddle-wheel steamer and romance your way along the rivers of south Bangladesh. (p28)

Sundarbans Head deep into the extraordinary Sundarbans on a four-day boat ride with a quality tour company. (p69)

Kaptai Lake Enjoy the splendid scenery and the awesome expanse of Rangamati's massive artificial lake. (p114)

Sangu River Securing a boat ride along this stunning river is challenging, but the reward is exceptional natural beauty. (p111)

City Rivers Hop on a rowboat at the main ghat of any city and simply cross to the other side. Try Dhaka's Buriganga River. (p42)

Top: Shiva Temple (p87), Puthia
Above: St Martin's Island (p120)

Hiking

Bangladesh isn't all as flat as a rice paddy. The hills to the east, in Sylhet and Chittagong, offer great hiking.

Hum Hum Falls Remote waterfall, deep inside the monkey-filled Rajkandi Forest Reserve; an adventurous day trip from Srimangal. (p136)

Boga Lake It's a two-day round trip from Bandarban (permits permitting), including a four-hour hike each way to the lake, where you can overnight. (p113)

Mt Keokradong One of Bangladesh's highest peaks (p108), and probably its most climbed; a three-day round trip from Bandarban (permit required).

Mowdok Taung The country's highest peak borders Myanmar; you'll need a good guide and a permit to make the seven-day round trip from Bandarban. (p109)

Wildlife

The human-eating tigers of the Sundarbans steal the headlines, but Bangladesh has plenty of other wildlife.

Royal Bengal Tiger The Sundarbans National Park has the world's largest single population of tigers – have fun trying to spot one. (p69)

Hoolock gibbons Bangladesh's only species of ape is sometimes spotted at Lowacherra National Park. (p133)

Elephants Visit Bangladesh's small population of wild elephants in the forested hills of the Teknaf Wildlife Sanctuary. (p122)

Birds The hard-to-get-to *haors* (wetlands) near Sunamganj in northwestern Sylhet are a magnet for domestic and migratory bird species. (p131)

Month by Month

January

Cool and dry, January
is one of the more
comfortable months,
although evenings can get
pretty chilly.

⭐ Bishwa Ijtema

The world's second-largest
gathering of Muslims, after
the Hajj in Mecca, takes
place in two three-day periods in mid- to late-January
in the north Dhaka suburb
of Tongi. Millions line the
streets.

☆ Chobi Mela

Asia's largest festival of
photography is a biennial
event organised by DRIK
gallery in Dhaka. The festival usually lasts for two
weeks towards the end of
January. There are events
planned for 2017. See www.
chobimela.org for details.

February

Similar weather to
January; cool and dry.
Locals might be wrapping
up in hats and scarves, but
for most Westerners it's
mild rather than cold.

⭐ Falgun

On the Bengali calendar, 13
February marks the begin-
ning of spring. The biggest
celebrations are at Dhaka
University (p39). Women
traditionally wear yellow.

⭐ International
Mother Language Day

Also called National
Mourning Day, this solemn
occasion on 21 February
remembers those killed
in 1952 during protests to
establish Bengali as an
official language of East
Pakistan. A large pro-
cession moves towards
Shaheed Minar, a memorial
in Dhaka University (p39).

March

The last month before the
weather really hots up,
March is still an OK time
to visit the Sundarbans,
the hill tracts and the
wetlands.

Holi

Known as Dol Purnima
in Bengali, Hinduism's
paint-throwing Festival of
Colours is best observed in
Dhaka's Shankharia Bazar
(p37). Will be held on 13
March 2017, 2 March 2018
and 21 March 2019.

☆ Lalon Festival

A three-day folk music
festival is held in Kushtia
(p77) during Dol Purnima
(Holi) in honour of Lalon
Shah, the legendary Baul
saint.

⭐ Independence
Day

On 26 March top political
leaders and hundreds of
visitors go to the National
Martyrs' Memorial (p58) in
Savar, just outside Dhaka,
to remember those who lost
their lives in the fight for
independence.

April

It's now too hot for some,
although travellers still
visit the Sundarbans for
honey-collecting trips,
and tea picking has begun
again in Sylhet.

✿ Bengali New Year

Known locally as Pohela Boishakh. Hundreds of thousands of people gather under the banyan tree in Dhaka's Ramna Park on 14 April to see in the new year before singing, dancing and various processions take place around the city and beyond.

🏃 Honey collecting

The honey-collecting season in the Sundarbans starts on 1 April, and visitors can join special tours that follow bee-sting-hardened honey harvesters into the mangrove forests.

✿ Boisabi

Celebrated by minority groups in the Chittagong Hill Tracts (p107), who all have different names for it, this three-day festival is held around Bengali New Year in mid-April and sees much eating, drinking (locally brewed rice beers are a favourite tipple) and merriment.

May

Really very hot now, with no cooling rains. Best to escape to higher ground in the east of the country if you can.

✿ Buddha Purnima

Sometimes called 'Buddha's birthday', this festival actually encompasses the birth, enlightenment and passing away of Gautama Buddha. Good time to be in the Chittagong Hill Tracts (p107). Dates match May's full moon, currently listed as 10 May 2017, 28 April 2018 and 18 May 2019.

✿ Nazrul Jayanti

The anniversary of the birth of national poet Kazi Nazrul Islam is celebrated with public readings and songs on 11 May.

✿ Rabindra Jayanti

The anniversary of the birth of Nobel Laureate Rabindranath Tagore is celebrated with public readings and songs on 25 May. It's an interesting time to visit the country's cultural capital, Kushtia (p77).

June

Bangladesh breathes a collective sigh of relief with the first rains in June, and the land explodes into life. It doesn't rain all day every day, but sporadic downpours cool the scorching temperatures.

✿ Ramadan

The Muslim month of fasting sees many restaurants either shut down or change to an *iftar* menu of traditional Ramadan snacks, eaten in the evening. Head to Old Dhaka's Chowk Bazar for evening atmosphere. Predicted to start on 27 May 2017, 16 May 2018 and 6 May 2019.

🍴 Mango Season

May and June is mango season in Bangladesh. Markets in west Rajshahi particularly overflow with them, but you'll find this queen of fruits everywhere.

July

Monsoon rains continue. It's a hit-and-miss time for travel, with unpredictable weather, but the fabulously moody clouds and oh-so-green scenery can be awesome. Tea picking in Sylhet is in full swing.

✿ Eid ul Fitr

The Muslim festival that celebrates the end of Ramadan is marked by alms-giving, prayer and feasting. Greet people with 'Eid Mubarrak!'. Predicted upcoming dates: 26 June 2017, 15 June 2018 and 4 June 2019.

✿ Rath Jatra

This Hindu festival celebrates Jagannath, lord of the world and a form of Krishna. Images are set upon a Jagannath Chariot and pulled through the streets. Head to Dhamrai (p58), just outside Dhaka. Upcoming dates are 25 June 2017 and 14 July 2018.

August

The hottest days have now passed, but along with September, this is flood season and huge swathes of Bangladesh disappear underwater, making travel extremely unpredictable.

✿ Day of Mourning

The 1975 assassination of Bangladesh's founder, Sheikh Mujib Rahman, is commemorated on 15 August. It's a national holiday when the Awami League is in power; at other times flags are flown at half-mast.

September

Flooding continues, although the worst of the monsoon rains are over. Sylhet's tea estates are lush and active. Temperatures are still hot, but not ridiculously so.

Eid ul Adha

The Muslim Festival of Sacrifice remembers Abraham's sacrifice of his son Ishmael, and is celebrated with mass morning prayers followed by the slaughter of a cow, sheep or goat. Expect blood-strewn streets. Upcoming dates are 1 September 2017, 20 August 2018 and 12 August 2019.

Janmasti

Sometimes in August, sometimes in September, this Hindu festival celebrates the birth of Krishna, an avatar of the god Vishnu. Thousands of devotees descend on Dhaka's Dhakeswari Temple (p37).

October

The start of the best time to visit. Late rains sometimes spoil plans but generally the weather is dry and comfortable. From now until March is ideal for the wetlands, the hill tracts and the Sundarbans.

Durga Puja

Loud and colourful six-day Hindu festival celebrating the worship of the Hindu goddess Durga. Effigies are built and paraded through Dhaka's Shankharia Bazar (p37) before being dumped

in the Buriganga River on the final day. Predicted dates are 11 October 2017 and 18 October 2018.

☆ Lalon Festival

The second of the two annual, three-day folk-music festivals held in honour of the greatest Baul of them all, Lalon Shah. This one marks the anniversary of his death. Head to Kushtia (p77) on 17 October.

November

Weather-wise, this is the best single month in which to visit Bangladesh. Temperatures have cooled and the rains have gone, but the landscape is still green and lush.

☆ Dhaka Festivals

The cool of November brings out the culture crowd in Dhaka, which hosts several great festivals (p43), including Dhaka Lit Fest, the Bengal Classical Music Festival, Dhaka International Folk Festival, and Jazz & Blues Festival Dhaka.

National Revolution Day

7 November commemorates the 1975 uprising that helped Major General Ziaur Rahman, the founder of Bangladesh Nationalist Party (BNP), rise to power. A national holiday when the BNP is in government, but not recognised by the Awami League.

Maha Raas Leela

This Hindu festival, which celebrates a young Lord

Krishna, attracts up to 200,000 pilgrims to the Kantanagar Temple (p97) near Dinajpur, and is held at full moon in November. It's also celebrated with fervour at Dubla Char, a remote island in the Sundarbans.

December

Getting cooler now, but still dry, December is also a very comfortable time to visit, although evenings start getting chilly towards the end of the month.

Eid Milad un Nabi

Celebrating the birth of the Prophet Muhammad, mosques around the country hold low-key events. Dates for upcoming years are 12 December 2016, 1 December 2017 and 20 November 2018.

Victory Day

A national holiday on 16 December, celebrated to mark the end of the 1971 Liberation War. Expect much flag-waving as well as events at the Liberation War Museum (p38).

Martyred Intellectuals' Day

Held on 14 December; remembers the murder of hundreds of journalists, doctors and academics that took place just days before the end of the Liberation War. Officials pay their respects at a mass gravesite in the outlying Dhaka neighbourhood of Rayer Bazar.

Itineraries

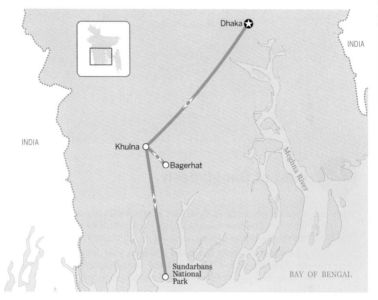

Sampling the Sunderbans

One week is just enough time to dip into Dhaka before going on the boat trip of a life-time through the tiger-filled mangrove swamps of the Sundarbans.

Ease yourself into **Dhaka** by spending your first day in the more upmarket neighbourhood of Banani before delving into the chaos with a sightseeing tour of Old Dhaka on day two. Don't miss Sadarghat for a rowboat trip on the Buriganga River.

You haven't got time to ride the Rocket paddle-wheel steamer (you'll need an extra two days for that). Instead, take an overnight bus to **Khulna** to meet up with your Sundarbans tour company, which you'll need in order to properly explore the **Sundarbans National Park**. Then relax on the deck of your boat and enjoy three days of tiger-tinged river adventure before floating back to Khulna.

Consider a day trip to **Bagerhat** before taking the bus back to Dhaka for one final day in the capital.

Note that you will need to have booked your Sundarbans trip at least three weeks in advance, so start planning this one from home.

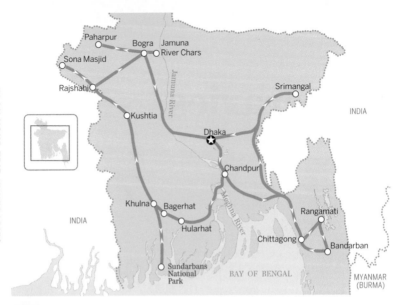

Best of Bangladesh

1 MONTH

Bangladesh is relatively small, so if you have a full month you can see pretty much all the main highlights. This tour takes in Dhaka, the Sundarbans and part of history-rich Rajshahi, plus the tea estates of Srimangal and the Chittagong Hill Tracts.

Your first job when you arrive in **Dhaka** is to book your cabin on the Rocket for your ferry ride the following evening. Tickets in hand, you can spend the rest of that day and the next taking in the sights of Old Dhaka before leaving on the 6pm boat.

Sit back and enjoy the lazy 16-hour river trip to **Hularhat**. Having disembarked mid-morning, grab a rickshaw to the bus stand, then a bus to **Bagerhat**. Spend the afternoon admiring Islamic ruins before hopping on another bus to **Khulna**, where you'll meet your Sundarbans tour company. Note: you will need to have booked your Sundarbans trip at least three weeks in advance.

The next morning, board your tour boat and enjoy three or four days of unrivalled river adventure as you track tigers in the mangrove forests of **Sundarbans National Park**.

Back in Khulna, take a bus north, pit-stopping in **Kushtia** – the cultural capital of Bengal – before continuing on to **Rajshahi**. Take a day trip to **Sona Masjid** to see the scattered ruins of the ancient city of Gaud before catching a bus to **Bogra**. There's not much to see here – although you could consider an unusual day trip to the sand **chars** on the Jamuna River – but Bogra is only a day trip away from the Unesco-protected Buddhist ruins of **Paharpur**.

Catch a bus from Bogra back to Dhaka, but don't dally; the next morning you'll be river-bound again, this time a morning ferry from Dhaka's Sadarghat to **Chandpur** before catching the train to **Chittagong**.

Sort out your permit for the hill tracts region with a tour company a week ahead of time, then spend four or five days exploring **Rangamati** and **Bandarban** before heading back to Chittagong.

Take the scenic day train to **Srimangal** where you can enjoy the surrounding tea estates, forest reserves and Adivasi villages before catching the train back to Dhaka.

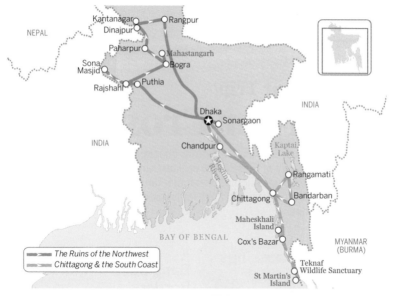

Kantanagar
Dinajpur
Rangpur
NEPAL
Paharpur
Mahastangarh
Sona
Masjid
Bogra
Rajshahi
Puthia
Dhaka
INDIA
Sonargaon
INDIA
Chandpur
Kaptai
Lake
Meghna River
Rangamati
Chittagong
Bandarban
Maheskhali
Island
BAY OF BENGAL
Cox's Bazar
MYANMAR
(BURMA)
Teknaf
Wildlife Sanctuary
St Martin's
Island

The Ruins of the Northwest
Chittagong & the South Coast

2 WEEKS The Ruins of the Northwest

This tour points you towards the older side of Dhaka before exploring the dusty ruins of history-rich Rajshahi and Rangpur.

Spend your first day visiting the museums and Raj-era architecture of central **Dhaka** before diving into the living history of Old Dhaka. Try to track down the hard-to-find ruins of Bara Katra and Chota Katra among the chaos of the bazaars. A day trip to **Sonargaon** makes an easy day three before you set off by bus to the temple-strewn village of **Puthia**, en route to **Rajshahi**.

Day trip from Rajshahi to **Sona Masjid**, to see the scattered ruins of the lost city of Gaud, before catching the bus to **Bogra**. The ruined settlement of **Mahasthangarh** makes a fun half-day trip before you head to the Unesco-protected Buddhist ruins of **Paharpur**, where you can stay the night.

From Paharpur, take a bus to **Dinajpur** (via Jaipurhat and Fulbari) so you can visit the stunning Hindu temple of **Kantanagar** before heading to nearby **Rangpur**, which has a sprinkling of Raj-era architecture, a top-class guesthouse and a daily train to Dhaka.

2 WEEKS Chittagong & the South Coast

The most diverse region of Bangladesh, Chittagong has mountains, forests, Adivasi villages, elephants and even beaches. This tour has the lot.

After a day visiting the must-see sights of **Dhaka**, hop on a morning ferry to **Chandpur**, from where you can catch a train to **Chittagong**. Apply for your permit for the hill tracts here before taking the bus to **Cox's Bazar** where you can rest up by the beach and even go surfing – but don't forget to visit **Maheskhali Island**.

Heading further south, catch a bus to **Teknaf Wildlife Sanctuary**, home to some of Bangladesh's few remaining wild elephants, before riding the waves to **St Martin's Island**.

Return to Chittagong to collect your travel permit, then head for laid-back **Rangamati** for a couple of relaxing days by Kaptai Lake. From Rangamati, take a bus to **Bandarban**, the heart of the Chittagong Hill Tracts, and the best place to base yourself for hiking.

There are buses from the Hill Tracts direct to **Dhaka**, but we'd suggest taking the scenic route back to Chittagong and then catching a train to Dhaka from there.

Plan Your Trip
Border Crossings

Bangladesh shares several border checkposts with its neighbour India, and many of these allow civilian transit between the two nations. Crossings such as Benapole, Tamabil and Akhaura remain popular with tourists, and have fairly good road transport networks on both sides.

Most Popular Crossings

Kolkata The twice-weekly train that connects Kolkata with Dhaka is comfortable and hassle-free. Apart from immigration formalities at the border, it's direct and nonstop.

Benapole Main border town on the road route to and from Kolkata. Has direct bus links to Dhaka, Khulna and Jessore.

Akhaura The other major border for India's northeast tribal states. Agartala on the Indian side has a domestic airport and a place to process Bangladesh visas. The Bangladesh side has a train station with links to Dhaka, Srimangal and Chittagong.

Burimari Bangladesh's gateway to Darjeeling, with transport links via the Indian town of Siliguri. Entering Bangladesh, most people head to Rangpur, but there is a night bus to Dhaka.

Tamabil Linking Sylhet with India's northeast tribal states, Tamabil isn't a place to linger, on account of the open mining that goes on around the border (cough! splutter!), but you're only two hours away from Sylhet by bus.

Bangladeshi–Indian Borders

There are numerous points in Bangladesh where you can cross the border with India, but only six or seven are set up with immigration facilities to service foreigners. At the time of research there was still no border crossing with Myanmar (Burma).

The same system is in place for all of these crossings (apart from the direct train to Kolkata), although differing levels of stringency are applied at each.

If you're leaving Bangladesh and entering India, the most important thing to remember is that you cannot get an Indian visa at any of the border towns, so you must have already sorted this out, preferably in your home country. Foreigners can try to get an Indian visa in Dhaka and Chittagong, but it's a bureaucratic nightmare, and many travellers leave the visa office empty-handed.

If you're coming into Bangladesh from India by land, note that you cannot get the same visa-on-arrival that you can get if you fly into Dhaka airport, but you can get Bangladesh visas in Kolkata and Agartala (Akhaura), as well as in New Delhi.

If you plan an overland departure from Bangladesh after your visa has been granted, you are supposed to pick up a change-of-route permit (p166) from the Immigration and Passport Office in Dhaka. In any case, crossing the border also requires you to pay a Tk 500 departure tax, which you can deposit in advance at select Sonali Bank branches in the country. The departure tax is critical, but the permit itself isn't asked for these days, so in practice you don't need it.

Be aware that visa regulations (p166) for Bangladesh change on a regular basis. For the latest information, double-check with the Bangladeshi embassy or consulate in your country.

Customs at land borders are fairly lax with foreigners. The same rules regarding what you can bring into the country (in the way of cigarettes and alcohol) apply at border crossings as at airports, though in practice a blind eye is usually turned to your luggage at land crossings.

Akhaura

This border (open 8am to 6pm) is the closest one to Dhaka and links Bangladesh with India's northeast states. There's a departure tax payment desk (10am to 3pm Sunday to Thursday) by immigration where you can pay your Bangladesh departure tax, and unofficial moneychangers operate on both sides of the border.

On the Indian side, the border is 3km from Agartala (rickshaw Rs 50), which has an airport, 12km away, with flights to Kolkata and Guwahati. Agartala's **Bangladesh visa office** (🖉 in India 0381-232 4807; Airport Rd, Kunjaban; ☺ application 9am-1pm Mon-Thu, 9am-noon Fri, collection same day 4pm) is about 2km north of Ujjayanta Palace.

On the Bangladesh side, the border is 4.5km from the town of Akhaura (shared auto-rickshaw Tk 20, rickshaw Tk 50), which has a train station with direct trains to Dhaka, Chittagong and Sylhet. The Sylhet trains all pass through Srimangal

(three hours). The Chittagong trains all pass through Comilla (two hours). If there's no reserved seating left, just buy a standing ticket and pile on. There are plenty of places to eat by the train station.

You can also get to Dhaka, Sylhet and Srimangal by bus via Chandura (shared auto-rickshaw Tk 60), a junction 20km away on the Dhaka–Sylhet Hwy.

There are direct buses to Chandura (Tk 120, three hours) from Dhaka's Sayedabad bus stand.

Benapole

The Benapole border (open 6.30am to 6.30pm) is on the main road route to and from Kolkata.

On the Bangladesh side, there's a departure-tax payment desk (Sunday to Thursday) by immigration. Once over the border you can pick up buses to Kolkata, or trains from nearby Bangaon.

Coming into Bangladesh, Benapole is about 2km from the border (shared CNG Tk 10, rickshaw Tk 20). The local bus stand has regular buses to Jessore (Tk 50, one hour) and one to Khulna (Tk 130, 2½ hours, 11.30am). Before you reach the bus stand, you'll see a handful of private coach companies on your left, with regular services to Dhaka (non-air-con/air-con Tk 600/1050, 9am to 9pm, eight hours). There's an AB Bank ATM opposite the bus stand. Otherwise, you'll see plenty of private moneychangers near the coach offices.

If you get stuck here, the **Parjatan Hotel** (🖉 01716-984262; Benapole; r without/with air-con Tk 1300/2100), just past the bus stand, away from the border, is decent and has a passable restaurant (mains Tk 100 to Tk 200; 7am to 10pm).

SELECTED TRAINS FROM AKHAURA

DESTINATION	TRAIN NAME	DEPARTS	ARRIVES	FARE (1ST/SHUVON)	OFF DAY
Chittagong	Mohanagar Provati	10.42am	3.40pm	Tk 180/80	none
Chittagong	Paharika Ex	3.25pm	8.20pm	Tk 180/80	Sat
Chittagong	Mohanagar Godhuli	7.27pm	12am	Tk 180/80	Sun
Dhaka	Upakul Ex	9.30am	1pm	Tk 130/75	none
Dhaka	Mohanagar Provati	11.38am	2.50pm	Tk 130/75	Sun
Dhaka	Upakul Ex	5.50pm	8.30pm	Tk 130/75	Wed
Dhaka	Mohanagar Godhuli	7.28pm	10.30pm	Tk 130/75	none
Dhaka	Turna Ex	3.40am	6.40am	Tk 130/75	none
Sylhet	Paharika Ex	1.05pm	6pm	Tk 155/90	Mon

Via Kolkata

In Kolkata, more than a dozen daily buses leave from Marquis St, bound for Dhaka (Rs 830 to Rs 1430, 13 hours), via Benapole, where you'll have to complete immigration formalities. Bus companies running the service include **Shohagh Paribahan** (www.shohagh.biz) and **Green Line** (www.greenlinebd.com).

The *Maitree Express* (Rs 520 to Rs 1355, 12½ hours) to Dhaka departs Kolkata (Chitpore) Station at 7.10am on Saturday and Wednesday. Buy tickets not from the station, but from a special desk at the **Eastern Railways Foreign Tourist Bureau** (☎033-2222 4206; 6 Fairlie Pl, Kolkata; ⊙Maitree Express Tickets 10am-5pm Mon-Thu, 10am-3pm Fri & Sat).

Burimari

This border (open 9am to 5pm) is used by travellers heading for Darjeeling.

Heading to India, most travellers come from Rangpur. First take a bus from Rangpur to Patgram (Tk 140, four hours) then take a CNG (Tk 20, 20 minutes) or bus (Tk 20) for the remaining 13km to the border. Pay your departure tax at Sonali Bank (p96) in Rangpur. You can change money unofficially on the Indian side of the border in Chengrabandha, from where there are regular buses to Siliguri (Rs 50).

Coming into Bangladesh, there's nowhere to change money; not officially, at least. There's one night bus to Dhaka (Tk 700, 11 hours, 6pm) run by **Shah Ali Paribahan** (www.shahaliparibahanbd.com), 200m past the border. Otherwise you need to catch a tempo to Patgram then a bus to Rangpur (last bus 7pm).

If you get stuck in Burimari, the very basic **Shekhar Plaza** (☎01918-457511; Burimari; r Tk 600), a green two-storey hotel on your left as you walk from the border, is the best you'll get. No English spoken.

Hili

This little-used border (open 9am to 5pm) is the closest to the Unesco-protected ruins of Paharpur. There's nowhere to pay the Bangladesh departure tax, except at the Sonali Bank (p96) in Rangpur.

Coming from Bogra, you need to catch a bus via Jaipurhat, from where it's Tk 40 by bus to Hili. Hili bus stand is a Tk 30 CNG ride from the border.

Coming from Rangpur, you have to catch a bus first to Fulbari (Tk 60, two hours) then to Hili (Tk 30, one hour).

The Indian side of the border is also known as Hili. You may be able to get onward transport to Kolkata (Rs 400, 12 hours) from the border, or else go via Balurghat, 20km away. The nearest train station is Malda.

Coming into Bangladesh, there's nowhere to change money. You need the Hili bus stand for Paharpur and Bogra (via Jaipurhat), but you can catch buses to Fulbari (for Rangpur) on the roadside, 200m past the border. **Shyamoli Paribahan** (www.shyamoliparibahan.com), 100m from the border, has four buses to Dhaka (Tk 450, seven to eight hours, 6.30am, 11am, 2.30pm and 10.30pm).

Sona Masjid (Gaud)

Another infrequently used border post (open 9am to 5pm), Sona Masjid is ideal if you want to explore the ruins of the ancient city of Gaud, which lie scattered on both sides of the border.

Leaving Bangladesh, you'll probably have to come from Rajshahi, where you'll also have to pay your Tk 500 departure tax at **Sonali Bank** (Saheb Bazar Rd; ⊙10am-4pm

---

DEPARTURE TAX

You must pay a Tk 500 departure tax (sometimes called a 'travel tax') if you're leaving Bangladesh via a land border. However, it isn't as easy as just handing over your last few taka as you pass through customs. It has to be paid into a branch of Sonali Bank. You will then be given a receipt as proof of payment, and it is this receipt that you hand over as you leave the country. Some border crossings have a small bank desk by immigration (such as Benapole and Akhaura), but they remain shut on Fridays and Saturdays. Otherwise, you need to pay the tax at a proper branch of Sonali Bank, although you can do this at any branch in the country.

Remember, banks in Bangladesh are always closed on Friday, and usually Saturday too.

The *Maitree Express*

Sun-Thu). Once you've had your fill of ruins on the Indian side of border, you'll be able to find onward transport from Gaud to Malda, 15km away, from where there are trains to Kolkata or Siliguri, for Darjeeling.

Entering Bangladesh, there's nowhere to change money. Buses to Rajshahi (Tk 150, three hours) leave from a small T-junction, 250m past the border.

Tamabil

The border checkpost (open 8am to 5pm) closest to Sylhet is busy, mostly with trucks filled with rocks and coal from the open mines around here, but a few travellers also cross. There's no departure-tax payment desk, but Sylhet has a number of branches of Sonali Bank (p129).

The border is a two-minute walk from where the bus from Sylhet drops you (walk up to your right). Once in India, it's a 2km walk to the town of Dawki (taxi Rs 50), from where buses run to Shillong (Rs 110, three hours).

Entering Bangladesh, buses to Sylhet (Tk 60, two hours) run from the main road just beyond the border post until around 8pm. There's nowhere to change money, but the guys in customs may be able to help you out.

Siliguri to Dhaka Direct

Some private agencies run direct buses from Siliguri to Dhaka (Rs 800, 16 hours). Try **Shyamoli** (☐ in India 9836583691; www.shyamolibusservice.com; Hotel Central Plaza Complex, Hill Cart Rd, Siliguri). You'll have to complete immigration formalities at Chengrabandha.

Plan Your Trip
Boat Trips

Bangladesh has more than 700 rivers, 8000km of navigable water-ways and possibly more types of boats than any other country. Taking a river trip is a quintessential Bangladesh experience, and we recommend you do it as often as you can, from hand-poled river ferries to the old paddle-wheel steamers known as Rockets.

Best Boat Trips

Best for Wildlife

Sundarbans (p69) Monkeys, wild boars, otters, crocodiles, river dolphins and more than 30,000 deer. Even if there weren't any tigers, this boat trip would be fun.

Best for Scenery

Sangu River (p111) This beautiful Hill Tracts river passes steep, tree-covered banks, rugged river cliffs and villages so remote you can only get to them by boat.

Best City Trip

Dhaka (p42) Bobbing across the Buriganga River – the lifeblood of Dhaka, if not the nation – on board a wooden rowboat, while triple-tiered ferries and oceangoing cargo ships charge past you is among the most surreal (and scary) experiences you'll have.

Best Boat

The Rocket Steeped in almost 100 years of history, Bangladesh's famous paddle-wheel steamer may not be the fastest thing on the waterways these days, but it gets more and more romantic each passing year.

Types of Boats

The Rocket

The Rocket is a generic name given to the four remaining paddle-wheel steamers that were built in the early 20th century and are run by the BIWTC (Bangladesh Inland Waterway Transport Corporation). Called Rockets because they were once the fastest thing on the waterways, they now plod along, diesel-powered, at a slower rate than more modern ferries and other other boats (which now also ply the same route).

The Route

All four Rockets follow the same set route. They used to go from Dhaka all the way to Khulna in a 30-hour epic trip to the edge of the Sundarbans, but at the time of research the last 10-hour stretch of the trip had been suspended indefinitely, so they were only travelling as far as Morrelganj.

FROM DHAKA (EVERY DAY EXCEPT FRIDAY)

Dhaka	6pm
Chandpur	midnight
Barisal	6am
Hularhat	10am
Morrelganj	2pm

TO DHAKA (EVERY DAY EXCEPT SUNDAY)

Morrelganj	9am
Hularhat	12.30pm
Barisal	6pm
Chandpur	1.30am
Dhaka	7.30am

The Classes

There are three main classes: 1st-class cabins are lovely, and well worth paying extra for. There are twins and singles. Both are carpeted and wood-panelled and come with fans, a TV, a small sink and crisp white bed linen. Shared bathrooms have showers. You also get access to the 1st-class dining room (although meals cost extra) and the wonderful 1st-class deck right at the front of the boat.

Second-class cabins are essentially a more basic version of 1st class. They are twin-bed cabins with bed sheets provided (although it's not quite so crisp and clean as in 1st), and are fan-cooled but have no TV or private sink and the shared bathrooms don't have showers. There are small side decks for you to sit out on, but you can often sneak onto the 1st-class front deck without being told off. Meals cost extra, but are generally pretty good.

Deck class is essentially a ticket onto the boat. It's then up to you to find a spot to sit or sleep on, on the lower, open-sided wooden deck. There are snack stalls down here, which all passengers can use. Deck class is fine for a daytime trip, but extremely uncomfortable if you're travelling overnight.

Launches

Private, more modern ferries – known as launches – ply the same route as the Rocket. The overnight ones tend to leave slightly later (from Dhaka between 7pm and 9pm) but are slightly quicker. There are also launches that leave Dhaka throughout the day for closer destinations, such as Chandpur, in Chittagong division.

Classes are similar to the Rocket, although you may also have the option of 'VIP cabins', with extra room and comfort, and private balconies.

Because there are more of them, you don't usually need to book your launch tickets too far in advance. Head down to Sadarghat (p36) – the main river ghat in Dhaka – and inquire about launches to wherever you want to go. If you turn up mid- to late afternoon, you should be able to bag a cabin on a boat that evening.

Country Boat

Smaller wooden boats, known as *nouka* (country boats), come in all sorts of shapes and sizes and ply the lesser rivers of the more remote regions of Bangladesh. Riding aboard one of these can be a magical experience. They are sometimes rowed and sometimes driven by a small engine. You'll find you often use them just to cross rivers, but you can take short trips on them all over the country. Even if you're not going anywhere in particular, you can just rock up at most river ghats and negotiate a fare with a boat-hand for a one-hour tour of the river. You'll have to have your best miming skills at the ready because it's very unlikely your boat-hand will speak any English... but it all adds to the adventure.

Top River Trips

Sundarbans National Park

The world's largest mangrove swamp (p69) is home to the largest single population of tigers found anywhere in the world, and boarding a boat to go in search of one of them is Bangladesh's undisputed number-one tourist attraction. It's possible to dip into the mangrove forest on a self-organised day trip from Mongla, but for a true adventure, book yourself onto a three- or four-day boat tour from Khulna.

Dhaka to Hularhat by Rocket

The first part of this 16-hour trip on the famous Rocket (p52) is overnight, so make sure you've booked a cabin! Try not to sleep in, though, because arriving at the large port at Barisal in the early morning mist is a sight worth seeing. Once the boat starts up again, sit back on the deck and lap up the scenery before hopping off at Hularhat and catching a bus to either Bagerhat or Khulna.

Buriganga River

For a fun, albeit slightly scary city-river trip, head to the rowboat ghat beside Dhaka's main ferry port at Sadarghat (p36)

THE HOLIDAY RUSH

During major national holidays such as Eid ul Adha, passenger ferries can become worryingly overcrowded as locals rush to get home to their families. Safety concerns can be a real issue at these times. Use common sense; if a ferry seems ridiculously packed (even by Bangladeshi standards), think twice about boarding it.

SEA VOYAGES

One side of Bangladesh opens out into the Bay of Bengal, so as well as all the amazing river trips outlined here, there are some short sea voyages you can take too.

St Martin's Island Large modern passenger ferries head south to laidback St Martin's Island (p120). Much of the two-hour trip follows the coastline of Myanmar (Burma).

Fatra Char You can take a day trip along the coast from Kuakata to Fatra Char (p81), a forested Island on the eastern fringes of the Sundarbans.

Swatch of No Ground Excellent tour operator Guide Tours (p42) can help you join a research boat to visit the Swatch of No Ground, a deep-water canyon south of the Sundarbans, where you can spot whales and dolphins.

and pay Tk 4 to cross the massive Buriganga in one of the many small wooden rowboats that shuttle passengers across the river. Watch as your tiny boat dodges triple-tiered ferries and cargo ships to get to the opposite bank. Then grab a cup of cha at a tea stall on the other side, take a deep breath and do it all again in reverse.

Sangu River

The scenery along most rivers is beautiful, but it's particularly special here, on the four- to five-hour stretch of the Sangu River (p111) running from Ruma Bazar to Bandarban. This is the Chittagong Hill Tracts, where you'll find dramatic rock faces rising from the water's edge, backed by forested hills teeming with wildlife. It's tough to sort out; you'll need a permit, and if you haven't brought a guide, you'll need your best miming skills because boatmen don't speak English here, but it's a small price to pay for breathtaking scenery and hours of peace and tranquillity.

Kaptai Lake

Formed when the Kaptai Dam was built in the 1960s, this enormous lake (p114), accessed from the super-relaxed town of Rangamati, offers numerous boating opportunities. The three-hour round trip to Shuvalong Falls is the most popular.

Maheskhali Island

With its village atmosphere and small collection of Hindu and Buddhist temples, the island of Maheskhali makes a wonderfully peaceful escape from the brash beach resort of Cox's Bazar, but it's the boat trip (p121) over to the island that's the real gem. You'll pass pirate-ship lookalike fishing boats, a huge and highly pungent fish market and a string of ice-making houses where huge blocks of ice slide down roller-coaster runners and into waiting boats, before you finally open out into the estuary that leads to Maheskhali.

China Clay Hills

Enlist the help of the staff at the YMCA in Birisiri to help arrange a relaxing three-hour boat trip along the Someswari River to the China Clay Hills (p62): exposed mounds of rock surrounding a picturesque turquoise lake. You'll have to walk the last bit, or take a rickshaw, but you can still do the whole round trip in a day.

Sunamganj Wetlands

The wetlands, or *haors*, of northern Bangladesh are a birder's paradise. Migratory birds flock here in winter and join the resident birds for one big feathered party. Tanguar Haor (p131), accessible from Sylhet, is one of the most popular wetland areas to visit.

Boat Tour Operators

Most of the trips mentioned here can be done independently, but using a tour operator saves you a lot of hassle, allows you added security and gives you the chance to hook up with other travellers.

Contic (p42) Has restored two traditional Bangladesh boats and runs top-end but informal multiday trips to various places. Highly recommended.

Guide Tours (p42) Bangladesh's most respected tour company runs day-cruises around the Dhaka area, plus multiday Sundarbans trips.

Bangladesh Ecotours (p102) Specialises in the Chittagong Hill Tracts and can help with river trips in hard-to-reach places in this region.

Tiger Tours Ltd (p42) Owns a small cruiser offering day and multiday trips from Dhaka.

Regions at a Glance

Bangladesh is relatively small, but unless you're spending a couple of months here, you'll still have to pick and choose which regions to visit.

The megacity of Dhaka sits conveniently at the centre of the country and acts as a gateway to almost everywhere.

Southwest of Dhaka is Bangladesh's biggest draw: the tiger-filled mangrove forests of the Sundarbans National Park.

To the northwest are the history-rich divisions of Rajshahi and Rangpur, home to forgotten kingdoms and dusty ruins, while the east of the country dispels the myth that Bangladesh is completely flat. Here you'll find the gently rolling hills of Sylhet's tea estates and, further south, the stunning forest-covered mountains of the Chittagong Hill Tracts.

Dhaka

Food
Culture
Chaos

Biryani & Kebabs

You'll almost certainly have your best food in Dhaka. Biryani houses rule the roost, but you'll also find some excellent kebab joints as well as some decent Western fare.

Galleries & Museums

Unsurprisingly, Dhaka also packs in the country's best museums, theatres and art galleries. Try to catch a show or an exhibition while you're in town or, at the very least, check out the National Museum.

Old Dhaka

For some it's too much to handle, but for others the mind-boggling chaos of Old Dhaka is what makes a visit to this most manic of megacities such an experience.

p34

Dhaka Division

Rural Vistas
Villages
History

Paddy fields

Especially in the far north, it's glistening paddy field after glistening paddy field as you bus it through this gloriously green region. Rural bliss.

Garo Settlements

There are around 25,000 villages in Dhaka division, including some in the far north where the population is predominantly Garo. Birisiri is a great place to start.

Ruins

This is no Rajshahi, but there is a smattering of crumbling ruins to explore in Dhaka division. The pick of the bunch are those at Sonargaon, although Muktagacha is also worth a trip.

p55

Khulna & Barisal

Wildlife
Scenery
Boats

Tigers

You'll see birds galore, spotted deer and maybe some monkeys in the Sundarbans, but the hardest creature to spot is also the one people are most keen to see – the Royal Bengal tiger.

Mangroves

Kuakata is a wonderfully natural beach, and the trip down there is full of lush farmland, but it's the pristine mangrove forests of the Sundarbans that steal the show.

The Rocket

Chances are you'll ride more boats in this river-drenched region than anywhere else in Bangladesh, but if you fall in love with any of them, it will be the old paddle-wheel steamer known as the Rocket.

p63

Rajshahi & Rangpur

History
Architecture
Humanity

Lost Kingdoms

History buffs get ready. The lost city of Gaud, the ruined kingdom of Mahastangarh and the remains of what was once the largest monastery south of the Himalaya.

Temples, Mosques & Monasteries

The ancient buildings of this region are an eclectic bunch. You'll find Bangladesh's most exquisite Hindu temple, its largest Buddhist ruins and some of the oldest and most unusual mosques.

Chars

Many of Bangladesh's poorest people make their homes on sand islands in Bangladesh's rivers, and visiting is a fascinating, challenging window onto their way of life.

p82

Chittagong Division

Adventure
Scenery
Adivasi Culture

Hiking

This region is full of off-the-beaten-track adventure. Whether it be searching for wild elephants or hiking to waterfalls and tribal villages, Chittagong is a place for those who love the outdoors.

Chittagong Hill Tracts

Chittagong has coastal beaches, enormous lakes, forest reserves and even a coral island, but it's the rugged mountains of the Chittagong Hill Tracts that dominate the landscape

Bandarban & Rangamati

Your chances of meeting Adivasi groups and learning about their ways of life are greater here than anywhere in Bangladesh.

p100

Sylhet Division

Scenery
Wildlife
Outdoor Activities

Tea Estates

Almost as diverse as Chittagong, Sylhet is home to thick forest reserves, bird-filled wetlands and the majority of the country's 163 tea estates.

Hoolock Gibbons

Birders will love the wetlands of Sunamganj, and there are a number of types of monkeys to be found in the forests around Srimangal, but the jewel in the crown of Sylhet's wildlife is the very rare Hoolock gibbon.

Boat Trips

Bangladesh's largest freshwater marshes at Ratargul are perfect to explore by boat – an easy day trip from Sylhet through the silent waterways of a rich tropical forest.

p125

On the Road

Dhaka

POP 16.9 MILLION / 🗐 02

Best Places to Eat

➡ Fakruddin (p48)

➡ Spaghetti Jazz (p49)

➡ Holey Artisan Bakery (p49)

➡ Dhaba (p49)

➡ Al-Razzaque (p48)

Best Places to Sleep

➡ Viator (p47)

➡ Sabrina's (p46)

➡ Radisson Blu Water Garden Hotel (p47)

➡ Hotel Pacific (p45)

➡ White House Hotel (p45)

➡ Lakeshore (p47)

Why Go?

Dhaka is not a quiet, retiring place. The city, bursting with nearly 17 million people (most of whom often seem to be stuck in the same traffic jam as you), is a gloriously noisy and chaotic place, bubbling with energy.

It's a city that can sometimes threaten to overwhelm the casual visitor, but once you climb into the back of one of its myriad colourful cycle-rickshaws, Dhaka's charm starts to slowly reveal itself. Life flows from the boats on the Buriganga River to its unexpectedly green parks and university campuses. Mughal and British monuments speak of its history, its mosques and Hindu temples of its spiritual side, and the thriving arts and restaurant scenes – plus the rush to build new roads and a metro railway system – give a glimpse of the direction of future travel.

Dhaka isn't without challenges, but sooner or later you'll start to move to its rhythm and truly embrace this furiously beating heart of Bengali culture.

When to Go
Dhaka

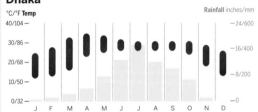

Jan–Mar Dry and cool; evenings can become slightly chilly.	**Apr** Getting hot, but Bengali New Year falls on the 14th, so cultural events abound.	**Nov & Dec** Monsoon rains are over, temperatures are cooler, and festival time begins.

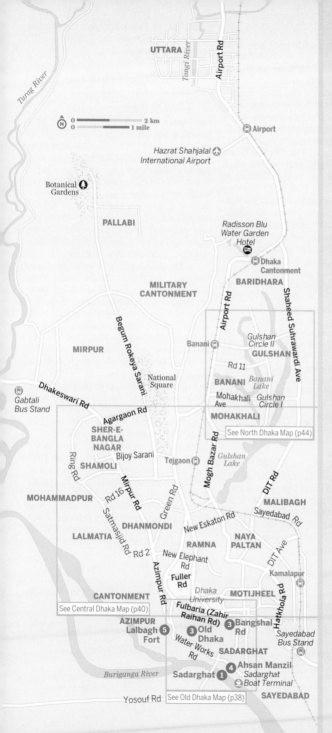

Dhaka Highlights

1 Sadarghat
(p36) Boarding a rowboat down at the gritty docks of Sadarghat and crossing the manic Buriganga River, the very lifeblood of this enormous city.

2 Cycle-rickshaws
(p51) See some of Dhaka's thousands of cycle-rickshaws being made – and buy a piece of rickshaw art for yourself on Bangshal Rd.

3 Old Dhaka
(p36) Getting lost wandering the fascinating, overcrowded alleyways of Old Dhaka (Puran Dhaka).

4 Ahsan Manzil
(p37) Poking around the museum at this charming pink palace.

5 Lalbagh Fort
(p37) Escaping Old Dhaka's hustle and bustle and exploring the ruins of this ancient fort.

History

Although there were settlements here from as early as the 7th century, ruled first by Buddhist kingdoms and later by Hindu dynasties, Dhaka only really came into its own in 1608 when it was taken over by the Mughals and installed as the capital of Bengal. It spent a glorious century under Mughal rule (its population swelling to near a million, with significant Portuguese and Armenian trading communities), but began to decline in the early 18th century when the capital was moved to Murshidabad in today's India.

The rise of the East India Company in Bengal saw Dhaka fall under British rule in 1793, but it was soon overshadowed by the rise of imperial Calcutta (Kolkata). At one stage the population was as low as 30,000. There were, nevertheless, some significant developments at this time. A modern water supply system was introduced in 1874. An electricity system followed in 1878. And in 1905, when Lord Curzon, the Governor-General of India, finalised the short-lived partition of Bengal, Dhaka was chosen as the capital of the new state of East Bengal and Assam.

The Partition of India in 1947 saw Dhaka installed as the capital of East Pakistan. A period of major upheaval for the city followed, with a large proportion of Dhaka's Hindus departing for India, while the city received a large influx of Muslims. And as the centre of regional politics, Dhaka saw an increasing number of strikes, demonstrations and incidents of violence.

On 7 March 1971 an estimated one million people attended the nationalist rally at Ramna Racecourse – now **Suhrawardi Park** (Map p40; ⊙6am-10pm) – which eventually led to the 26 March declaration of Bangladesh's independence. Nine months of bloody civil war followed before the Pakistani surrender on 16 December, again at Ramna Racecourse, which saw the birth of an independent Bangladesh.

◉ Sights

◉ Old Dhaka

Sadarghat   RIVER
(River Ghat; Map p38) Running calmly through the centre of Old Dhaka, the Buriganga River is the muddy artery of Dhaka and the very lifeblood of both this city and the nation. Exploring it from the deck of a small boat from Sadarghat (shod-or-ghat) is to see Bangladesh at its grittiest. The panorama of river life is fascinating. Triple-towered ferries leer over pint-sized canoes, and country boats bump against overladen barges with barely an inch of clearance above water.

On the foreshores, stained with grease and mud, you'll find children fishing with homemade nets in the lee of rusting tankers. Further out, repairmen busy themselves crashing, bashing and scrubbing ship hulls while floating on planks of wood.

Among all the large ships are the tiny wooden ones you can hire. These are available almost everywhere along the waterfront, though most people hire them from around Sadarghat boat terminal (p52). If you walk along the jetty here, English-speaking boatmen will find you and offer you a one-hour tour of the river. If you can barter the price down to Tk 30 you'll be doing well.

Alternatively, walk slightly west to the **small rowing-boat landing** (Map p38); from here wooden rowing boats ferry passengers across the river all day for a set price of Tk 5 per person. The opposite riverbank is of no particular interest – it's packed with clothes shops, though there are some snack stalls and tea stands, too – but it's the trip there and back that's the attraction.

ORIENTATION
....

For simplicity, we divide the city into three areas: Old Dhaka (Puran Dhaka), Central Dhaka and North Dhaka.

Old Dhaka is a maze of bustling bazaars and incredibly crowded narrow streets and is by far the most interesting part of the city for tourists. It's packed with historic sights but hotel facilities are somewhat lacking.

The larger, more modern, Central Dhaka begins about 2km to the north, with its commercial heart in the district of Motijheel (moh-*tee*-jeel).

North Dhaka includes the more upmarket suburbs of Banani and Gulshan, home to embassies, expats and Dhaka's nicest guesthouses and restaurants – although there's little in terms of sights.

Ahsan Manzil   PALACE
(Pink Palace; Map p38; Ahsanullah Rd; foreigner/local Tk 100/10; ☺9.30am-4.30pm Sat-Wed & 2.30-7.30pm Fri Oct-Mar, 10.30am-5.30pm Sat-Wed & 3-8pm Fri Apr-Sep) Dating from 1872, the must-see Pink Palace was built on the site of an old French factory by Nawab Abdul Ghani, the city's wealthiest zamindar (landowner). Some 16 years after the palace's construction, it was damaged by a tornado, then altered during restoration, becoming even grander than before. Lord Curzon stayed here whenever he was in town.

After the death of the nawab (prince) and his son, the family fortune was dispersed and the palace eventually fell into disrepair. It was saved from oblivion by massive restoration in the late 1980s, aided by photos of each of the 23 rooms, taken during the high point of the palace's history. The photos are still on display, as are various family portraits and the skull of Nawab Abdul Ghani's favourite elephant, Feroz Jung.

Lalbagh Fort   FORT
(Map p38; foreigner/local Tk 200/20; ☺Mon noon-5pm, Tue-Sat 9am-5pm Oct-Mar, Mon noon-6pm, Tue-Sat 10am-6pm Apr-Sep) The half-completed Lalbagh Fort and its well-tended gardens are an excuse to escape Old Dhaka's hustle and bustle for an hour or so. The fort is particularly atmospheric in the early morning light. Construction began in 1677 under the direction of Prince Mohammed Azam, Emperor Aurangzeb's third son, although he handed it to Shaista Khan for completion. However, the death of Khan's daughter, Pari Bibi (Fair Lady), was considered such a bad omen that the fort was never completed.

Three architectural monuments within the complex were finished: the Mausoleum of Pari Bibi (in front of you as you enter), the Diwan, or Hall of Audience (to your left) and the three-domed Quilla Mosque (to your right) all date from 1684.

The only monument you can enter is the Diwan, an elegant two-storey structure containing a small but excellent museum of Mughal miniature paintings, coins, carpets and calligraphy, along with swords and firearms. In the same building, a massive arched doorway leads to the *hammam* (bathhouse). Outside is a huge disused bathing tank.

The Mausoleum of Pari Bibi is unusual because of its materials of construction: black basalt, white marble and encaustic tiles of various colours have been used to decorate its interior, while the central chamber, where Pari Bibi is buried, is entirely veneered in white marble.

Dhakeswari Temple   TEMPLE
(Map p38; Bakshi Bazar) Dhakeshwari Temple is the centre of the Hindu faith in Bangladesh. It is dedicated to Dhakeswari, the protector of Dhaka and an incarnation of the goddess Durga. Although modern in construction, there has been a temple on this spot for nine centuries. Visitors are welcome at any time (remember to remove your shoes on entering).

Every year in September (exact dates vary according to the Hindu calendar), the temple and surrounding streets throng with thousands of celebrants for Durga Puja, the goddess' annual festival, a particularly colourful, noisy and joyful time to visit.

Shankharia Bazar   STREET
(Map p38) Clouds of incense and a bursting paintbox of colours signal a welcome to so-called **Hindu Street**. Lined on either side with old houses, garlands of lurid orange marigolds, and dark doorways leading to matchbox-sized shops and workshops, this can be an extremely photogenic part of Old Dhaka, as the *shankharis* (Hindu artisans), whose ancestors came here over 300 years ago, busy themselves creating kites, gravestones, wedding hats and bangles carved out of conch shells.

The area is particularly flamboyant during Hindu festivals, but colourful year round.

Star Mosque   MOSQUE
(Sitara Masjid; Map p38; Armanitola Rd) This unusual mosque, with its striking mosaic decoration, dates from the early 18th century, although it has been radically altered. It was originally built in the typical Mughal style, with four corner towers. Around 50 years ago a local businessman financed its redecoration with Japanese and English porcelain

Old Dhaka

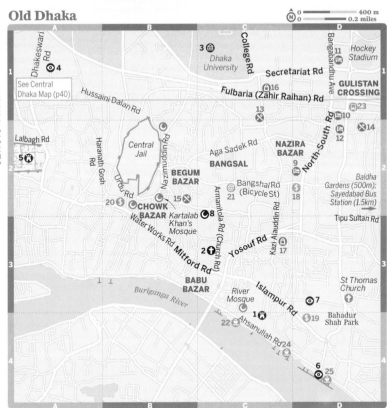

tiles, and the addition of a new verandah. If you look hard you can see tiles illustrated with pictures of Mt Fuji!

Armenian Church of the Holy Resurrection
CHURCH

(আর্মেনিয়ান চার্চ; Map p38; Armanitola Rd) This small area is known as Armanitola, and is named after the Armenian colony that settled here in the late 17th century. The white-and-lemon-painted Armenian Church of the Holy Resurrection, dating from 1781, is the soul of this now almost extinct community, and is a tranquil spot. Check out the many beautiful gravestones with Armenian inscriptions. Donations welcomed.

The caretaker, who lives in a house within the grounds, has done much to restore the church and delights in giving personal tours. In any case, you'll need him to let you in as the gates are always locked.

Central Dhaka and Beyond

National Museum
MUSEUM

(জাতীয় যাদুঘর, Jatio Jadughar; Map p40; Kazi Nazrul Islam Ave; foreigner/local Tk 100/10; ⊙9.30am-4pm Sat-Wed, 3pm-7.30pm Fri Oct-Mar, 1hr later later Apr-Sep) The excellent National Museum, sprawling over several floors, begins with the geological formation of Bangladesh, whisks you through a rundown of the nation's flora and fauna, saunters through a Buddhist and Hindu past, and brings you up to date with the War of Liberation and the creation of the modern state. Highlights include lively 6th century terracotta Hindu plaques, Buddhist statuary, vignettes of village life and the 'how did they get it inside?' wooden river racing boat.

Liberation War Museum
MUSEUM

(মুনিযুদ্ধ যাদুঘর, Mukti-juddha Jadughar; Map p40; ☎02-955 9091; 5 Segun Bagicha Rd; Tk 100; ⊙10am-5pm Mon-Sat) Housed in a beauti-

Old Dhaka

ful whitewashed colonial-era building, this small museum chronicles the 1971 War of Independence, one of the 20th century's more deadly wars. Though it might not make for happy holidays, this museum is a useful stop for those hoping to understand modern Bangladesh. The shaded courtyard out back has a tea stall and a small stage where cultural events are held from time to time. There's also a small bookshop.

Be warned: displays start off tame enough but gradually become more graphic before culminating in a room full of personal items (each of which comes with a short story on the owner's life); a large pile of human skulls and bones; and some very disturbing photos of rotting corpses with bound hands being eaten by dogs and vultures.

To get here from Topkhana Rd, head north up Segun Bagicha Rd and it's on the second street on the right.

National Assembly Building ARCHITECTURE
(জাতীয় সংসদ ভবন, Jatio Songsod Bhabon; Map p40; www.parliament.gov.bd/index.php/en/visit-parliament; guided tour per person Tk 500; ⊙ Sun-Thu 9am-5pm) In 1963 the Pakistanis commissioned Louis Kahn, a world-renowned American architect, to design a regional capitol for East Pakistan. Due to the liberation movement and ensuing war, the National Assembly Building wasn't completed until 1982. The building often features in books on modern architecture, and is regarded as among Kahn's finest works. It's a huge assembly of concrete cylinders and rectangular boxes, sliced open with bold, multi-storey

circular and triangular apertures instead of windows.

You can enter the building only on a pre-arranged four-hour guided tour, which you must book in advance. You can pick up a booking form at the front gate, or download it from the parliament website. You also need to bring two copies of your passport and visa.

Dhaka University HISTORIC BUILDING
(ঢাকা বিশ্ববিদ্যালয়, Dhaka Bisso Biddayaloy; Map p38) Dating from 1921, Dhaka University, or just DU, has some fine old buildings. The architectural masterpiece is the red-brick **Curzon Hall** (Map p40; Dhaka University, High Court St), a highly impressive example of the European-Mughal style of building erected after the first partition of Bengal in 1905. Local students will often approach you to chat if you're wandering the grounds.

Old High Court HISTORIC BUILDING
(পুরাতন হাই কোর্ট; Map p40) The imposing old High Court, once the governor's residence, is just north of Dhaka University's main campus. It is the finest example in Dhaka of the European Renaissance style.

Baldha Gardens GARDENS
(Tk 20; ⊙ 9am-5pm) At the eastern end of Tipu Sultan Rd, and a block south of Hatkhola Rd, the Baldha Gardens are a relaxing corner in busy Dhaka. The two walled enclosures, Cybele and Psyche, were once the private gardens of Narendra Narayan Roy, a wealthy zamindar (landlord), whose grandson gave them to the government in 1962 as a tribute to his family.

Central Dhaka

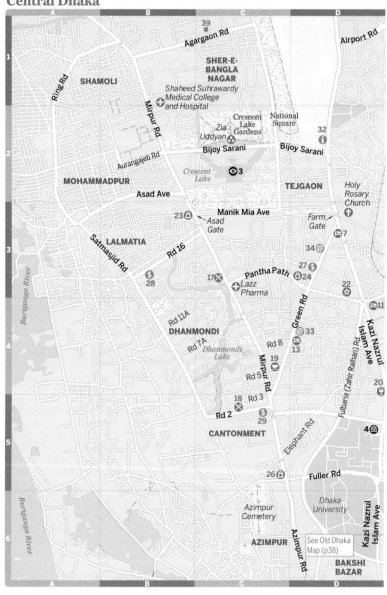

Botanical Gardens GARDENS
(Mirpur; foreigner/local Tk 100/10; ☉9am-5pm)
The shady, tranquil botanical gardens,
stretch over 40 hectares and contain over
1000 species of local and foreign plants, as
well as lots of birdlife that flock to its several lakes and ponds (particularly in winter).
Some way from the centre of Dhaka, it's a
nice respite from the city's mass of humanity. In the distance you'll see the Turag River.

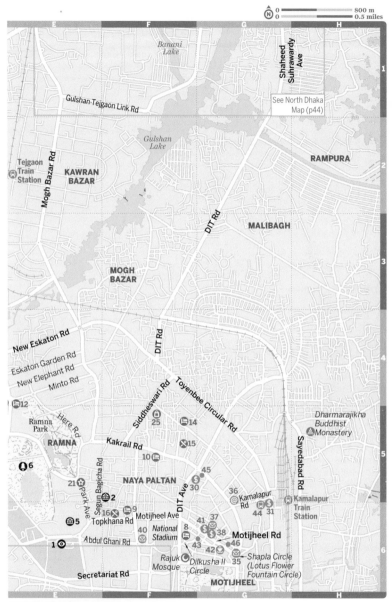

Activities

Taking a guided tour around the city – particularly Old Dhaka – can be a great way to get the most out of the city's unexplored corners. It's also possible to arrange boat trips along the river.

Rickshaw Rides

One of the best ways to see the sights of Dhaka is by cycle-rickshaw, but although taking a rickshaw for a straightforward trip from A to B is easy enough, trying to arrange a city tour with a non-English-speaking

DHAKA ACTIVITIES

Central Dhaka

rider is well-nigh impossible, and finding English-speaking riders is tough. One trick is to hang around outside five-star hotels, where English-speaking riders congregate. Alternatively, wait until you chance upon one who speaks some English and collar him for a future tour. Locals say you can hire rickshaws for around Tk 50 per hour, but you'll do well to get one for less than Tk 100. Expect to pay around Tk 400 for a half-day tour; more if the rider speaks very good English and can therefore also act as a guide. Tour operators can also sometimes arrange sightseeing by rickshaw.

River Trips
You can take a public row boat from Sadarghat across the Buriganga River for just Tk 5, but if you want something a bit more organised, try a guided tour.

Guide Tours   BOAT TOUR
(Map p44; ☏02-988 6983; www.guidetoursbd. com; Flat B1, House 2E, Rd 29, Gulshan I) Offers full-day cruises along the Shitalakkhya River on its yacht, SB *Ruposhi*, with pick-up

and drop-off at its office in Gulshan. Prices range from Tk 4200 to Tk 13,000 per person, depending on how many are in your group. Also offers day tours of Dhaka, as well as the Sundarbans and Chittagong Hill Tracts.

Tiger Tours Ltd   BOAT TOUR
(Map p44; ☏02-883 4653; www.tigertoursbd. com; 5th fl, Rob Supermarket, Gulshan Circle II, Gulshan) A relatively new guiding company offering boat tours from Dhaka on the MV *Tangaur Haor*, from day cruises to multiday excursions. Also offers tours within Dhaka and Dhaka division.

Contic   BOAT TOUR
(☏02-881 4824; www.contic.net; 3/F 87 Shaheed Suhrawardi Ave, Baridhara) Contic has two large but elegant handmade wooden boats, with cooking facilities and accommodation on board, and organises all-inclusive half- and full-day rides as well as overnight trips. Prices start at US$45 and US$55 per person for half- and full-day trips.

Note that they need at least six passengers to run a trip and passengers must book, and pay a 50% deposit, at least one week in advance.

🖝 Tours

Urban Study Group WALKING TOUR
(📱 02-967 5222; usg.dhaka@gmail.com) Unique walking tours of Old Dhaka run by an energetic group of architect activists, highlighting the hidden treasures of Dhaka's built heritage and the struggle to preserve them in an ever-changing urban environment.

Group tours are usually run on a Friday or Saturday; donations requested.

Royal Bengal Tours TOUR
(📱 01714-075718; www.royalbengaltours.com) Friendly guide company offering excellent tours of Dhaka and surrounds, as well as further afield.

Bengal Tours TOUR
(Map p44; 📱 02-883 4716; www.bengaltours.com; house 45, Rd 27, block A, Banani) Offers half- and full-day city tours. The half-day tours focus on Old Dhaka, while the full-day tour spins you around both the commercial city and Old Dhaka.

✨ Festivals & Events

In the cooler winter months, Dhaka comes alive with a host of festivals.

Dhaka Lit Fest LITERATURE
(www.dhakalitfest.com; ⊘ Nov) A highpoint of Dhaka's cultural calendar, this gem of a festival raises the banner high for free-thinking in a country where it is sometimes under threat. Expect a lively programme of talks featuring writers and thinkers from Bangladesh, the Indian subcontinent and farther afield. Entrance is free, but attendees must register online in advance.

Bengal Classical Music Festival MUSIC
(www.bengalfoundation.org; ⊘ Nov) A highlight of the musical calendar, this four-day festival brings out the best in Bengali classical music.

Dhaka Jazz and Blues Festival MUSIC
(http://bluescomm.com/jazz; ⊘ Nov) Three nights of top jazz and blues, usually attracting some big names from the international scene.

Dhaka Comicon CULTURAL
(www.dhakacomicon.com; ⊘ Dec) Proving that Bangladesh is very much part of the world that the geek shall inherit, Dhaka's Comicon

is an ever-growing gathering for fans of pop culture, from comics and movies to video games and anime.

Dhaka International Folk Fest MUSIC
(www.dhakainternationalfolkfest.com; ⊘ Nov) A popular three day musical celebration of folk music, with artists from Bangladesh, the Indian subcontinent and beyond.

Pahela Baishakh CULTURAL
(Bengali New Year) Celebrated on 14 April, the Bengali New Year, also known as Pahela Baishakh, is a big deal in the capital, with a huge parade of sculptures of toys and masks made by students from the University of Dhaka, symbolising the right of women and children to live lives free from violence.

🛏 Sleeping

The town centre has plenty of accommodation, but many of the best options are north of town in Gulshan and Banani.

🛏 Old Dhaka

Many of the very cheapest hotels in Old Dhaka still refuse to accept foreign tourists (although some can be persuaded with a friendly smile and a bit of Bengali), although all the places that we recommend do.

Hotel Baitus Samir International HOTEL $
(Map p38; 📱 02-716 2791; 155 Shahid Sayed Nazrul Islam Sarani; s/d from Tk 450/650) Brightly lit, clean rooms with pokey bathrooms (some with squat toilets) represent decent value for Dhaka's minimum-budget travellers. Rooms are on upper floors so they're relatively quiet despite the hectic streets below.

Hotel Shadman HOTEL $
(Map p38; 📱 02-711 3591; 164 Nawabpur Rd; s/d from Tk 450/700) Tiled corridors lead to basic but spacious rooms with TV, attached bathroom and natural light (a luxury you don't always get in budget digs in Old Dhaka). Rooms are on the upper floors of a tower block so it's much quieter than at rival hotels. No hot water, no air-con, and squat toilets only.

Hotel Al-Razzaque International HOTEL $
(Map p38; 📱 02-956 6408; 29/1 North-South Rd; s/d Tk 400/750, with air-con Tk 600/1000; ❄) A good-value budget option that puts you as close to the Old Dhaka action as you can get. Al-Razzaque has small but tidy rooms with very clean bathrooms. Most have external windows. The restaurant next to the

North Dhaka

Hazrat Shahjalal
International Airport
(5km)

Rd 63

Rd 70

Rd 79

43

17

United Nations Rd

Gulshan Ave

Banani
Graveyard

BANANI

Kurmitola
Golf Club

Rd 27

Rd 58

Rd 59

Rd 59

33

44

36

Rd 86

47

9

1

Rd 55

45

40

8

Rd 16

Rd 18

Rd 50

Rd 51

Rd 83

North Ave

Rd 23

Rd 4

Rd 20

4

50

22

Banani
Train
Station

Rd 24

Rd 10

Rd 27

Gulshan
Circle II

3

Rd 96

Kemal Ataturk Ave

@

Rd 99

Rd 16

Rd 8

Rd 10

Rd 12

12

Rd 103

21

Rd 44

Amusement
Park

30

Airport Rd

Rd 11

Rd 42

Gulshan
Central
Mosque

7

10

Rd 4

BANANI

See Enlargement

6

39

13

35

Rd 5

Rd 38

5

18

Rd 1

14

37

Rd 35

Rd 32

Rd 113

Rd 24

Banani
Lake

2

31

Rd 116

Rd 23

16

Mohakhali Ave

South Ave

49

Gulshan
Circle I

32

Clothes
Market

42

See Central Dhaka Map (p40)

Rd 8

Gulshan Ave

Rd 2

38

Rd 137

Mogh Bazar Rd

Rd 1

Rd 143

41

Mohakhali
Bus Station

28

Gulshan
Lake

Gulshan-Tejgaon Link Rd

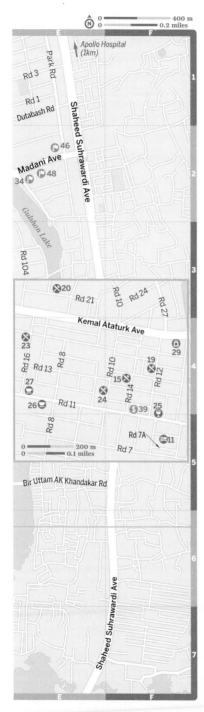

entrance is excellent; reception is on the third floor.

Hotel Ramna
HOTEL $

(Map p38; ☏02-956 2279; 45 Bangabandhu Ave; s/d/tr from Tk 750/1200/1950; ✴) Average hotel with bright, spacious rooms and communal balconies overlooking the busy streets below. It's clean for the price, but still pretty basic. No hot-water showers and squat toilets only.

Central Dhaka

Central Dhaka, particularly the Motijheel area, has a good number of midrange accommodation options, and is just a short rickshaw ride from the sights and sounds of Old Dhaka.

★ White House Hotel
HOTEL $$

(Map p40; ☏02-832 2976; www.whitehouse hotelbd.com; 155 Shantinagar Rd; s/d from Tk 3000/3500; ✴@☎) This modest hotel is very welcoming, its pleasant rooms containing rattan furniture and comfortable mattresses. A couple of the rooms facing the road are a bit noisy, but there are plenty of quiet ones to choose from, including some pleasantly bright and airy rooms. The hotel restaurant is pretty good if you want to eat in.

★ Hotel Pacific
HOTEL $$

(Map p40; ☏02-958 7671; www.hotelpacificdhaka. net; 120B Motijheel; r without/with air-con from Tk 1400/2900; ✴@☎) Pacific is about as close to a backpackers hotel as you get in this part of Dhaka. Staff members are welcoming, very helpful and speak decent English. The cheapest rooms are windowless and slightly musty, so it's worth paying Tk 100 more for a window. Hot showers and sit-down toilets are standard, and most rooms also come with a fridge.

SEL Nibash
HOTEL $$

(Map p40; ☏02-966 1017; www.selnibash.com. bd; 30 Green Rd, Dhanmondi; s/d Tk 3500/4000, ste from Tk 6000; ✴@☎) If you need to base yourself in Dhanmodi, you could do a lot worse than laying your head at this midrange business hotel. It's efficient rather than plush, but fair value for the money.

Hotel Royal Palace
HOTEL $$

(Map p40; ☏02-716 8978; www.hrpalace.com; 31D Topkhana Rd; s/d Tk 1400/2500, with air-con Tk 1900/2900; ✴@☎) A slightly knocked-about-the-corners hotel, but down a relatively quiet

North Dhaka

lane off the main street. There are clean and spacious rooms, wi-fi and a restaurant. And if you're in need of a traditional shave, there's even a barber shop next to reception.

Hotel Farmgate   HOTEL $$
(Map p40; ☏ 02-911 8538; www.hotelfarmgate. com; 82 West Tejturi Bazar, Farmgate; s/d Tk 1500/2000, with air-con Tk 2200/2500, without bathroom Tk 500/700; 🅰) Small but spotlessly clean rooms are good value in this straightlaced budget hotel. The restaurant on the ground floor is very popular, and there's a rooftop garden with fabulous views. The hotel is a bit isolated from the main sights, but the area is lively, especially come early evening.

Hotel Victory   HOTEL $$$
(Map p40; ☏ 02-935 3088; 30A VIP Rd, Naya Paltan; s/d from Tk 2800/4100; 🅰@🛜) This is a small, informal hotel close to the centre of Dhaka. It's a reliable option rather than a fabulously exciting one, but it's clean, com-

fortable and the free airport transfer and fruit basket are welcome offerings.

🛌 North Dhaka

Banani and Gulshan, in North Dhaka, are two of the city's most upmarket residential districts, although most of the best-value hotels and guesthouses are concentrated in Banani. Prices are higher here than elsewhere, but the streets are quieter and generally more pleasant to wander around. It's also an area where you can find Western-friendly treats such as international cuisine, Internet cafes and modern supermarkets. This is still very much the real Bangladesh, but it's not quite as in-your-face as the mesmerisingly hectic streets of Old Dhaka.

⭐ **Sabrina's**   HOMESTAY $$
(Map p44; ☏ 02-885 6968, 01911-758668; sabhhl @gmail.com; Apt C1, House 137, Rd 4, block A, Banani; dm/r Tk 1800/3500; 🅰🛜) A homely apartment converted into a backpacker hostel by a Chi-

nese expat. There are only four rooms (so make sure you book), two with en suite, one without and another converted into a bunk-bed dormitory. All rooms are lovingly cared for and there's great Chinese home cooking available. Contact in advance as we heard Sabrina's is soon to move location.

★**Viator**   GUESTHOUSE **$$$**
(Map p44; ☑ 01717-925272, 02-987 1434; http://viatorbd.com; House 60, Rd 7A, block H, Banani; s/d Tk 2720/3530; ❋ @) A relaxed and friendly guesthouse, Viator has spotless rooms, which come with bags of space, plenty of natural light and comfortable, quality furniture. Breakfast is included. Meals can be ordered in advance, but it's walking distance from plenty of Gulshan restaurants and cafes. The fair-trade handicrafts shop on the ground floor is perfect for souvenirs.

★**Lakeshore**   HOTEL **$$$**
(Map p44; ☑ 02-885 9991; www.lakeshorehotel.com.bd; House 46, Rd 41; s/d from US$186/230; ❋ @ 🛜 ☒) Everything about this small but top-quality hotel, from the modern glass bathroom fittings to the rooftop pool and the excellent restaurant, is simply magnificent. 'We're security-cleared for the American embassy,' their management proudly told us. If you fit into this price category then it's worth every penny.

★**Executive Inn**   HOTEL **$$$**
(Map p44; ☑ 02-988 5639; www.executiveinnbd.com; 155/A North Gulshan Ave; r from US$200) This brand new hotel markets itself for the business crowd but is tricked out like a funky boutique number. Stylish furniture and wall decorations give a sophisticated vibe, while a wall of fame offers inspirational quotes courtesy of CEOs like Steve Jobs.

It sounds unlikely, but it all hangs together well – something new and exciting for Dhaka's hotel scene.

Hotel Golden Deer   HOTEL **$$$**
(Map p44; ☑ 02-882 6259; www.hotelgoldendeer.com; Rd 35/A, House 31/B; s/d from Tk 5400/7800; ❋) Tucked down a leafy lane is the enigmatically named Golden Deer. This creature offers plush white-tiled rooms, but the attraction are the views of Banani Lake. It's rare to get a cityscape view in Dhaka, so insist on a room at the front when booking.

Tropical Daisy   HOTEL **$$$**
(Map p44; ☑ 02-989 5211; www.tropical-daisy.com; 31/B Road 35, Gulshan II; r Tk 4300) A slightly gloomy lobby belies brighter rooms at this Gulshan hotel tucked away down a quiet street. Accommodation is very spacious, and a couple have small kitchenettes.

Green Goose Guesthouse   GUESTHOUSE **$$$**
(Map p44; ☑ 02-882 1928; ggoose@citech-bd.com; Rd 38; r from Tk 7400) Super-sized rooms with bizarre, but kind of cool, wood panelling over the walls. The little kitchenettes make this a good one for long-stay guests (but avoid the few rooms with internal windows). It's on a quiet side street, with a pleasantly green roof terrace. Free airport transfers are included.

Royal Park   HOTEL **$$$**
(Map p44; ☑ 02-881 5945; www.royalparkbd.com; House 85, Rd 25A, block A, Banani; r from US$140; ❋ @ 🛜 ☒) Refitted from top to toe in 2014, this small business hotel offers good facilities and excellent service. Rates include wi-fi, airport pick-up, as well as use of the gym and pool. The art on the walls tries to confuse you into thinking you're in Renaissance Italy rather than Bangladesh.

DHAKA'S FIVE-STAR HOTELS

The following offer familiar, international-standard, five-star facilities and services. At the time of research, Hilton and Marriott were also rumoured to be planning hotels in Dhaka.

Westin (Map p44; ☑ 02-989 1988; www.starwoodhotels.com/westin; cnr Gulshan Ave & Rd 45; r from US$239; ❋ @ 🛜 ☒) The pick in terms of quality and its Gulshan location.

Radisson Blu Water Garden Hotel (☑ 02-875 4555; www.radissonblu.com/hotel-dhaka; Airport Rd, Dhaka Cantonment; r from US$195; ❋ 🛜 ☒) Best for the airport.

Pan Pacific Sonargaon (Map p40; ☑ 02-814 0401; www.panpacific.com; 107 Kazi Nazrul Islam Ave; r from US$350; ❋ @ 🛜 ☒) Distinguished. Rates drop to around US$150.

Ruposhi Bangla Hotel (Map p40; ☑ 02-833 0001; www.ruposhibanglahotel.com; 1 Minto Rd; r from US$260; ❋ @ 🛜 ☒) Former Sheraton, with plans to reopen as an Intercontinental. Rooms discount to US$150.

Eating

Dhaka's restaurant scene is pretty lively, particularly around Gulshan and Banani. Keep up to date with new openings via **Dhaka Foodies** (http://thedhakafoodies.com).

Old Dhaka

★Al-Razzaque
BANGLADESHI $
(Map p38; 29/1 North-South Rd; mains Tk 80-200; ⊙6am-1am) Wildly popular with the locals, and rightly so, Al-Razzaque does delicious curries, biryanis and Bangladeshi breakfasts, but the pièces de résistance here are the plate-sized flaky rotis, which are absolutely magnificent. No English menu, but some English spoken.

Nana Biryani
BANGLADESHI $
(Map p38; Abul Khairat Rd; biryani Tk 90; ⊙7am-1am) One of those central Dhaka places with no English sign or menu, barely any English spoken, but worth persevering with for some tasty chicken or mutton biryani. They also do some tasty mutton-tikka cakes as a side dish.

Hotel Star
BANGLADESHI $
(Map p38; BCC Rd; meals Tk 130; ⊙6am-2am) Very popular, no-nonsense restaurant with dependable curries and biryanis, though the speciality here is kebabs.

Haji Biryani
BANGLADESHI $$
(Map p38; Kazi Allaudin Rd, Nazira Bazar; biryani Tk 130; ⊙4.30-9.30pm) An Old Dhaka institution, Haji only does one dish – mutton biryani – but does it exceedingly well. This place is tiny, so you'll almost certainly have to share a table: squeeze in, sit down and just wait for your biryani to arrive.

Do as the locals do and drip some lime juice over it before you tuck in, then chomp on a fresh chilly in between mouthfuls. No English sign, but it's next to a mosque, and its green metal shutters are noticeable.

Central Dhaka

Star Hotel & Kebab
BANGLADESHI $
(Map p40; Rd 2, Dhanmondi; mains from Tk 120; ⊙5.30am-midnight) One of the most popular of Dhaka's Star Kebab chains, this one does a mutton leg roast to die for, plus the usual tasty biryanis and curries, and good dhal-and-roti breakfasts. The place is packed out at lunchtimes so you might need to share a table, but don't believe waiters who tell you that they don't have an English menu.

Dhaka Roti House
BANGLADESHI $
(Map p40; off Inner Circular Rd, Naya Paltan; mains around Tk 120; ⊙7am-midnight) A good central choice for kebabs. The beef *sheekh kebab* (grilled meat on a skewer) and the grilled chicken are sumptuous, and the rotis sure aren't bad either. Also does biryani and a few curry dishes. No English sign or menu, but some English spoken. Take the lane down the side of the cinema and it's the first restaurant on your right.

New Café Jheel
BANGLADESHI $
(Map p40; ☎02-955 2255; 18/1 Topkhana Rd; mains Tk 80; ⊙6am-midnight) Thick, fiery curries at this bright and clean favourite – one of several cheap eateries all of a piece along this stretch of road, though few have English signs. For Tk 120 you can get you a curry, rice and naan bread.

Santoor
INDIAN $$$
(Map p40; House 2, cnr Rd 11 & Mirpur Rd; mains from Tk 300; ⊙noon-3pm & 6-10.30pm) Named after an Indian stringed instrument and billed as a 'symphony of dining', Santoor serves up mouth-watering Indian dishes. The tandoor kebabs are good, but the south Indian favourites such as *dhosa* (rice pancake), *idli* (lentil and rice cake), *vada* (fritters) and *uttapam* (thick crepe) are really the dishes that shouldn't be missed.

North Dhaka

★Fakruddin
BANGLADESHI $
(Map p44; 37 Bir Uttam AK Khandakar Rd, Gulshan Circle I; mains Tk 120-200; ⊙noon-10pm) It might sound like sticking our necks out, but we reckon this no-nonsense joint probably serves the best biryani in Dhaka, plateful by massive plateful. Or maybe it's not a gamble at all: this place is always packed by locals who know a good thing when they taste it. There's an English menu.

Star Kebab & Restaurant
BANGLADESHI $
(Map p44; House 15, Rd 17, block C, Banani; mains from Tk 120; ⊙6am-midnight) Part of the hugely popular Star Kebab chain, this is a hit with the local student population, and does dependable, affordable local nosh in a clean, bright and bustling environment. Portions are huge, and it's excellent for Bangladeshi breakfasts. Expect to share a table.

★Dhaba
INDIAN $$
(Map p44; House 104, Rd 12, block E, Banani; mains from Tk 100-300; ⊙11.30am-10.30pm) Indian

street food served in a clean, trendy, air-con restaurant. Everything here is delicious, but the *chaat* (spicy snacks, Tk 50 to Tk 70) are excellent value. Choose a couple of those, washed down with a fresh fruit juice and you won't need a main course.

Roll Xpress
CAFE $$

(Map p44; House 34, Rd 21, Banani; lunch around Tk 200; ☺11am-10.30pm; 🛜) A very pleasant coffee shop in a quiet, refined courtyard. The coffee isn't super-cheap (around Tk 140) but it's good and you can get great light lunches of wraps and south Indian *dhosas* (rice pancakes), while you hang out with the cool kids from the nearby universities checking their social-media profiles.

Tarka
INDIAN $$

(Map p44; mains from Tk 180) A small but chic new Indian restaurant, with modern cream-and-black fittings and an offbeat line in menus made from laser-inscribed wood. Luckily, the food doesn't rely on gimmicks, but offers good quality Indian classics. Try the *paneer* (cheese) dishes – the cheese is made in-house.

Istanbul
TURKISH $$

(Map p44; ☑01981-761401; mains from Tk 200; ☺noon-10.30pm) Head here for a big plate of Turkish kebabs. It's a popular lunchtime spot, and if you're not keen on meat there are plenty of great salads and meze, too. At night, direct yourself towards the scale replica of the Bosphorus Bridge covered in fairy lights – you won't be able to miss it.

Pan Tau
THAI $$$

(Map p44; House 42, Rd 12, block E, Banani; mains from Tk 580; ☺noon-3pm & 6-11pm) Pan Tau has established itself as a trusted place for great Thai curries, a refined atmosphere and excellent service, all washed down with their mocktails. Note that the air-conditioning is frequently set to Antarctic.

Samdado
JAPANESE $$$

(Map p44; ☑02-882 8400; Rd 35, Gulshan II; sushi plates from Tk 800; ☺11am-11pm) Sushi is relatively new in Dhaka, but Samdado is one of the city's oldest Japanese restaurants. The dark wood and bamboo decor here lends an appropriate atmosphere to the freshly prepared sushi and sashimi. The menu also features plenty of noodle and teriyaki dishes, plus a smattering of Korean and Thai standards.

★ Holey Artisan Bakery
BISTRO $$$

(Map p44; ☑01969-200200; www.holeybread.com; House 5, Rd 79, Gulshan II; mains Tk 600-1200, sandwiches Tk 600) Upscale bistro with a pleasant lawn area that takes its name from the (Italian-run) artisanal bakery on site. If there's better bread available in Dhaka, we'd like to know about it. Prices attract the well-heeled and international crowd, enjoying stone-baked pizzas, lovely salads and classy sandwiches. There's also a shop for breads and cakes to take home.

Bamboo Shoot
CHINESE $$$

(Map p44; RM Centre, 2nd fl, Gulshan Ave; mains Tk 650-900; ☺noon-3.30pm & 6-10.30pm) Bamboo Shoot is Dhaka's most reliable outpost for authentic Chinese cuisine and well worth a splurge. It's in the same building as **Agora supermarket** (Map p44; RM Centre, ground fl, Gulshan Ave; ☺9am-8pm) – a useful landmark for helping rickshaw drivers navigate. Sing your heart out afterwards in one of the karaoke rooms.

★ Spaghetti Jazz
ITALIAN $$$

(Map p44; ☑02-882 2062; 43 North Gulshan II; mains from Tk 640; ☺12.30-3pm & 6.30-10.30pm) A stylish and intimate setting for probably the best pizza and pasta you'll find anywhere in Bangladesh. The antipasti and fish and meat courses are also strongly recommended. The entrance is tucked away a bit – it's on the back road behind Gulshan II Circle.

🍷 Drinking & Nightlife

Apart from top-end hotels, which have hideously expensive bars, and the embassy clubs, which you need to be invited to by members, Dhaka's only drinking options are a handful of dark, seedy, smoky bars, frequented almost entirely by men. They're an experience to visit, rather than a place for a pleasurable drink, but can be fun if you get a group together. Drinks are mostly cans of beer plus spirits such as whisky, tequila and vodka. They all do food, too (they are, strictly speaking, restaurants). All are closed on Fridays.

Cafe Mango
CAFE

(Map p40; Rd 5, off Green Rd, Dhanmondi; ☺10am-10pm; 🛜) One of the coolest cafes in town. Trendy deco in an old house and excellent coffee (from Tk 100) and scrummy Western food.

Blue Moon Recreation Club BAR
(Map p44; 3rd floor, 67/D Rd 11, Banani; ⊙11am-11pm Sat-Thu) Extremely smoky venue modelling itself on the sports-bar experience, although the most recreation going on here is ordering another whisky. The Blue Moon refers to the surfeit of neon lighting. Food is available, and there's often live music of sorts on Wednesday and Sunday nights.

Coffee World COFFEE
(Map p44; House 98, Rd 11, Banani; ⊙9am-midnight; 🛜) Part of a Dhaka chain, this small coffee shop is bright, comfortable, does OK coffee (from Tk 100), reasonable slices of cake, and opens earlier than most.

Sakura BAR
(Map p40; off Kazi Nazrul Islam Ave; ⊙noon-3pm & 5.30-10.30pm Sat-Thu) Dark, smoky and women-free, but popular. Local beers from Tk 20 and imported beers from Tk 250. Located on 2nd floor of a small handicrafts market opposite Ruposhi Bangla Hotel (p47). After trading hours, you have to enter from around the back of the market.

Club Gelato CAFE
(Map p44; House 50, Rd 11, Banani; coffee from Tk 100; ⊙10.30am-11.30pm) Club Gelato is a good replica of an Italian cafe, serving posh coffee and possibly the best ice cream in Bangladesh (from Tk 120) – real gelato!

☆ Entertainment

The best place to find what's on is through the listings website **Dhaka Happenings** (www.dhakahappenings.wordpress.com).

Although *hadudu* (traditional Bengali wrestling, also known as *kabaddi*) is the national sport, it's cricket that the locals go crazy for. The Dhaka Dynamites, the city's Twenty20 Bangladesh Premier League team, plays at the **Sher-e-Bangla Stadium** (📞01714-546965; Mirpur), which also hosts test internationals. Visit www.bdcricteam.com for more information.

★ Jatra Biroti LIVE MUSIC
(Map p44; 📞02-890 0840; http://jatrabd.com/jatra-biroti; 60 Kemal Ataturk Ave, Banani; ⊙Thu-Sun) Dhaka's coolest music and arts lounge, Jagra Biroti hosts regular live music and spoken word events. Brightly painted walls, soft lights and billowing fabrics create a magical caravan atmosphere. Thursday nights typically feature folk music, Fridays are open-mic and Saturdays are 'electro-acoustic'. A small restaurant is also planned for the venue. A real Dhaka gem.

Shilpakala Academy LIVE PERFORMANCE
(Map p40; 📞02-956 2836; www.shilpakala academy.org; 14/3 Segunbagicha, Ramna) The best place in Dhaka for cultural performances is Shilpakala Academy, the national academy of fine art and the performing arts.

Star Cineplex CINEMA
(Map p40; 📞02-913 8260; www.cineplexbd.com; tickets Tk 150-250) On the top floor of the massive shopping centre Bashundhara City (p50), this cinema has English-language options for the latest Hollywood blockbusters, as well as the best in Bollywood.

🛍 Shopping

There are very few things you can buy in Bangladesh that you can't buy in Dhaka, and Dhaka is certainly the place with the largest selection of Bangladeshi souvenirs. The **Bashundhara City** (Map p40; www.bashun dhara-city.com; Pantha Path; ⊙10am-8pm) mall is the biggest and most modern shopping centre in the city.

Aranya CLOTHING
(Map p44; 60 Kemal Ataturk Ave; ⊙10am-10pm) Traditional hand-woven Bangladeshi garments of superior quality and design. Certainly not the cheapest, but definitely among the most stylish.

Kumudini CLOTHING & HANDICRAFTS
(Map p44; 74 Gulshan Ave; ⊙10am-8pm) Three floors of top-quality traditional Bengali clothing and handicrafts, including some lovely children's clothes and toys, fabulous embroidery as well as a variety of jute products.

Banga Bazar MARKET
(Map p38; College Rd; ⊙closed Fri morning) Large, hectic clothing market with seconds, and factory overruns that would otherwise have been heading for European and American brands, providing plenty of scope for bargain hunting for the persistent fashionista.

★ Jatra HANDICRAFTS
(Map p44; 60 Kemal Ataturk, Banani; ⊙10am-10pm) Charming folk handicrafts and clothes with a funky modern twist. You'll find the best brightly painted toy rickshaws here, and if you've time to order in advance you can even get yourself inserted into your own lurid Dhallywood film poster like the ones

CITY ON THE EDGE

Dhaka is one of the world's megacities. It has an estimated population of nearly 17 million, and sucks people in from across the country with a seemingly inexhaustible appetite: over 2000 people move to the city every day. Many of the arriving migrants are leaving the country due to loss of farm land through salination of their soil (by rising sea levels) combined with increased seasonal flooding (caused by the melting Himalayan glaciers that give Bangladesh's rivers life). Dhaka also finds itself increasingly prone to flooding and – ironically – water shortages due to overburdened infrastructure. The UN has predicted that by 2030 Dhaka will have a population of 27 million people, putting the city very much in the front line of climate-change challenges.

that decorate the counter – a unique souvenir of Bangladesh!

Aarong CLOTHING, HANDICRAFTS
(Map p44; www.aarong.com; Gulshan-Tejgaon Link Rd, Gulshan I; ⊙10am-8pm, closed Sun) A good place for all your Bangladesh souvenirs under one roof. Aarong is the biggest name in quality Bengali clothing and handicrafts, and is the retail branch of the Bangladesh Rural Advancement Committee (BRAC), which aims to create employment for economically and socially marginalised people through the promotion of traditional Bangladeshi handicrafts. There's another branch in **Mirpur** (Map p40; www.aarong.com; 1/1, block A, Mirpur Rd; ⊙10am-8pm, closed Thu).

Folk International HANDICRAFTS
(Map p44; www.folkinternational.webs.com; House 19, Rd 108, Gulshan; ⊙10am-8pm) A non-profit handicrafts centre, offering a good selection of souvenirs.

Words 'N' Pages BOOKS
(Map p44; Rd 7, Gulshan I; ⊙10am-8pm) This place has decent stock of English-language books and magazines, and a nice cafe to relax in after browsing.

First Chain Bookshop BOOKS
(Map p40; www.pbschain.com; Shantinagar Rd, Naya Paltan; ⊙10am-9pm) Large bookshop with good range of English-language books, especially kids books, and music CDs. It has a small cafe and juice bar, and free wi-fi. You can buy online, too.

New Market MARKET
(Map p40; Mirpur Rd; ⊙closed afternoon Mon & all Tue) Dhaka's largest market, and that's saying something. Sells pretty much anything you can imagine. Keen shoppers and browsers could lose a day here (and there are plenty of food concessions to restore flagging spirits).

Bangshal Rd RICKSHAWS
(Map p38; Bicycle St; ⊙Sat-Thu) This street in Old Dhaka, and the adjoining Kazi Alauddin Rd, is the place to buy rickshaw parts, rickshaw art or even rickshaws themselves. The art is painted on thin strips of tin (later attached to the back of rickshaws), which can be rolled up to fit nicely inside most suitcases or rucksacks. Expect to pay around Tk 200. Bargaining is required, of course.

ⓘ Information

DANGERS & ANNOYANCES

Considering its massive size, Dhaka is a remarkably safe city and few travellers experience any problems in terms of crime (although you should always take extra care of your belongings in overly crowded places such as markets and train and bus stations).

The biggest danger is road safety. Road accidents are all too common and you should be extra vigilant when crossing the city's hectic streets. In fact, in Dhaka you should even have your wits about you when walking along pavements – potholes are not uncommon, nor are low-hanging electricity cables.

One major annoyance, of course, is air pollution, which can be horrendous, particularly if you are prone to allergies.

Hartals (strikes) are common. Violence at this time isn't unknown, so it's sensible to avoid demonstrations wherever possible.

INTERNET ACCESS

Wif-fi is almost standard in any cafe or midrange and above hotel. In addition, there are the following:

Cyber Cafe (Map p44; Golden Plaza Market, Gulshan Ave, Gulshan Circle II; per hr Tk 40; ⊙10am-8pm) Next door to SEL Nibash Hotel.

Cyber Cafe (Map p40; Green Rd, Dhanmondi; per hr Tk 30; ⊙9am-11pm) Inside a small electronics market, just off Gulshan Ave.

E-Park Cyber Cafe (Map p40; Toyenbee Circular Rd, Motijheel; per hr Tk 25; ⊙10am-9pm) A short walk from the main train station.

SM Cyber Cafe (Map p38; Bangshal Rd, Old Dhaka; per hr Tk 40; ⊙10am-11pm) Up a narrow staircase to the 2nd floor.

MEDICAL SERVICES

Apollo Hospital (☑ ambulance 01714-090000, ambulance 02-840 1661, appointments 02-884 5242; www.apollodhaka.com; Plot 81, block E, Bashundhara Residential Area, off Pragati Ave) Probably the best hospital in Dhaka.

International Centre for Diarrhoeal Disease Research in Bangladesh Hospital (ICDDRB; Map p44; ☑ 01730-019695, 02-989 9620; www.icddrb.org/clinic; 68 Shahid Tajuddein Ahmed Sharani, Mohakhali; ⊙ 8.30am-5pm Sun-Thu) The travellers' clinic here is excellent for travel health advice and travel-related issues such as vaccinations. A consultation costs Tk 1000 (Tk 4000 if you have medical insurance). You should make an appointment, but if you have an emergency, such as needing a rabies jab, they will see you on the spot.

Shaheed Suhrawardy Medical College and Hospital (Map p40; ☑ 02-308 0019; www.suhrawardyhospital.gov.bd; Sher-e Bangla Nagar) Medical college hospital, with an emergency department.

MONEY

For money-changing services, try **HSBC** – with branches in Chowk Bazar (Map p38; ☑ 02-966 0547; www.hsbc.com.bd; Water Works Rd; ⊙10am-4pm & 6-8pm Sun-Thu, 2-4pm Sat), Gulshan (Map p44; cnr Gulshan Ave & Rd 5, Gulshan Circle I; ⊙10am-4pm & 6-8pm Sun-Thu, 2-4pm Sat) and Motijheel (Map p40; Motijheel Rd; ⊙10am-4pm & 6-8pm Sun-Thu, 2-4pm Sat) – or **Standard Chartered Bank** (Map p40; ☑ 02-833 2272; www.standardchartered.com/bd; Motijheel Rd, Motjheel; ⊙10am-4pm & 6-8pm Sun-Thu, 2-4pm Sat). There are also lots of private moneychangers on Gulshan II Circle.

Most ATMs accept foreign bank cards, including the following:

AB Bank ATM (Map p40; Rd 16, Dhanmondi)

AB Bank ATM (Map p40; Green Rd, Farmgate)

AB Bank ATM (Map p40; Kamalapur Rd, Motijheel)

AB Bank ATM (Map p40; DIT Ave, Naya Paltan)

AB Bank ATM (Map p40; Rd 2, Cantonment)

AB Bank ATM (Map p38; North-South Rd, Nazira Bazar)

AB Bank ATM (Map p38; Islampur Rd, Sadarghat)

HSBC ATM (Map p44; North Ave, Gulshan II)

HSBC ATM (Map p44; Rd 11, Banani)

POST

DHL (Map p40; ☑ 02-955 3511; 93 Motijheel Rd; ⊙9am-9pm)

FedEx (Map p40; ☑ 02-956 5113; 95 Motijheel Rd; ⊙9am-10.30pm)

Main Post Office (Map p40; ☑ 02-955 5533; cnr Abdul Ghani & North-South Rds; ⊙9am-6pm Sat-Thu) Near Baitul Mukarram Mosque. Parcel-wallahs (who sew up large parcels) can be found in a small shelter on the left of the building.

ⓘ Getting There & Away

AIR

Dhaka is served by numerous international airlines, including **Emirates** (Map p40; ☑ 02-989 2801; www.emirates.com; SA Tower, Road 134, block SE (A), Gulshan South Ave, Gulshan I) and **Singapore Airlines** (Map p44; ☑ 02-985 1881; www.singaporeair.com; Casablanca, 5th flr, 114 Gulshan Ave, Gulshan II). Domestic routes are served by such companies as **Biman Bangladesh Airlines** (Map p40; ☑ 02-956 0151; www.bimanairlines.com; Dilkusha II Circle, off Motijheel Rd, Motijheel; ⊙9am-5pm) and the reliable **Regent Airlines** (Map p44; ☑ 02-895 3003; www.flyregent.com; SA Tower, Bir Uttam AK Khandakar, Gulshan Circle I). Destinations include Chittagong, Cox's Bazar, Sylhet, Rajshahi and Jessore.

BOAT

You're supposed to book 1st-class Rocket (paddle-wheel) tickets at the **Bangladesh Inland Waterway Transport Corporation head office** (BIWTC; Map p40; ☑ 02-891 4771, 02-955 9779; 141-143 Motijheel; ⊙ Sun-Thu 9am-4.30pm) in Motijheel. Second-class tickets should be bought at the much-harder-to-find **Badamtoli office** (☑ 02-739 0691; ⊙8am-4pm) close to the **Badamtoli boat terminal** (Map p38), although with a smile and some persistence you may be able to persuade the guys at the head office to sell you 2nd-class tickets, too. Deck-class tickets are bought on board, but are hard to come by for the overnight trips which start in Dhaka.

The Rocket departs at 6pm from the **Sadarghat Boat Terminal** (Map p38; Ahsanullah Rd) every day except Friday. Note that currently, the boat only goes as far as Morrelganj, not all the way to Khulna.

Private ferries, known as launches, also leave the Sadarghat Boat Terminal daily. Tickets are just bought from the boat in question. Long-distance trips leave in the evening, from around 7pm, and travel overnight. Shorter trips leave throughout the day.

BUS

The bus system in Bangladesh seems mind-bogglingly chaotic at first, but you soon get used to it. Dhaka has several bus stations serving different destinations, each made up of a series of ticket counters selling tickets to different destinations. None has signs in English. To find the right counter, just mention the name of your destination to the first few people you stumble across, and you'll soon be ushered towards the correct ticket counter or, at smaller stations, towards the bus itself. Note: a ticket counter is sometimes just a wooden table.

It's often the case that a number of companies run buses on the route you want, and ticket prices vary slightly from company to company.

Also note that bus stations are generally referred to as 'bus stands'.

Gabtali Bus Stand

Dhaka's largest bus station, Gabtali is a madhouse; be on guard for pickpockets (particularly after dark), but in general people are very friendly and helpful. Buses leave regularly on the following routes from around 7am until at least 5pm. The following fares are shown as non-AC/AC.

Barisal Tk 450/650, six to nine hours
Bogra Tk 380/500, five hours
Dhamrai Tk 50, one hour
Dinajpur Tk 600/1400, 10 hours
Jessore Tk 480/1000, seven hours
Khulna Tk 575/1100, eight hours
Rajshahi Tk 450/1000, six hours
Rangpur Tk 500/1000, seven hours

Sayedabad Bus Stand

Sayedabad (Hatkhola Rd) is a huge station used mostly for accessing places to the east of Dhaka. All of the main coach companies have offices in and around this station, so it's tempting to pay a bit extra for more legroom. Destinations include:

Comilla Tk 200 (non-AC only), three hours, 5.30am to 10.30pm
Chittagong Tk 480/1250 (non-AC/AC), six hours, 5am to midnight
Sylhet Tk 470/950 (non-AC/AC), five hours, 5am to 11.30pm

Gulistan (Fulbaria) Bus Stand

Hectic **Gulistan** (Map p38; Gulistan Crossing, Nawabpur Rd), just north of Old Dhaka, is basically just a series of roadside bus stops. Destinations include Sonargaon (Tk 40, one hour).

Mohakhali Bus Stand

Mohakhali (Map p44; Mogh Bazar Rd) serves places in north Dhaka division. If you take a rickshaw from Banani to here (Tk 40), you'll have to walk the last stretch, along Mogh Bazar Rd. All buses are non-AC. Destinations include:

Birisiri Tk 300, five to six hours, 7.30am
Mymensingh Tk 220, four hours, 6am to 9pm
Tangail Tk 150, two hours, 6am to 8pm

BRTC International Bus Terminal

This small and orderly **international bus terminal** (Map p40; ☎ 02-935 3882; Kamalapur Rd) has two daily morning buses to Kolkata (Tk 1700, 11 hours). It's best to book a couple of days in advance if you can. Also has daily buses to Siliguri (Tk 1500, 10 hours) and thrice-weekly buses to Agartala (Tk 350, four hours, Monday, Wednesday and Thursday).

COACH

The major coach companies have offices dotted around the city, but two places where there's a concentration of them are on the fringes of Sayedabad bus stand and along **Toyenbee Circular Rd** (Map p40), just north of Motijheel. Expect to pay about twice as much as for a normal bus, and three or four times as much if you opt for air-con. The most popular companies are

SELECTED TRAINS FROM DHAKA

DESTINATION	TRAIN NAME	DEPARTS	ARRIVES	FARE (1ST SEAT/ SHUVON)	OFF DAY
Chittagong	Mahanagar Provati	7.40am	3.40pm	Tk 425/320	none
Chittagong	Chittagong Mail	10.30pm	8.10am	Tk 635/425/320*	none
Dinajpur	Ekota Ex	10am	7.40pm	Tk 855/570/360*	Tue
Khulna	Sundarban Ex	6.20am	5.20pm	Tk 620/390	Wed
Khulna	Chittra Ex	8.30am	6.20pm	Tk 920/620/390*	Mon
Mymensingh	Balaka Commuter	10.40am	2.50pm	Tk 175/110	none
Rajshahi	Silkcity Ex	2.40pm	9.05pm	Tk 725/315	Sun
Sylhet	Parabat Ex	6.40am	1.40pm	Tk 395/245	Tue
Sylhet	Upaban Ex	9.50pm	5.30am	Tk 590/395/245*	Wed

*1st berth/1st seat/shuvon

Green Line (always air-con), Soudia, Hanif and Shohagh Paribahan, but there are many others.

TRAIN

Dhaka's main train station, **Kamalapur** (www.railway.gov.bd; Off Outer Circular Rd, Kamalapur), is relatively well organised and easy to manage – especially if you've just come from India! Many trains to and from here also stop at the smaller Banani and Airport train stations, both of which are more convenient if you're staying in North Dhaka.

Tickets are sold up to five days in advance and sell out quickly, so it's worth trying to buy them as soon as they're released. You can buy tickets in advance from Banani train station ticket office (Dhaka–Mymensingh Highway, Banani) even if your train won't be stopping there.

Most Chittagong trains go via Akhaura (1st seat/shuvon Tk 195/125, two to three hours), for the India border, and Comilla (1st seat/shuvon Tk 250/160, three to four hours). All Sylhet trains go via Srimangal (1st berth/1st seat/shuvon Tk 445/295/185, five hours). All Khulna trains go via Jessore (1st berth/1st seat/shuvon Tk 840/560/350, eight hours).

Twice a week (Wednesday and Friday, 8.10am), there is a direct *Maitree Express* train to Kolkata (1st class/AC chair/non-AC chair Tk 1800/1100/650, 13 hours), in India. The train leaves from **Dhaka Cantonment train station** (Tongi Diversion Rd), but you have to buy your tickets at a designated **ticket counter** (◷ 9am-5pm) at Kamalapur Train Station. You'll need your passport and copy of Indian visa.

🛈 Getting Around

Dhaka's traffic is famously terrible. Raised expressways are being built to ease congestion, but don't expect the traffic jams to ease any time soon. Always plan on journeys taking longer than expected.

TO/FROM HAZRAT SHAHJALAL INTERNATIONAL AIRPORT

Hazrat Shahjalal International Airport (☏ 02-819 4350; www.caab.gov.bd) is 20km north of the centre of Dhaka. Top-end hotels often include airport pick-up in their room rates. Most midrange hotels will have a pick-up service for a charge (expect at least Tk 1500 to a hotel in Banani).

It's cheaper, of course, to take a taxi. There's a fixed-rate taxi booth just outside the airport exit. Expect to pay between Tk 800 and Tk 1000, depending on where you are heading. If you walk out to the car park or beyond, you'll be able to negotiate slightly cheaper fares yourself.

It's cheaper still to catch a CNG (auto-rickshaw). Expect to pay Tk 250 to Tk 300 to Banani (North Dhaka), and about twice that to Motijheel (Central Dhaka). Your bargaining position will increase if you walk further out of the airport towards the main road, where there will be more CNGs to choose from.

Local buses do run from the main road into the city, and are very cheap (Tk 10), but are extremely difficult to negotiate for non-Bengali speakers, and are always packed.

Cycle-rickshaws aren't allowed at the airport or on the main highway leading to it.

BUS

Cheaper than cheap, local buses have no English signs, and their numbering is in Bengali. They are always overcrowded, so boarding between major bus stops is no mean feat. Fares vary, but around Dhaka you rarely need to pay more than Tk 10.

CNG

Auto-rickshaws run on compressed natural gas and hence are known as CNGs, or otherwise as baby taxis. All have meters, but it's rare to find a driver willing to use one, so get ready for some hard bargaining. Travel by CNG can be hairy – it seems no gap is too small for a CNG to squeeze through! Here's a rough guide to the sort of fares you can expect:

Airport to Banani Tk 250
Airport to Motijheel Tk 300
Banani to Gabtali bus stand Tk 200
Banani to Gulistan Crossing Tk 140
Banani to Sadarghat Tk 200

RICKSHAW

Dhaka's fantastically colourful rickshaws (which in Bangladesh means cycle-rickshaws) are a tourist attraction in their own right and you should go for a spin in them as often as you can. You will find them everywhere (there are around 500,000 of them on the streets on any one day), and when traffic is crowded (as it usually is) they're not much slower than anything else that moves. Rickshaws are restricted from moving right across the city by traffic regulations and sheer distances, so you can usually travel only short distances, within a particular neighbourhood. Prices are negotiated. We find that Tk 10 per kilometre is normally about right.

TAXI

Two types of taxis operate on the roads of Dhaka. The yellow Navana taxis are more spacious, have air-con and are usually cleaner than their black counterparts, but you pay for the difference. Meters in yellow taxis clock more quickly and at a higher rate than the black taxis, but this is often irrelevant because most drivers are reluctant to use the meters. Dhaka also has a radio taxi service called **Toma Taxi** (☏ 01866-667070; www.tomataxi.com.bd), which has about 200-odd cabs plying the greater Dhaka area.

Dhaka Division

Best Places for History

➡ Sonargaon (p57)

➡ Mymensingh (p59)

Best Landscapes

➡ China Clay Hills (p62)

➡ Someswari River by Birisiri (p62)

➡ Sonargaon (p57)

Why Go?

Enveloping the city of Dhaka, and including some destinations that make great day trips from the capital, Dhaka division stretches for more than 250km from south to north, reaching right up to the border with the Garo Hills in India.

It's a rural wonderland, comprising some 25,000 villages, and much of the region is given over to radiant rice paddies, filling your vision with more hues of green than you ever knew existed. A smattering of wonderfully romantic, slowly decaying ruins also lends a historic air to the region, but it's the land in the far north of Dhaka division that has perhaps the greatest pull. Here, the green carpet of paddy fields gives way to dappled forests, great rivers and hilly panoramas, and the indigenous culture of the Garo people awaits the more adventurous traveller.

When to Go
Mymensingh

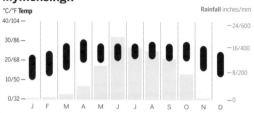

Oct–Mar The dry season means off-the-beaten-track trips in the far north.

Jun & Jul Dhamrai has chariot-pulling during the Rath Jatra festival.

Jun–Sep Monsoon brings boggy roads, but the landscape is a sight in itself.

Dhaka Division Highlights

1 Sonargaon (p57)
Exploring charmingly dilapidated ruined mansions, little-visited ancient mosques and a stunning rajbari-turned-museum in Bangladesh's one-time capital.

2 Birisiri (p62) Plugging yourself into the Adivasi way

of life at this remote forested village.

3 China Clay Hills (p62)
Hiking, boating or riding a rickshaw to the small but stunning turquoise lake by the hills.

4 Mymensingh (p59)
Wandering the old-town

market streets and enjoying tree-shaded riverside walks in this laidback town.

5 Dhamrai (p58)
Meeting the craftspeople at the unusual metalcraft workshops of this Hindu village.

Sonargaon

Sonargaon was the eastern capital of Bengal at various times in history. It slipped into decline when Muslim rulers decided to move their capital to Dhaka in the 17th century, and is now little more than a couple of villages with a scattering of ruins. It makes an excellent day drip from Dhaka, though, combining countryside, culture, archaeology and adventure in one easily accessible bundle.

◉ Sights

Painam Nagar   RUIN
(admission Tk 100) Constructed almost entirely between 1895 and 1905 on a small segment of the ancient capital city, the tiny settlement of Painam Nagar consists of a single street, lined with around 50 (now dilapidated) mansions built by wealthy Hindu merchants. The once-elegant town is busy fighting a losing battle with nature, and with every passing year the trees and vines drape themselves a little further over the decaying houses, creating a delightful ghost-town quality where the buildings appear to hang like exotic fruits from the trees.

Many of the original merchant owners fled to India at the time of the Partition, leaving their elegant homes in the care of poor tenants, who did nothing to maintain them. Most of the remaining owners pulled out during the anti-Hindu riots of 1964, which led to the 1965 Indo–Pakistan War. Despite the rot, a few people continue to live in some of the houses and their bright shades add a technicolour tint to the village.

Sadarbari   MUSEUM
(Folk-art Museum; admission Tk 100; ◎ 9am-5pm Fri-Tue) Built in 1901, this stunning rajbari (Raj-era mansion) is an appropriate building for a folk-art museum, and was undergoing a massive renovation at the time of research. When finished it will be full of handicrafts from the 17th century onwards. Currently, a new building nearby houses the collection, which is strong on carved wood, pottery, jewellery and even bed-sized treasure chests.

Your ticket gives entry to both museums and the grounds, where the rajbari's beautiful water-soaked gardens are another highlight, and perfect picnic territory.

Sadarbari is a popular destination for visitors from Dhaka, and throngs at weekends. It takes about 30 minutes to walk here from where the bus drops you off. Rickshaws (Tk 10 to Tk 20) are also widely available.

Goaldi Mosque   MOSQUE
Built in 1519, and now virtually hidden behind thick bamboo groves and clusters of mango and jackfruit trees, the graceful, single-domed Goaldi Mosque is the most impressive of the few extant monuments of the original capital city. It's a fine example

BANGLADESH'S GOLDEN CITY

The ancient capital of Sonargaon (or 'Golden City' in Hindi) flourished as the region's major inland port and centre of commerce during the pre-Muslim period. By the 13th century it was the Hindu seat of power. With the Muslim invasion and the arrival of the sultan of Elhi in 1280, its importance magnified as the region's de facto Islamic capital. Some 42 years later, the first independent sultan of East Bengal, Fakhruddin Mubarak Shah, officially established his capital in Sonargaon.

For the next 270 years, Sonargaon, known as the 'Seat of the Mighty Majesty', prospered as the capital of East Bengal, and the Muslim rulers minted their money here. An envoy from the Chinese emperor visited Sultan Ghiyasuddin Azam Shah's splendid court here in 1406, and he observed that Sonargaon was a walled city with broad streets, great mausoleums and bazaars where business of all kinds was transacted. In 1585, famous traveller Ralph Fitch noted that it was an important centre for the manufacture and export of *kantha* (traditional indigo-dyed muslin), the finest in all of India. Ancient Egyptian mummies were reportedly wrapped in this *kantha* exported from Bengal.

When the invading Mughals ousted the sultans, they regarded Sonargaon's location along the region's major river as too exposed to Portuguese and Mogh pirates from the Rakhine coast of Burma. In 1608 they moved the capital to Dhaka, thus initiating Sonargaon's long decline into oblivion. Yet its legendary fame for incredibly fine muslin fabric continued undiminished until foreign competition from the British (and their import quotas) ruined the trade.

Sonargaon

Sonargaon

◉ **Sights**

of pre-Mughal architecture and one of the country's oldest surviving mosques.

Few people know about the mosque (including some rickshaw-riders), so it's probably best to take the lovely 15-minute walk through farmland from Painam Nagar; just keep asking for 'Goaldi Masjid'.

 Eating

If you don't bring your own picnic, you can grab lunch from any one of a cluster of roadside restaurants opposite Sadarbari. Expect to pay between Tk 100 and Tk 200 for a simple rice-and-curry meal.

Kolapata Restaurant   BANGLADESHI $$
(opposite Mograpara bus station; mains Tk 100-350) One of the few decent dining options in Sonargaon, Kolapata serves up healthy portions of Bangladeshi curries, biryanis and

bhajis (vegetable dishes), in neat and clean surroundings. It's next to the flyover opposite the bus station – look for the banana leaf logo that gives this restaurant its name.

ⓘ Getting There & Away

Buses (Tk 40, one hour) leave frequently from Dhaka's Sayedabad bus stand and drop you at the Mograpara **bus station** at the crossroads on the main Dhaka–Chittagong Hwy, from where rickshaw-wallahs will be keen to show you to the sights. The area also makes for pleasant walking.

Dhamrai

This predominantly Hindu village with a few surviving metalcraft workshops makes an unusual day trip from Dhaka and is particularly rewarding during major Hindu festivals. The main strip is a busy market street, but it also contains a dozen or so extravagant century-old houses built by the wealthy Hindu families who once lived here.

Dhamrai is a good place to experience the Hindu festival of Rath Jatra (every June or July according to the Hindu calendar). At the far end of town and in the middle of the road sits the **Jagannath Chariot**, a multi-storey chariot adorned with painted images from Hindu mythology, which is paraded down the street during the festival.

Buses to Dhamrai pass the **National Martyrs' Memorial** (Jatiyo Smriti Saudha; pronounced 'jat-ee-yo shmree-tee shod-oh'), a tapering 50m-high memorial to the millions who died in the struggle for independence and which is housed in well-kept gardens. The memorial is on the outskirts of the industrial town of Savar.

◉ Sights

Dhamrai Metal Crafts Workshop   WORKSHOP
(☏ 01713-003136; Main Rd) The most accessible of three workshops in the village that have revived the ancient lost-wax technique of making brass and bronze statues. The owner, Sukanta Banik, speaks excellent English and is happy to give visitors a guided tour of his family's beautiful old house and its fascinating workshop. There is no pressure to buy anything, but there are a number of objects on sale that make excellent souvenirs.

Just beyond the workshop is an alleyway on your left, which leads to the village's principal Hindu temple, built close to an ancient Shiva temple, which is now being swallowed by the undergrowth.

Eating

Dhamrai has a few places in the centre of town where travellers can get a biryani in surroundings of somewhat dubious hygiene.

ℹ Getting There & Away

Buses (Tk 35, one hour) leave frequently from Dhaka's Gabtali bus stand and drop you at a junction on the main road. Turn right (north) here and walk for a few hundred metres until you reach Dhamrai village. Keep walking straight to get to the workshop. Buses between Dhamrai and the National Martyrs' Memorial cost Tk 5.

Mymensingh

☎ 091 / POP 407,800

A leafy city built on the banks of the mighty Brahmaputra River, Mymensingh has a sprinkling of Raj-era buildings and one of the most interesting old quarters in the country. It also acts as an ideal launchpad for off-the-beaten-track trips further north – a rarely visited region dotted with Garo villages and swathed in lush, green landscapes.

◉ Sights

Old Town Bazaars   MARKET

The original alleyway-riddled core of the town, located between the train station and the waterfront, is a fascinating place in which to get lost. The lanes are filled with market stalls selling all manner of goods; keep an eye open for the gold workshops where people hammer down minuscule gold pieces found in the riverbed in order to make jewellery. The town has a large Hindu minority and there are several noticeable Hindu shrines in the old town area.

Riverbank Parks   PARK

(River Rd) The thin stretch of parkland on the waterfront at the western edge of town makes up one of the most enjoyable public spaces in this part of Bangladesh. Late every afternoon, locals head here to loll about in the shade of trees and watch boats crisscross the river. Cricket matches are held in the fields just behind the parkland.

Should you want a closer look at the other side of the river, one of the small wooden boats will take you over (Tk 2). From the far bank, set off across this rural scene towards one of the many little villages, whose locals are likely to be very welcoming. It's a perfect setting in which to create your own adventure.

Mymensingh Rajbari   HISTORIC BUILDING

Built between 1905 and 1911, this well-kept former mansion in the city centre is now occupied by an organisation that trains female teachers, but much of the original structure remains. An ornamental marble fountain lies just beyond the arched gateway entrance. Behind the main building is the Jal-Tungi, a small two-storey bathhouse once used as the women's bathing pavilion.

You can politely ask the guard for admittance to the grounds, but it's doubtful whether you'll be granted a glimpse of the building's interior.

Botanical Gardens   GARDENS

(বোটানিকাল গার্ডেন; admission Tk 5; ☺ 9am-5pm)
Three or four kilometres east of town, next

ADIVASI FOCUS: THE GAROS

Name They call themselves the A-chik Mandi (literally 'hill people'), although most outsiders refer to them as Garos.

Population Around two million in total, of which around 100,000 to 200,000 are thought to live in Bangladesh.

Current region Largely in and around the Garo Hills of India.

Original homeland The Garo are thought to have migrated from the Tibetan plateau more than 2000 years ago.

Religion Thanks to the efforts of 19th-century missionaries, most Garos are now Christians, though they often maintain aspects of a traditional belief system known as Sangshareq.

Language A-chick in India, A-beng in Bangladesh. A surprisingly large number of Garo people also speak English.

Unusual fact The Garo have a matrilineal society – titles and land ownership are passed down through the women of the family, and when a man marries he moves into his wife's house. They are not matriarchal; men still tend to govern Garo communities and manage the properties that the women own.

Mymensingh

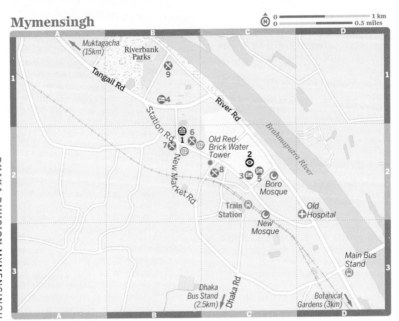

Mymensingh

⊙ Sights

🛏 Sleeping

✗ Eating

to the Agriculture and Fisheries College, are these large and peaceful gardens. Well laid out, although not particularly well maintained, they make a decent place to relax on a bench with a book. You can also get boats across the river from here. A rickshaw from the town centre costs around Tk 40.

🛏 Sleeping

Mymensingh doesn't have an enormous array of sleeping options, but enough for it to be a worthwhile base.

Nirala Rest House   HOTEL $

(☑ 091-67384; 67 Chotto Bazar; s/d from Tk 300/600) A basic but acceptable budget option, Nirala has rooms that are small but clean enough and that come with their own small attached bathrooms (squat loo only). Coming from the train station, take the first of the two roads on your left opposite the Boro mosque. The hotel is then on your left. Limited English.

Hotel Mustafiz International   HOTEL $$

(☑ tel/fax   091-63870;   www.mymensinghhotel mustafizintl.com; 6/3B Gangadas Guha Rd; s/d Tk 1100/1400, with air-con Tk 1580/2200; ❄ 🛜) The Mustafiz International does a good job of offering reliable midrange business-style accommodation to the Mymensingh scene. It has a conference room but some bedrooms are large enough to host meetings in – and even throw in a sofa or two.

Hotel Amir International   HOTEL $$

(☑ 01711-167948, 091-51500; www.hotelamirbd. com; Palika Shopping Centre, 46 Station Rd; s/d TK 1150/1440; ❄ 🛜) Lots of shiny tiled floors and wood-panelled walls make this a neat and welcoming place to stay. The clean rooms come with wi-fi and satellite TV. The manager speaks some English. A comfortable and trustworthy choice.

Eating

The road leading from the train station toward the riverfront and Boro Mosque is a good place to head for cheap joints offering rice, curry and kebabs.

Sarinda Park Cafe   CAFE **$**
(River Rd; mains from Tk 120; ⊙6am-11pm) Sarinda offers Bengali and Indian food plus a few Chinese dishes, but of equal draw here is the well-maintained garden – a lovely place to rest up. The kebabs are good, as are the local snacks such as *shobji* (mixed vegetable curry, pronounced 'sabzee'). The menu is in Bengali only, and not much English is spoken.

Rom III Restaurant   BANGLADESHI **$**
(1st fl, 25 Shaymachoron Roy Rd; mains from Tk 120; ⊙7am-midnight) Tasty curries and delicious kebabs. Portions are enormous – perfect for sharing, or ask for a half-plate of rice if you're on your own. On the opposite side of the road, the related ROM III Sweets & Bakery will answer cravings for Bengali sweets.

Sarinda   BANGLADESHI **$$**
(CK Ghosh Rd; mains from Tk 170; ⊙9am-11pm) Kebabs, roast chicken, fish and biryani in one of the town's smartest restaurants. Popular with families.

China Green Restaurant   CHINESE **$$**
(☑091-53331; Station Rd; mains Tk 150; ⊙11am-11pm) This place offers average Chinese fare.

ⓘ Information

Check email at **Toyal Cyber Cafe** (Station Rd; per hour Tk 25; ⊙9.30am-9.30pm) or **E-View Cyber Café** (Station Rd).

The **Old Hospital** has basic services; go to Dhaka if you have the choice.

ⓘ Getting There & Away

The Dhaka bus stand, 2km south of town, only serves Dhaka (Tk 240, four hours). Buses depart from dawn and throughout the day. Buses to most other destinations leave from, or at least pass through, the extremely hectic **Main bus stand** by the bridge crossing; destinations include Birisiri (Tk 80, 3½ hours) and Bogra (Tk 150, six hours). Buses to Muktagacha (Tk 25, 30 minutes) leave from the **Tangail bus stand**.

Around Mymensingh

Muktagacha

A wonderful decaying 300-year-old rajbari, and a traditional sweet so lip-smackingly delicious that it's famed across the country, make the quiet village of Muktagacha a worthy half-day trip from Mymensingh.

◎ Sights

Muktagacha Rajbari   HISTORIC SITE
Spread over 10 acres, the rajbari here is a special estate, even in disrepair. The main structure is bedecked with Corinthian columns, high parapets and floral scrolls in plaster, while the grounds encompass several shrines. The caretaker speaks broken English and will probably offer you a guided tour. He's quite a character and well worth the baksheesh he'll ask for (about Tk 50 is fair).

Inside you'll find, among other things, a former treasury with the last of 50 safes and a room that the caretaker quaintly describes as the 'finishing room', but is actually a less quaint execution chamber. The main audience chamber here has the remnants of a rotating dance floor.

The Rajeswari temple and the stone temple, believed to be dedicated to Shiva, are just two of the finer shrines within the complex, while just outside are the former stables for the rajbari's 99 elephants (now occupied by the local police).

The rajbari is signposted from the main road where the bus stops.

....

SELECTED DAILY TRAINS FROM MYMENSINGH

DESTINATION	TRAIN NAME	DEPARTS	ARRIVES	FARE (1ST/SHUVON)
Dhaka	Jamuna Ex	4.40am	8.20am	Tk 175/110
Dhaka	Jamalpur Commuter	7.10am	10.30am	Tk 175/110
Dhaka	Brahmaputra Ex	9.23am	12.40pm	Tk 175/110
Dhaka	Hawr Ex	11.15am	3.10pm	Tk 175/110
Dhaka	Balaka Ex	3.15pm	7.25pm	Tk 175/110
Dhaka	Aghnibina	7.17pm	10.45pm	Tk 175/110

WORTH A TRIP

BHAWAL NATIONAL PARK
··
Located at Rajendrapur, and only one hour north of Dhaka, **Bhawal National Park** (admission per person Tk 6, per car Tk 30, per minibus Tk 50) is where city types come to remember what a lungful of fresh country air feels like. While no means an untouched wilderness, its forest walks, angling and lake boating make it a favourite weekend haunt with the inhabitants of Dhaka. In recent years, the forest department have created a 'silent zone' where music is banned, and have reintroduced peacocks, spotted deer, fishing cats and pythons.

✖ Eating

Gopal Pali Prosida Monda
Sweet Shop   DESSERTS $
(📋 01711-707909; monda platter Tk 10; ⊙ closed Fri morning) This much-loved place makes the best *monda* (grainy, sweetened yogurt cake) in the country. Settle back in the tasting room, where a silver plate with a few tasters of *monda* will be presented for you to try.

To find the shop, walk straight ahead as you exit the rajbari, then turn right at the end of the lane and the shop will be on your left. Look for the lion motif over the door. It's one of the most famous sweet shops in Bangladesh, so anyone will be able to direct you.

────────────────────

Birisiri & the China Clay Hills

Birisiri is a quiet, welcoming Garo village, set in a small forest close to the Someswari River. It offers little in terms of tourist sights, but the journey here, across lush farmland, is extremely picturesque and the village is within striking distance of the highly photogenic China Clay Hills. Most interestingly perhaps, Birisiri offers travellers the chance to meet and learn more about the Garo people.

◉ Sights

China Clay Hills   HILL
(Cheena Mati Pahar) The cool turquoise waters beside the China Clay Hills (really little more than low mounds) make for an extremely photogenic spot, and a lovely place for a tree-shaded picnic, though the main reason to venture this far north is for the journey itself. Take a tranquil three-hour rowboat trip up the Someswari River, or else a bone-rattling, but fun two-hour rickshaw ride, crossing the river on a small wooden ferry before passing through a number of remote villages en route.

English-speaking staff at Birisiri's YMCA or YWCA can help arrange either a boat or a rickshaw to the China Clay Hills. Expect to pay around Tk 800 for a rowboat (three hours one way) or Tk 1600 for a motorboat (one hour, one way). Note that boats can't take you all the way to the China Clay Hills because the site isn't beside the river. They will likely drop you at Ranikhong, from where you'll have to walk or pick up a rickshaw for about a 15-minute ride. Hiring a rickshaw for the day from Birisiri costs around Tk 500.

Tribal Cultural Academy   MUSEUM
The only 'sight' in Birisiri, this small research museum is worth a look. You may have to ask around to get someone to unlock the doors, but once you're in you'll find exhibits displaying the culture and traditions of local ethnic minorities such as the Garo. The museum is a short walk north along the main road from the centre of Birisiri.

🛏 Sleeping & Eating

Your only food options are the no-frills roadside restaurants on the main street where the bus drops you off – expect simple chicken and rice and the like for about Tk 100.

YWCA   HOSTEL $
(📋 01712-042916; Birisiri; dm/s/d from Tk 400/750/900) This well-looked-after hostel has clean, tidy rooms that overlook an attractive garden with a bamboo pergola. Very friendly, but sometimes fully booked because of training days held here. Follow the signs down a track from the main road where the bus drops you off and keep walking for a few hundred metres.

YMCA   HOSTEL $
(📋 01743-306230, 09525-56266; Birisiri; dm from Tk 200, r from Tk 450) The YMCA has pretty basic rooms, with squat-toilet bathrooms, but they overlook a huge garden, which houses the even more basic dorms. Not be confused with the nearby YWCA, although it's on the same lane from the bus stop.

ⓘ Getting There & Away

Buses to Mymensingh (Tk 80, 3½ hours) leave throughout the day from the main road. One bus continues all the way to Dhaka (Tk 240, seven to eight hours). It usually leaves at around 3pm, but it's worth checking this when you're here. Coming here from Dhaka, there is one direct bus, which leaves from Mohakhali bus stand at 7am.

Khulna & Barisal

Best Places to Eat

➡ Garden Inn (p79)

➡ Shokal Shondha (p79)

➡ Goon Goon Coffee
Shop (p67)

Best Places to Sleep

➡ Banchte Shekha (p75)

➡ Western Inn
International (p65)

➡ Hotel Grand Park (p79)

Why Go?

A land of savage beauty where man still battles nature for everyday survival, unexplored Khulna comes top on the bucket list of intrepid adventurers. Comprising in large parts of nothing but marshlands, waterlogged jungles and rivers, this archetypal explorer country is not easy to navigate, but it promises to leave you with some of your most abiding memories of Bangladesh.

The star attraction around here is the Sundarbans, the world's largest mangrove forest and home to the largest single tiger population on earth. If you organise only one trip in Bangladesh, make sure it's a trip to the Sundarbans.

Jungles apart, the area is also known for its secluded beaches, historic mosques and a mesmerising network of rivers to explore. Talking of rivers, it's also the best place to hop onto a riverine vessel and enjoy some of the most iconic boat trips this water-laden country has to offer.

When to Go
Jessore

Nov–Feb Mildest and most pleasant time to visit the Sundarbans.

Mar Thousands of pilgrims descend on Kushtia to pay their respects at the shrine of Lalon Shah.

Apr Trek through the Sundarbans in the honey-harvesting season.

RAJSHAHI
DIVISION

DHAKA

Pabna

Kuthibari
Kushtia 5

Padma River

Jamuna River

Faridpur

Narayanganj

CHITTAGONG
DIVISION

DHAKA
DIVISION

Shariatpur

Chandpur

Jessore

Narail
Gobra
Noapara

Kashiani

KHULNA
DIVISION

Benapole

**Rocket
Riverboat** 3

Baleshwar River

Satkhira

Khulna

Banaripara

Bhomra

Khatakhali

Bagerhat
2

Barisal

Bhola

Hularhat

Jhalokati

Megna River

*Karamjal
Forest
Station*

Mongla

Morrelganj

**barisal
division**

Burigoalini

*Harbaria
Forest
Station*

Patuakhali

Char
Fasson

INDIA
(WEST BENGAL)

**Sundarbans
National
Park**
1

Kotka

*Hiran
Point*

Kunga River

Dublar
Char

Fatra
Char

Haringhata River

Kazal River

Misripara

Kuakata 4

Gangamati
Mangrove
Forest

Shahbazpur Channel

BAY OF BENGAL

Khulna & Barisal Highlights

1 **Sundarbans National
Park** (p69) Floating through
the forests in search of the
elusive Royal Bengal tiger or
joining in the seasonal wild
honey harvest.

2 **Bagerhat** (p73)
Visiting the magnificent
mosques of this sleepy town
before exploring its forested
villages.

3 **Rocket Riverboat**
(p68) Riding this vintage
paddle-wheel steamer,
Bangladesh's most iconic
riverboat.

4 **Kuakata** (p81)
Travelling to this remote
beach on the eastern fringes
of the Sundarbans.

5 **Kushtia** (p77)
Contemplating the poetry
of Rabindranath Tagore or
the folk songs of the Fakir
musician Lalon Shah in this
teeny cultural town.

KHULNA DIVISION

Most people arrive in the southwestern division of Khulna with the primary intention of organising a boat trip deep into the Sundarbans, to spy on Royal Bengal tigers in their mangrove habitat. That apart, the biggest draw of the region are the Islamic ruins of Bagerhat, which is now a Unesco World Heritage Site.

Until some years ago, arriving here by the Rocket steamer via the river route from Dhaka used to be yet another *raison d'être* for travellers in Bangladesh. The silting of the river curtailed the journey by a third in recent times, but the part-ferry, part-bus journey from Dhaka via Barisal can still be very exciting.

Travellers heading to (or coming from) Kolkata in India will also pass through Khulna – the land border at Benapole is one of Bangladesh's busiest – while Kushtia makes an interesting cultural stop if you're on your way north to the history-rich division of Rajshahi.

Khulna

📞 041 / POP 660,000

Khulna, the capital of Bangladesh's southwestern province, serves as a launchpad for organised trips into the Sundarbans, and is hence an important dot on the country's tourist map. A boom town with a considerable Hindu population (West Bengal in India is barely 40km away as the crow flies), the town itself offers few worthy sights, although its surrounds are home to a few interesting historical monuments and activities.

The local culture here has a tangible Indian flavour to it, and the frontier sensation hangs heavy in the air. Many people talk about having relatives across the international border, and have been to India on frequent visits. The regional dialect here has a greater linguistic overlap with West Bengal than eastern or northern Bangladesh, while the cuisine, peppered with cross-border cooking traditions, also has its own distinct identity.

◎ Sights

Rabindranath
Memorial Museum   HISTORIC BUILDING

(Dakhin Dihi Village; Tk 100; ⊙10am-5pm Tue-Thu & Sat-Sun, 2.30-5pm Fri & Mon) A picture of poise and prettiness, this recently restored building belonged to the in-laws of Benga-li poet and Nobel Laureate Rabindranath Tagore. It's said that Tagore visited the house only on the day of his wedding and reportedly never returned here. Nonetheless, locals have carefully preserved the building, the interiors of which have now been converted into a pictorial museum. Located in a pastoral setting and fronted by gulmohars (flowering trees) and hedges, the building appears straight out of a fairy tale.

Buses plying the road between Khulna and Jessore can drop you at Dakhin Dihi (Tk 30, one hour). From the main road, you can take a rickshaw for Tk 50, or simply walk for about 20 minutes.

Madhu Kunj   HISTORIC BUILDING

(Sagordari Village; Tk 100; ⊙10am-5pm Tue-Thu & Sat-Sun, 2.30-5pm Fri & Mon) This well-kept building and garden complex was the family home of revered 19th-century Bengali poet Michael Madhusudan Dutt (1824–73), who is known to have introduced blank verse to Bengali poetry and is credited with some of the most intricate verses ever written in the language. The main mansion where he was born and grew up before moving to Kolkata for higher studies is now a museum of family memorabilia. The surrounding gardens and orchards are particularly photogenic.

To get here, take a Satkhira-bound bus to Chuknagar (Tk 30, 40 minutes, 7am to 5pm) and then change for Keshabpur (Tk 20, 20 minutes, every hour). From Keshabpur, hire a 'van-rickshaw' (a battery-operated rickshaw with a seating board attached) to Sagordari for Tk 300. Alternatively, drive from Khulna in a hired car. The journey takes about an hour.

🛏 Sleeping

Hotel Jalico   HOTEL $

(📞041-725912; www.hoteljalico.com; Jessore Rd; s/d from Tk 500/750, with air-con from Tk 950/1200; ❄) Run by a friendly manager who personally oversees housekeeping operations, Jalico is one of the best-value hotels in Khulna, with large, spotless rooms. Air-con and fan rooms are essentially the same; you can choose not to use the air-con and pay a cheaper rate. The access is through the ground-floor passage of a shopping mall (follow the English signage).

Western Inn International   HOTEL $$

(📞041-810899; http://western-inn.com; Jessore Rd; s/d incl breakfast from Tk 1500/1800; ❄@🛜) Clearly the best hotel in Khulna, this place

Khulna

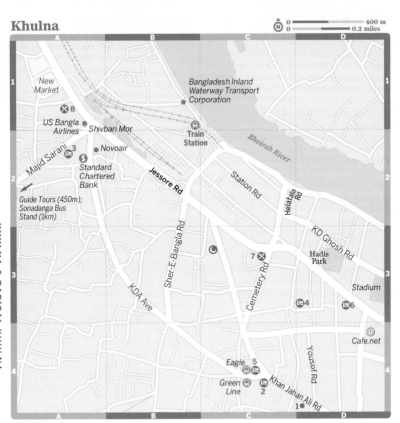

Khulna

Activities, Courses & Tours

Sleeping

Eating

has huge suite-like rooms that feature soft beds and spotless bathrooms with sit-down loos and bathtubs. The sleeping areas have windows and balconies overlooking a tree-shaded residential block; you can get sweeping views of the town looking out. The hotel's restaurant is highly recommended for Bangladeshi meals, and the English-speaking staff is helpful.

Hotel City Inn HOTEL $$
(☎ 01711-298501; www.cityinnltd.com; Majid Sarani; s/d incl breakfast from Tk 1800/2400; ❄ @ 🛜 ☒) A new establishment that opened its doors in 2015, this smart hotel has spacious rooms and clean bathrooms with bathtubs and sit-down loos. Single women were seen checking out here, which is always a good sign as far as safety is concerned. The restaurant does decent Bangladeshi and Chinese food, and the complementary breakfast is both wholesome and tasty.

Hotel Royal International HOTEL $$
(☎ 041-721638; www.hotelroyalintl.com; KDA Ave; s/d incl breakfast from Tk 1200/2000; ❄ @ 🛜) Clearly a shadow of its stately past, this upscale place has a good offering of rooms, many of which are done up in snazzy

FISHING WITH OTTERS

Fishing with otters has been taking place for at least 1000 years and was once fairly widespread across the world; in the UK, it didn't die out until 1880. There are two techniques employed by the fishers; one involves the otters individually catching fish and returning them to the fishers while the other (employed in Bangladesh) involves a net being lowered into the water and 'shuffled' along the river bed or against clumps of water plants to disturb the fish, which the otters then chase into the net.

Guide Tours (☑041-731384; www.guidetoursbd.com; 88 Sonadanga Rd 2; ☺9am-5pm) and **Bengal Tours** (☑041-724355; www.bengaltours.com; 236 Khan Jahan Ali Rd; ☺9.30am-5pm Sat-Thu) organise day trips and overnight trips from Khulna to villages such as Hariar, where this ancient fishing practice can still be found. For any semblance of authenticity, you need to book yourself on an overnight trip because fishing with otters is a nocturnal practice. Daytime demonstrations are laid on for tourists, but can feel overly contrived.

Even though it's technically possible, don't try to go to these villages by yourself. Unless you speak good Bengali, it's extremely difficult to arrange either a daytime demonstration or a night's stay on a fishing boat, let alone finding your way to the main areas of interest. Besides, rural public transport is patchy in these parts, so you may waste a lot of time trying to get here, and chances of getting stranded at dusk are high.

Expect to pay Tk 10,000 for a day trip from Khulna organised through a tour operator, or as much as Tk 30,000 for an all-inclusive overnight trip. If you still decide to turn up on your own (in which case it's strongly recommended that you hire a car for the day from Khulna), fishers will ask for as much as Tk 10,000 for a daytime fishing demonstration. You may be able to get them down to around Tk 4000, but that will require good bargaining and language skills.

faux-muslin upholstery. It's clean and well kept, but service can vary from prompt to lacklustre. There's a travel agency in the lobby where you can make arrangements for car rental as well as guided trips to the Sundarbans.

Hotel Castle Salam HOTEL **$$**
(☑041-720160; www.hotel-castlesalam.com; cnr KDA Ave & Khan Jahan Ali Rd; r incl breakfast from Tk 1200; ❋@☎☒) The rooms here are fairly spacious and well-appointed, though some of the cheaper ones are surprisingly low on ventilation. Nonetheless, it's one of Khulna's popular hotels, and the staff speak good English. As well as a good restaurant and coffee shop, it also has a bar (open from 7pm to 10pm) accessible to foreign guests, and a rooftop swimming pool.

✖ Eating

Two of the best restaurants in town are attached to two of Khulna's best hotels, Western Inn (p65) and Castle Salam (p67). Both are open to nonguests, and serve a good selection of Bangladeshi, Indian and Chinese dishes, from around Tk 100 upwards per dish. Both are open from around 7am to 3pm and 7pm to 11pm.

Aloka Restaurant BANGLADESHI **$**
(Jessore Rd; mains from Tk 90; ☺7.30am-10.30pm) Extremely popular with locals, this place whips up delicious, no-nonsense main courses (biryanis, curries and set meals) plus hearty breakfasts (dhal, fried egg, paratha), and is run by a friendly manager who speaks decent English. No English menu, but the staff will help you choose. It's on the first floor of a building at the corner of Jessore and Cemetery Rds.

Grillhouse BANGLADESHI **$**
(New Market; mains Tk 100-140; ☺10am-11pm; ▣) The kebabs (served from 4.30pm) at this smart eatery are simply mouthwatering, although on most evenings, they will have been gulped down by eager diners before you've arrived. Kebabs aside, the menu has a decent selection of Bangladeshi and Chinese dishes, and the friendly English-speaking manager ensures a cordial atmosphere.

Goon Goon Coffee Shop CAFE **$**
(Hotel Castle Salam, cnr KDA Ave & Khan Jahan Ali Rd; snacks Tk 100-140; ☺9am-3pm & 7-11pm; ▣) This modern eatery stocks an assortment of pastries, sandwiches and cakes and, most importantly, presses fresh coffee. You could also try the tasty shawarma rolls, although

ℹ️ GETTING TO KHULNA BY ROCKET

Until recently, one of the most popular and iconic boat journeys in Bangladesh used to be from Dhaka to Khulna aboard the Rocket, a vintage paddle-wheel steamer harking back to the early 20th century. The name Rocket derived from the fact that the maritime relic was – at the time of its induction – the fastest thing on the rivers (modern-day steamers now travel at a much quicker pace).

While the service is still operational from Dhaka, the last stretch leading up to Khulna along the Bhairab River has been suspended due to heavy silting of the riverbed, which prevents heavy-hulled boats from cruising the river's inland channel. If you want a slice of this classic cruising experience, your only option is to travel by the Rocket from Dhaka as far as Hularhat (1st/2nd class Tk 1420/855, 16 hours, 6pm, no service Sunday), and then catch a bus to Khulna. Buses go via the historic town of Bagerhat, a place you'll probably want to visit, too.

Note that Hularhat isn't the last stop on the Rocket (that's Morrelganj), but it is the most convenient hop-off point for onward transport to Bagerhat and Khulna.

When you get off the boat at Hularhat, take a shared electric rickshaw (per person Tk 30) to the Khulna bus stand (make it clear you want a bus to Khulna or Bagerhat be-cause there is a closer local bus stand, too). From the Khulna bus stand, regular buses go to Khulna (Tk 100, two hours, until 5pm) and Bagerhat (Tk 50, one hour, until 6pm).

Also note that the Dhaka–Barisal section of the Rocket trip is overnight, so you're only able to appreciate the scenery during the three-hour stretch from Barisal to Hularhat the next morning.

they are far from authentic. Floor-to-ceiling windows on the far end afford good street views. It's located on the 1st floor of Hotel Castle Salam, but is open to nonguests.

ℹ️ Information

Cafe.net (2/2 Babu Khan Rd; per hour Tk 50; ⏰10am-10pm) This is a cyber cafe with a real cafe attached to it. Connections are reliable and quick.

Standard Chartered Bank (KDA Ave; ⏰10am-4pm Sat-Thu) This efficient bank changes money and has an ATM.

ℹ️ Getting There & Away

AIR

The nearest airport is at Jessore, from where **Novoair** (☎017-55656660; www.flynovoair. com; KDA Ave) and **US Bangla Airlines** (☎017-77777788; www.us-banglaairlines.com; Ibrahim Miah Rd) have daily flights (from Tk 3200) to Dhaka. Both airlines offer a shuttle bus service (Tk 200) that picks up passengers from their respective offices in the town centre four hours prior to departure.

BOAT

In the past couple of years the much-loved Dhaka–Khulna paddle-wheel steamer service hasn't reached as far as Khulna due to oversilt-ing upriver. The **Bangladesh Inland Waterway Transport Corporation** (BIWTC; ☎041-721532; www.biwtc.gov.bd), the regional authority for

the service, indicated at the time of research that there was a strong possibility that the old services to Khulna would never resume. Be sure to check with one of the BIWTC offices before you make any plans for Khulna that revolve around a trip on the Rocket.

BUS

The main bus station is Sonadanga bus stand. It's Tk 30 to Tk 50 in a CNG from the town centre. Destinations include Mongla (Tk 70, 90 minutes, 5am to 6pm), Bagerhat (Tk 60, one hour, 6am to 8pm) and Jessore (Tk 90, 90 min-utes, 6am to 6pm).

Private coach companies that run services to Dhaka include **Green Line** (www.greenlinebd. com; KDA Ave; air-con Tk 1200, eight hours, 10am and 10.15pm) and **Eagle** (KDA Ave; non-air-con/air-con Tk 600/1200, eight hours, hour-ly from 4am to 4pm and 8pm to 11pm), both of which have offices by Hotel Castle Salam.

TRAIN

Almost all trains from Khulna go through Jes-sore, but buses are much more frequent.

Trains to Dhaka (1st berth/1st seat/shuvon Tk 930/620/390) include the *Chitra Express* (11 hours, 8.30am) except Monday, and the *Sundar-ban Express* (11 hours, 7.30pm) except Tuesday.

Trains to Rajshahi (1st seat/shuvon Tk 425/180) include the *Kapotaksha Express* (seven hours, 6.30am) except Saturday, and the *Sagordari Express* (seven hours, 2.50pm) except Monday.

Sundarbans National Park

A shroud of mystery and danger looms over the Unesco-protected Sundarbans National Park, the largest mangrove forest in the world. Bleak and haunting at the same time, the wilderness here comprises an enormous network of interconnected waterways, stretching inland for about 80km from the Bay of Bengal. This is truly wild terrain, and a three- or four-day boat trip into the heart of this magnificent part of south Asia often ranks as the chief highlight of a trip to Bangladesh.

Plants & Wildlife

The Sundarbans is home to some unique subcontinental wildlife, though spotting it in the thick mangrove forests is difficult. Most visitors report seeing little, but many argue that it is the pristine environment and not the wildlife that is the real attraction. It's hard to overstate the thrill of floating through the mangrove swamps, and sleeping overnight on board a boat, knowing that out there, somewhere, there are Royal Bengal tigers!

ROYAL BENGAL TIGERS

The creature everybody wants to see (and the one that you really have very little chance of sighting) is the magnificent Royal Bengal tiger. Tigers have a life span of around 16 years and, in these parts, they prey predominantly on spotted deer (chital), or sometimes wild boar. It is only in old age, when they have lost their physical agility and canine fangs, that they are thought to turn to easier prey – local humans.

There are estimated to be around 4000 wild tigers left in the world, with the Sundarbans officially being home to around 10% of that number. It's notoriously difficult to count tigers, even more so when they're lurking behind thick and hopelessly inaccessible mangrove forests. Figures published in 2009 estimated that the Sundarbans supported between 300 and 500 tigers. However, these figures were extrapolated from the archaic pugmark counting method as well as the mapped territorial range of just two tigers who were tagged with GPS tracking collars. If a fresh census conducted in 2015 (using the more precise camera-trap method) is to be believed, the forests here may only have about 100-odd tigers left.

Although the Royal Bengal tiger is the most numerous of the world's five remaining subspecies of tiger, it is still very much on the endangered list. Threats to the Sundarbans tiger population include environmental degradation (illegal logging, river pollution, and the continued rise of salinity levels in the mangrove swamps), reduction in prey (spotted deer are threatened by poaching and environmental degradation) and human conflict, including retaliation killings (on average three a year) and, of course, poaching.

Conservation is clearly key to sustaining the environment of the Sundarbans, and its tiger population in particular. In 2009, the government-backed Bangladesh Tiger Action Plan was hatched. Its long-term vision is to protect the country's tiger regions to the extent that they are able to sustain the optimum number of tigers, although initially the aim is to simply stabilise the current tiger population. Devised by a group of leading conservationists, and backed not only by the Bangladesh government but also by key environment groups such as the Zoological Society of London (www.zsl.org), it does offer cause for optimism. For more information, check the tiger conservation section of the ZSL website, or the website of the conservation program called Wild Team (www.wild-team.org).

CROCODILES

Less popular among tourists than Royal Bengal tigers (but equally important to wildlife conservationists) are the three crocodile species that live in the Sundarbans. Of these, the snout-nosed, fish-eating gharial is a critically endangered creature, while the hulk-sized saltwater crocodile and estuarine crocodile are more common. It's hard to ascertain their individual populations, but the combined headcount of all three species is roughly around 200. The crocodile breeding centre in Karamjal Forest Station (p71), downstream from Mongla, is a key initiative on part of the forest department to breed and release crocodiles into the waters so as to stabilise their numbers.

BIRDS

Over 300 different bird species have been recorded in this region, including about 95 species of water birds and 35 species of birds of prey. Birds found here include snipes, white and gold herons, kingfishers, woodcocks, coots, yellowlegs, sandpipers, common cranes, golden eagles and the *madan-tak* (adjutant bird).

OTHER WILDLIFE

Apart from tigers and crocodiles, 31 other species of mammals also call the Sundarbans home, including spotted deer (an estimated 30,000 live here, and they are relatively easy to spot), wild boars, clawless otters and monkeys. The region also has 35 species of reptiles, including large cobras and pythons. There are also eight species of amphibians and numerous river dolphins.

One interesting creature to seek out, particularly during honey-harvesting season, is the giant and very aggressive honey bee.

MANGROVES

Of course, the one thing you're guaranteed to see on a trip into the forests of the Sundarbans is trees, chief among which are mangroves. Of the 54 species of mangroves in the world, 26 are found in the Sundarbans. Extremely resilient and highly adaptive, mangroves need to be able to tolerate broad ranges of salinity, temperature and moisture because of the tidal sea water that surrounds them. They also play a key role in protecting the coastline from erosion, storm surges, cyclones and tsunamis. Their massive root systems – which grow as vast networks of vertical stumps peering out of the submerged earth like periscopes – help dissipate wave energy and slow down tidal water so that sediment is deposited as the tide comes in. In this way, mangroves can be said to build their own environment.

Tours

Unless you are just engaged on a day trip from Mongla, the only way to enter the forest is as part of an organised tour with a recognised travel agency. It will take care of all logistics for you.

Most companies offer fairly similar packages and all concentrate on the far southeast of the swamp, typically reaching as far as Kotka, where there is a beach. Boat quality and environmental awareness varies between operators. The less you pay, the less you will get.

Guide Tours (p67) in Dhaka or Khulna knows these forests like nobody else and is heavily involved in conservation and research projects here. It gets fantastic reports for its tours, and its guides are walking founts of information. The more people in a group, the less you'll pay, but to increase your chances of seeing wildlife, try to go on a small-group tour. The cheapest four-day trip will cost around Tk 10,000 per person on the largest boats, while the small-group tours cost around Tk 16,500 per person. Fees include all food, accommodation and transport, but you will need to pay an additional Tk 800 per person per day for permits.

Guide Tours can also arrange any transport you might need from Dhaka or Jessore to Khulna.

LIFE IN THE SUNDARBANS

No permanent settlements are permitted inside the forest other than camps built by the forest department, coast guard or navy, plus a few government camps housing registered labour force for the extraction of timber. Infrastructure within the forest is generally limited to the buildings of these camps, plus some tourist facilities such as walkways and watchtowers.

However, some semi-permanent fishing communities operate at the southern edge of the forest. These fishers use forest timber for firewood and to construct jetties, shelters and fish-drying racks.

Things change drastically from November to mid-February as thousands of fishers from Chittagong converge on **Dublar Char**, at the mouth of the Kunga River, a Sundarbans estuary, to harvest the schooling shrimp that come here to breed, and to catch fish and sharks. Dublar Island is further inundated with visitors for three days between late November and early December, when thousands of Hindus from Khulna, Barisal and Patuakhali come to the island for the Maha Raas Leela festival. They set up statues of deities in makeshift temples, bathe in the holy waters and release or sacrifice goats. During the festival, sweetmeats, dried fruit, toys, hookahs, wooden clogs and religious paraphernalia are sold in an adjoining temporary fairground. A few weeks after the festival-goers depart, the fishers also return to Chittagong. For the next nine months the island is deserted.

Bengal Tours (p67) in Dhaka or Khulna offers trips that are similar to those of Guide Tours. They cover the same areas and are equally responsible and knowledgeable.

Mongla

📞 04658 / POP 58,000

Flanked by mighty tropical rivers and silted over by annual floods, Mongla is a small river-port town where tourists who can't afford (or haven't had time) to prearrange a multi-day Sundarbans tour from Khulna can dip into the mangrove forests on a last-minute day trip. The Sundarbans begins just 5km south from here and the longer, better-organised tours from Khulna will pass through here before they delve deeper into the forests.

The environment in Mongla is bleak, to say the least. Ravaged by floods, hit by frequent cyclones and in constant dearth of fresh potable water, humanity here is caught in an eternal struggle for survival against the elements. Of course, you will face none of it on a boat trip or during your stay here, as tourists are always considered a priority.

◎ Sights & Activities

St Paul's Catholic Church CHURCH
(সেন্ট পলস ক্যাথলিক চার্চ) Built only in 1992, St Paul's is an unusual piece of architecture: a Catholic church disguised as a mosque, with touches of Buddhist artwork. Embroidered wall hangings depict a Bangladeshi Christ and there are some bold (but plain) stained-glass windows. You'll notice statues of Christian saints, but also depictions of the Buddhist lotus-flower symbol as well as the crescent of Islam. The church forms part of St Paul's School, which was founded by Italian missionaries in 1954.

◉ Boat Trips

Despite Mongla's proximity to the Sundarbans National Park, Khulna remains the better place to organise a boat trip if you really want to explore and appreciate the forest in any depth. If, however, you just want a cheap and cheerful day trip and haven't been able to book a trip from Khulna in advance, then Mongla is the best place to start.

In recent years, the forestry department has banned any independent boats from Mongla (and other towns) from taking tourists on overnight trips into the Sundarbans. This rule was introduced after a couple of nasty incidents involving lost boats. Nowadays, no matter what boatmen in Mongla may tell you, the only legal way to travel independently into the Sundarbans from Mongla is on a day trip to the Karamjal Forest Station.

Private tour operators organising boat trips will find you soon after you arrive in Mongla. Shop around for quotes, and be clear on what is included in the price, where the boat will go and how long it will go for. And never pay everything up front. Offer an advance and settle the balance after the trip.

For trustworthy advice on boat trips, seek out **Abdul Malek** (📞 01717-150990; amalek034@gmail.com), the manager at Parjatan Hotel (p72). He doesn't run his own trips, but can help you arrange one. He quotes Tk 2000 for a half-day return trip (four hours) to Karamjal, and Tk 5000 for a full-day return trip (8am to 5pm) to the outlying and less-visited **Harbaria Forest Station**, via Karamjal. Prices don't include entry fees at Karamjal or food and water (take your own).

Note that you need permits to enter the area beyond Karamjal, hence the full-day trip being more expensive. Also note that prices will fall if you book as a group because some costs (boat hire, for example) can be shared. A single boat can easily take up to 10 people.

Karamjal Forest Station WILDLIFE WATCHING
(admission Tk 300; ⊙10am-4pm) The only legal way to travel independently into the Sundarbans from Mongla is on a day trip to the Karamjal Forest Station. With raised walkways and viewing platforms, the Karamjal Forest Station is hardly the back of beyond, but surprisingly in recent years it's been one of the best places to actually see a tiger.

Think of it as a fun boat trip rather than an off-the-beaten-track safari adventure and you won't leave disappointed. If you do see a tiger, consider it an unexpected bonus.

Within the forest station is a **crocodile breeding centre** managed by the forest department, which aims to restore the previously threatened croc population in the region's rivers. The star crocodiles here are Romeo and Juliet and their offspring Pilpil, who live in a secured lake, respond to calls and gulp down live chicken twice a week.

Mongla

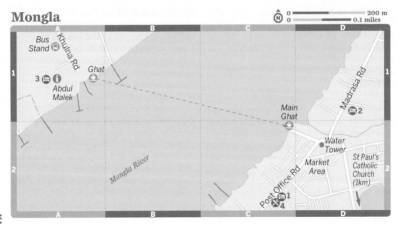

N 0 —————————— 200 m
0 —————————— 0.1 miles

Mongla

🛏 Sleeping
1 Hotel Bangkok.......................................C2
2 Hotel Habib International D1
3 Parjatan Hotel A1

✖ Eating
Royal Bengal Restaurant.............(see 3)
4 Sureswar Hotel & Restaurant.............C2

🛏 Sleeping

Hotel Habib International HOTEL $
(☑ 01711-281658; Madrasa Rd; s/d Tk 600/800) A newish place on the top floors of a commercial building, Habib has a busy location but boasts fantastic river views from the common balconies. Rooms are small but well-kept for the price, and a few have windows that strangely open onto corridors. That said, it's the best budget option in Mongla. Hot water is supplied in buckets.

Hotel Bangkok HOTEL $
(☑ 01711-397531; Post Office Rd; r Tk 600, without bathroom Tk 300) This charmingly disorganised place has small rooms with deep-green walls, some of which face the river. Run by a friendly man who speaks some English, it strangely makes you feel at home despite its stark and cheap interiors. Bring your own sheets if you can.

Parjatan Hotel HOTEL $$
(☑ 01773-044470; www.parjatan.gov.bd; Khulna Rd; r without/with air-con Tk 1200/2000; ❄ 🗺) Also known as Hotel Pashur, this is the nicest place to stay in Mongla. It's across the river (Tk 3 by ferry) from town, by the main bus stand. Set in peaceful gardens, the rooms here are bright and clean, though visibly musty. There's wi-fi at the lobby, wholesome food in the restaurant, and the resourceful manager speaks good English.

Pashur also has Mongla's only licensed bar located in an annexe, where you can drink upon producing your passport. Beers are Tk 400.

✖ Eating

Mongla isn't overflowing with eating options. Most places cater to locals and passing sailors who come from the nearby port, and border on squalid.

Sureswar Hotel & Restaurant BANGLADESHI $
(Post Office Rd; mains Tk 60; ⊘ 5am-1am) This local favourite located on the main drag stocks the standards and has a handy 'food catalogue' painted onto the wall in English. It's a good place for an early morning dhal-and-roti breakfast.

Royal Bengal Restaurant BANGLADESHI $$
(Parjatan Hotel, Khulna Rd; mains Tk 100-150; ⊘ 7am-10pm; 📷) Located across the river within the premises of Parjatan Hotel, this clean and well-serviced restaurant has a very good selection of simple yet tasty Bangladeshi and Indian options in a quiet environment. The fish, chicken and beef curries are thoughtfully tempered for global palates and make for a very enjoyable meal. Has an English menu.

ℹ Getting There & Away

BOAT

Rocket paddle-steamer services to and from Mongla have been suspended indefinitely due to the silting of the river, and it is unlikely they will resume anytime soon. If you still take the Rocket from Dhaka, you will have to get off at Hularhat, three hours away, and then travel to Mongla by bus via Bagerhat (Tk 100, 8am to 5pm).

BUS

From the **bus stand** (Khulna Rd), buses for Khulna (Tk 60, 90 minutes, 7am to 5pm) leave every 15 minutes and go via the T-junction known as Khatakhali (Tk 40, one hour) where you can change for Bagerhat.

Bagerhat

✒ 0401 / POP 48,500

A fantastic open-air museum of medieval architectural heritage, Unesco-protected Bagerhat sends a shiver of excitement down the spines of archaeology buffs. Hidden among the green folds of the surrounding countryside of this sleepy town are more ancient mosques and mausoleums than anywhere else in Bangladesh (except Dhaka).

Bagerhat was built in the 15th century by one of the most revered saints in Bangladeshi history, Khan Jahan Ali, and is a significant cradle of Islam in Bangladesh. The crowning jewel of its fabulously little-known architectural collection is the Shait Gumbad Mosque – a multi-domed medieval masterpiece. Several other mosques and mausoleums, complemented by a spectacular landscape of tranquil paddies, tropical trees, ponds and birds, are a joy to explore.

The town, about 4km from the main sights, lacks decent hotels and restaurants, so it's sensible to visit Bagerhat as a day trip from Khulna, which is a short bus ride away.

◎ Sights

Many of Bagerhat's monuments are actively used for daily worship, and are thus more popular with pilgrims than travellers. While you are more than welcome to visit these latent gems, don't expect much in terms of tourist infrastructure. Guides are hard to find, and in most cases, you will simply have to ask locals for directions to nearby structures (the Bengali word for mosque is *masjid* or, colloquially, *morjid*, while mausoleum is *mazar*). Schedule an entire day for the treasure hunt. Most places are open to visitors between dawn and dusk.

★ Shait Gumbad Mosque · · · · · · · · · MOSQUE

(Tk 200; ◎ 9am-5pm Tue-Sat & 2.30-5pm Mon Oct-Mar, 9am-6pm Tue-Sat & 2.30-6pm Mon Mar-Sep)
Built in 1459 (the same year Khan Jahan Ali died), the famous Shait Gumbad Mosque is the largest and most magnificent traditional mosque in the country. Shait Gumbad means 'the Temple with 60 Domes' – a misnomer considering there are actually 81. This fortress-like structure has unusually thick walls, built in the tapering brick style, and is a hugely impressive sight. The overall architectural influence is unmistakably Turkish, and the arches within the main hall are a graceful exercise in geometry.

Bagerhat Museum · · · · · · · · · · · · · · · MUSEUM

(◎ 9am-5pm Tue-Sat & 2.30-5pm Mon Oct-Mar, 9am-6pm Tue-Sat & 2.30-6pm Mon Mar-Sep)
This small, neatly arranged museum, located within the grounds of the Shait Gumbad Mosque (admission is covered by the mosque entrance fee), contains relics from the surrounding area. It's a good place to familiarise yourself with Bagerhat's local history before wandering off on your explorations. Don't forget to check out the carefully preserved skin of one of the legendary crocodiles that once lived in Thakur Dighi

---

THE CROCODILES OF THAKUR DIGHI

The mausoleum complex of Khan Jahan Ali (p74) overlooks a placid pond known as **Thakur Dighi**, which until recently was home to two gigantic crocodiles reportedly more than 100 years old. Fondly named Dhalapahar and Kalapahar (literally 'white mountain' and 'black mountain' respectively), these languid creatures were a hit with camera-toting tourists as well as pilgrims, who fed them live chicken in return for divine blessings. Following their deaths in 2011 and 2014, local authorities released a fresh family of crocodiles in the water with the objective of keeping the fanfare alive. However, the new reptiles quickly earned a reputation for snapping at humans. Do not step into the water at any time.

Bagerhat

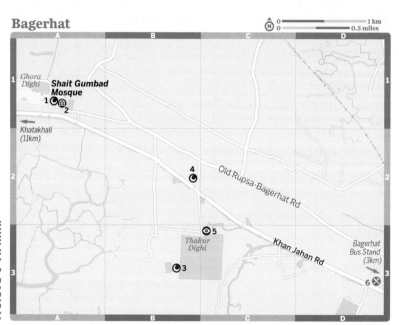

pond. The place shuts between 12.30pm and 2pm for lunch.

Tomb of Khan Jahan Ali   MAUSOLEUM
(Mazhar Khan Jahan Ali; ⊙ dawn-dusk) A place of active worship, Khan Jahan Ali's Tomb is the only monument in Bagerhat that still retains its original cupolas (domed ceilings). The cenotaph at the entrance is covered with tiles of various colours and inscribed with Quranic verses, but it is usually covered with a red cloth embroidered with gold threads. The single-domed **Dargah Mosque** is enclosed within the same complex by a massive wall, with short towers at each corner and archways to the front and rear.

The mausoleum is a popular pilgrimage site and therefore has a little more colour and flair than some of the other monuments in the region. During the annual Urs celebrations in early December, marking the anniversary of the saint's death, the complex sees thousands of visitors turning up to pay their tributes and partake in fete-like festivities.

Ronvijoypur Mosque   MOSQUE
Located on the street that leads directly north from the turn-off to Thakur Dighi, this splendidly chunky 15th-century mosque is singularly impressive. It contains the largest mosque dome in Bangladesh, spanning 11m and supported by 3m-thick brick walls. The mosque's interior is plain, but the main *mihrabs* (niches) are decorated in some graceful floral patterns.

Nine-Domed Mosque   MOSQUE
(Noy Gombuj Masjid; নয় গম্বুজ মসজিদ) On the western bank of Thakur Dighi, a short walk from the mausleum of Khan Jahan Ali, is the recently repaired Nine-Domed Mosque (also called Noy Gombuj Masjid). It's an impressive structure, with eight small domes surrounding one larger central dome. The *mihrabs* (niches) are embellished with terracotta floral scrolls and foliage motifs,

with chain-and-bell terracotta motifs in the centre.

🛏 Sleeping & Eating

Consider staying the night in Bagerhat only if you're badly stuck. The place has few lodging options that meet acceptable standards.

Bagerhat's sights and their surrounding villages and ponds make great spots for a picnic, but you'll have to bring food supplies from Khulna or Mongla (bottled water is readily available though). There are a number of cheap, no-nonsense local restaurants by the bus stand where you can grab a fish-curry-and-rice meal for around Tk 100.

Dhansiri Restaurant   BANGLADESHI $$
(Khan Jahan Rd, Dashani; mains Tk 100-130; ⊙ 7am-10pm) A popular dining place among locals, this fast-moving restaurant does a few good fish platters (try the fresh and tasty prawns from neighbouring hatcheries), and hygiene standards are probably the best you'll find in Bagerhat. No English spoken, but waiters are friendly and patient.

❶ Getting There & Away

Buses shuttling from Khulna (Tk 60, one hour, hourly until 8pm) bring you to Bagerhat through some enchanting countryside, passing the Shait Gumbad Mosque on the left and then stopping briefly at the turn-off to Thakur Dighi pond (on the right). While returning to Khulna, you may be able to wave down a passing bus from here itself, but to ensure you have a seat, you may have to board from the Bagerhat bus stand, around 4km southeast of Thakur Dighi.

There are no direct buses to Mongla. You have to catch a Khulna-bound bus to the T-junction a few kilometres north of Bagerhat. This junction is known as Khatakhali. Annoyingly, you'll be expected to pay the full Khulna fare. From the Khatakhali T-junction, you can wave down a Khulna–Mongla bus for Mongla (Tk 40, one hour, hourly until 6pm). Don't expect a seat, though.

If you're planning to take the Rocket paddle-wheel steamer back to Barisal or Dhaka, take a bus to Hularhat from the bus stand (Tk 40, one hour, until 6pm) and then take a shared auto-rickshaw (per person Tk 30, 20 minutes) to the ferry ghat. The Rocket leaves Hularhat at 12.30pm.

❶ Getting Around

The bus stand is about 4km southeast of the Shait Gumbad Mosque, along the main Khan Jahan Rd. Coming from the bus stand, expect to pay about Tk 60 for a rickshaw, or else hop in

a shared CNG (per person Tk 20). Once you've explored Shait Gumbad Mosque and its outlying relics, take another CNG to get to Thakur Dighi Pond (Tk 20), where the other major cluster of monuments are located.

Jessore

📞 0421 / POP 740,000

Mercantile Jessore (pronounced Joshor) is a quintessential Bangladeshi small town characterised by bustling yet manageable street-markets, narrow winding streets, roadside stalls and a plethora of tea stands. Being an authentic, non-touristy place, it makes for a good wander and offers a great opportunity to sample local proletarian culture at its most undiluted form. There's little to see or do here as such, but logistically speaking, the town acts as a good transit point between Khulna and the Indian border at Benapole.

◉ Sights

Chachra Shiv Mandir   HINDU TEMPLE
(Khulna Rd, Chachra Village) About 3km down the road to Khulna, this quaint and delightful 18th-century temple is certainly worth an excursion out of Jessore's urban mess. Dedicated to the Hindu god Shiva, the temple is built in the Bengal style with a two-tier vaulted roof crowning its arched brick walls lined with intricate terracotta panels. The village behind the temple, thrown around a tiny pond, is inhabited by friendly people and is a nice place to sample some rural sights and sounds.

To get here, take a CNG from town and expect to pay about Tk 150 for a return trip (including waiting).

🛏 Sleeping

Banchte Shekha   GUESTHOUSE $
(📞 01732-223240; www.banchteshekha.org; off Airport Rd; r without/with air-con Tk 575/1150; ❄) Helping fund a local NGO-run women's training centre, this welcoming guesthouse on the peaceful outskirts of town is easily the nicest and best-value place to stay in Jessore. Apart from two air-con units with attached bathroom, the dorm-like rooms are simple, fan-cooled and share bathrooms. Scrumptious canteen-style meals (breakfast/lunch/dinner Tk 60/140/160) made from garden-fresh produce are served upon prior notice.

Jessore

Jessore

🛏 Sleeping
1 Hotel Hasan International....................A2

✖ Eating
2 New Nuru Hotel......................................B2
3 Rose Garden...B2

Some rooms here have two beds, some four, but they all cost the same, are kept spotlessly clean and overlook a flower- and vegetable-filled courtyard with a fishpond. To get here, hop in a CNG and say 'Arabpur' (the name of this part of town) or 'Airport Rd'. Once you're close, start asking for 'Banchte Shekha' (pronounced bach-teh shay-kah). A ride from the town centre costs around Tk 30.

Hotel Hasan International   HOTEL **$$**
(☏ 0421-67478; Keshoblal Rd; s/d from Tk 1260/1680; 🅰️🌐📶) Clearly the best hotel in town (for lack of adequate competition), this central place has large air-con rooms, hot water, in-room wi-fi and satellite TV. Rooms out front suffer from some road noise, but it's much quieter compared to other hotels. The restaurant does passable Bangladeshi, Indian and Chinese fare.

✖ Eating

New Nuru Hotel   BENGALI **$**
(MK Rd; mains Tk 100; ⊘ 6am-10pm) The unchallenged curry king of Jessore, this place does a very popular mutton curry (Tk 90) that's best eaten with plain rice and an assortment of *bhorta* and *bhaji* on the side. The fiery kebabs and the simple dhal-and-naan breakfasts also hit the spot. No English menu; not much English spoken either.

Rose Garden   CHINESE **$$**
(Jess Tower, MK Rd; mains Tk 120-200; ⊘ 11.30am-10pm; 🍽) This is a clean and friendly restaurant with an extensive Chinese menu, tucked away on the upper floors of a small shopping centre. It seems extremely popular with Jessore's locals as a place for family outings and meals. For the quality of food, however, the prices are a bit over the top. There's an English menu.

ℹ Information

City Bank (MK Rd) City Bank has an ATM that accepts foreign cards.

Oishi Online (off Shahid Sarak Rd; per hour Tk 50; ⊘ 10am-8pm) Decent connections are available at Oishi Online, but the electricity may play truant at times.

Queen's Hospital (☏ 0421-68355; Jail Rd) This is a good private hospital for round-the-clock emergency and out-patient treatments.

ℹ Getting There & Away

AIR

A CNG from the town centre to the airport (45 minutes) is around Tk 100. From Banchte Shekha guesthouse, it's around Tk 60. **Novoair** (☏ 01755-656660; www.flynovoair.com) and **US Bangla Airlines** (☏ 01777-777788; www.us-banglaairlines.com) both operate daily flights to Dhaka, with fares starting from Tk 3200.

BUS

A rickshaw from the town centre to Monihar Bus Stand should be Tk 20. Expect to pay around Tk 30 to the other two bus stands.

Monihar bus stand primarily serves Dhaka (from Tk 360, seven hours, 6am to 10pm). From Benapole bus stand, buses go to Benapole (Tk 50, one hour, 5am to 8pm). Destinations from Shankapur bus stand include Khulna (Tk 90, 90 minutes, 6am to 6pm) and Kushtia (Tk 140, three hours, 6am to 6pm).

Apart from public buses, you can also get **Green Line's** (☏ 0421-68389; MK Rd) luxury air-con coaches to Dhaka from its ticket office in the town centre (Tk 570, six daily, eight hours).

TRAIN

There are 10 daily trains to Khulna (1st seat/ shuvon Tk 85/55; two hours), although it's much easier to take the bus instead.

Two trains go to Dhaka (1st berth/1st seat/ shuvon Tk 840/560/350, nine hours). The *Sundarban Express* leaves at 9pm and arrives in Dhaka at 5.40am. It doesn't run on Tuesdays. The *Chitra Express* leaves at 9.55am and arrives at 6.20pm. Its day off is Monday.

Kushtia

📞 071 / POP 85,000

Kushtia is steeped in cultural history. This tiny town was once the home of Nobel-laureate poet Rabindranath Tagore, who penned some of his most influential works while living in his family mansion here. Kushtia is also the final resting place of the great mystic musician Lalon Shah; a hugely popular folk-music festival is held here in his honour twice a year.

⊙ Sights

Kuthibari   MUSEUM

(Tk 100; ⊘9am-5pm) Kuthibari is the former residence of Bengal's most famous poet, Rabindranath Tagore. It was built in the mid-19th century and Tagore lived here for over 10 years from 1880, composing some of his immortal poems, songs and short stories. He returned here from Kolkata in 1912 for several years, translating his works into English

and earning the Nobel Prize for Literature (1913) in the process. The house has been turned into a museum dedicated to Tagore's life and works.

The building is set among landscaped gardens, where musicians sometimes gather to perform in his honour. There are a few snack stalls outside the entrance to the house, where you can grab lunch, but bringing a picnic to eat in the grounds isn't a bad idea. To get here, you can hitch the 16km ride in a tempo (Tk 30) from the centre of town.

Shrine of Lalon Shah   SHRINE

(Lalon Shah Rd) For both foreigners as well as Bangladeshi tourists, the white onion-domed shrine of musician and poet Lalon Shah is the main reason for visiting Kushtia. Lalon Shah is one of the most famous mystic personalities in Bangladesh, and the serene shrine is a fascinating peek into the spiritual side of Bangladeshi life. The shrine centres on the holy man's tomb and that of his adopted parents, while around the perimeter of the shrine are the tombs of various local dignitaries.

Behind the tomb complex is a covered area where musicians sometimes play and sing Lalon Shah's songs, while pilgrims burst into dance. In mid-March and mid-October, the **Lalon Festival** is held on the grassy maidan, overlooking the river nearby. It's a five-day folk-music extravaganza and attracts

---

LALON THE SINGING SAINT

Bauls and Fakirs are mystic minstrels who constitute both a quasi-religious sect and a strong musical tradition in Bengal. Following similar principles to Sufism, their music celebrates celestial love, but does so in very earthy terms rather than spiritual ones, and Baul ideology is thus said to transcend religion.

Lalon Shah is regarded as the most important poet-practitioner of the Baul tradition, and is treated as a saint, mystic poet, song composer, social reformer and secular thinker all rolled into one. No one is quite certain when or where he was born. He claimed to have merely 'arrived'; suffering from smallpox at age 16, he was found by a local farmer floating in the river near Kushtia. As the boy recovered, it became clear that he was possessed of great wisdom and he quickly attracted many followers.

Lalon was a humanist and was vehemently opposed to all distinctions of religion and caste. Throughout his long life, he said nothing of the time before his discovery and nobody has ever been able to prove whether he came from an Islamic or Hindu background. Although he often spoke positively on aspects of all religions, he encouraged people to look 'into themselves' for answers and, being a talented poet and musician, he used music to get his messages across.

An iconic figure for preaching religious tolerance and secularism, his philosophy, articulated in songs, has inspired and influenced many poets and social and religious thinkers, including Rabindranath Tagore, who references the tradition in much of his writings.

Lalon died in 1890 and is believed to have reached the ripe old age of 116!

thousands of pilgrims, itinerant vendors and marijuana-smoking holy men who travel from all across the subcontinent to commemorate Lalon Shah's birth (March) and death (October).

Sleeping

Noor International
HOTEL $

(☑ 01778-897792; Rajdhani Complex, Upazila More; s/d from 500/600, with air-con from 1200/1600; ❄ @ ☎) Shiny and newly commissioned, this mint-fresh place (as of now) has airy and bright rooms done up in colourful upholstery. The toilets with sit-down loos and round-the-clock hot showers are the best you'll find in town. Wi-fi and breakfast come free with the air-con rooms. To find it, walk five minutes south from the lotus-flower roundabout past the DC Court complex.

Hotel Rose View
HOTEL $$

(☑ 01730-912343; NS Rd; d from Tk 1400; ❄ @ ☎) Easily the smartest place by Kushtia's standards, this hotel on the upper floors of a commercial building has a string of home-style rooms that are clean, well-appointed and generally pleasant to stay in for a couple of nights. To get to it, walk for about 500m due east from the lotus-flower roundabout along NS Rd, keeping to your left.

Eating

There are a number of cheap and cheerful local restaurants by the Dhaka Bus Stand, most of which open early for breakfast. Expect dhal, roti and fried egg.

Mouban
BANGLADESHI $

(NS Rd; mains from Tk 80; ☺ 7am-10pm) A very popular roadside restaurant, this place makes unending platters of kebabs, biryani and extremely tasty fried chicken that hit the spot. There's also a lip-smackingly good selection of sweets in an attached shop. English sign, but no English menu. From the lotus-flower roundabout, walk about 500m along NS Rd and you'll find it on your left.

Karamai
CHINESE $$

(NS Rd; mains Tk 150-200; ☺ noon-3pm & 6-10pm; ▥) This place does a sort of quasi-Chinese selection that is far from authentic, but is nonetheless tasty and wholesome. It's housed in clean surrounds on the 1st floor of a building on the northern side of NS Rd, a few hundred metres east of the lotus-flower roundabout. There's an English menu.

❶ Getting There & Away

The Dhaka bus stand (not really a bus stand, but rather just a place where buses stop) is close to the main drag (NS Rd). To get to NS Rd from the bus stand, walk across the railway line, bear right then turn right at the lotus-flower roundabout. A number of companies with ticket offices at this bus stand have regular services to Dhaka (non-air-con/air-con Tk 320/600, five to six hours).

The Terminal bus stand is about 2km south of town (rickshaw Tk 20) and has services to Jessore (Tk 180, three hours, 6am to 6pm) and Rajshahi (Tk 180, two hours, 7am to 5pm).

BARISAL DIVISION

The river-laden division of Barisal is very much off the radar for the average tourist, but an off-the-beaten-track journey here makes for a wonderfully authentic riverine experience. Barisal has little in the way of must-see sights, but its maze of waterways, luxuriously green farmland and quiet village life make it a beautiful place to travel around.

The small, charming city of Barisal has a busy port, and is a convenient place to base yourself for forays into other parts of the division. You can also catch ferries, including the Rocket, and ride the region's extensive waterways. If you head further south, to Kuakata, you can even catch boats to the eastern fringes of the Sundarbans National Park, which is an unusual alternative to the more popular tours that run from Khulna.

Barisal

☑ 0431 / POP 210,000

Surrounded by turbid rivers and hemmed by unending tracts of greenery, Barisal (bor-ee-shal) is a major port city and one of the gateways to the waterworld that is Bangladesh. It's strangely isolated from the rest of the country, and is interestingly much easier to reach by boat than road (although buses to and from Dhaka are straightforward enough). Barisal is one of the more pleasant outposts in the country, with several ponds in the city centre and handsome buildings from the Raj era, crumbling away in quiet backstreets. But it's the busy river port, constantly humming with life, that is the real hub, and to arrive here by boat in the early-morning mist (as you do if you catch the Rocket from Dhaka) is an unforgettable experience.

🛏 Sleeping

Hotel Athena International
HOTEL $

(☎01712-261633; Katpatty Rd; s/d Tk 500/800, with air-con Tk 1100/1300; ❄🛜) Athena makes you an offer you simply can't refuse for the price. The rooms with comfy beds and sit-down loos are well-maintained, and the English-speaking management makes sure that all your requirements are satisfactorily met. The reception is on the 1st floor, and the access is marked by an English sign.

Hotel Sedona International
HOTEL $$

(☎01705-293878; www.hotelsedonabd.com; Sadar Rd; s/d incl breakfast from Tk 1700/2200; ❄@🛜) A welcome addition to Barisal's midrange segment, this place opened shop in 2015 and has a string of small but well-appointed rooms with plenty of light, air, tasteful woodwork and most importantly, sparkling clean sit-down loos. The rooms are low on street noise and offer pleasant views of town which you can savour from your bedside windows.

Hotel Grand Park
HOTEL $$$

(☎01777-735160; www.hotelgrandparkbarisal. com; Port Rd, Chandmari; s/d incl breakfast Tk 8000/10,000; ❄@🛜🏊) Somewhat incongruous for a place like Barisal, this gigantic operation conjures images of Las Vegas right in the heart of this tropical waterworld. Rooms are extremely smart and luxurious, and service is impeccable. However, it's located about 1.5km out of the town centre, where the surrounds are peaceful but you feel strangely disconnected from the buzz.

🍴 Eating

Shokal Shondha
SWEETS $

(Sadar Rd; mains from Tk 50; ⏰6am-10pm) This is a good place to buy yourself a platter of sticky local sweetmeats. It's more clean and hygienic compared to most sweet shops, and the early morning breakfast of dhal and paratha is also eminently hearty. There's no English sign or menu. Look for white lettering on a green sign, under the NCC Bank.

Garden Inn
BANGLADESHI $

(Sadar Rd; mains from Tk 100; ⏰11am-10pm) Located deep inside a commercial building, this place probably does the best local food in town. Try the delicious *haleem* (meat and lentil soup) with naan for dinner, or go for

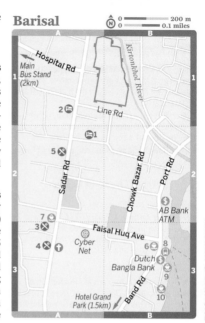

Barisal

an aromatic, slow-cooked *kachchi* biryani. There's an English sign leading you to the place, but no menu at all. The enthusiastic staff will help you choose the kitchen's best offerings.

Rose Garden Restaurant
BANGLADESHI $

(Sadar Rd; mains Tk 80-120; ⏰7am-11pm) This place is clearly a locals' favourite. It's a bit dark and dingy for comfort, but the food (biryanis, fried chicken, kebabs) speaks for itself. Avoid the Chinese dishes, unless you're really keen to sample some full-on fusion. There's an English menu rife with spelling errors.

ℹ Information

There's an **AB Bank ATM** (Port Rd) near the launch ghat that accepts foreign cards. The bank has another ATM just before the main bus stand, on Hospital Rd.

Cyber Net (Faisal Huq Ave; per hour Tk 50; ⌚10am-9pm) Offers speedy internet access on the 2nd floor of a commercial building.

Dutch Bangla Bank (Band Rd) Has an ATM by the piers that accepts foreign cards.

ℹ Getting There & Away

AIR

US Bangla Airlines (☎ 01777-777788; www. us-banglaairlines.com) has three weekly flights (Tk 3200) connecting Barisal to Dhaka, on Sunday, Tuesday and Thursday.

BOAT

The Rocket runs from Barisal's **Rocket Ghat** (Band Rd) to either Dhaka, in one direction, or Morrelganj in the other. It used to run all the way to Khulna, but silting of the riverbed has made the river too shallow for the vessel to travel beyond Morrelganj. If you want to go as far as Khulna, you can catch the Rocket up to Hularhat, then take a bus to Khulna from there.

Note, the Rocket to Dhaka stops for half an hour in the small fishing town of Chandpur (Tk 650, seven hours), from where you can get to Chittagong by bus (Tk 380, four hours) or train (1st seat/shuvon Tk 280/120, five hours, 5am and 1.50pm).

For daytime Rocket trips, just buy your ticket on board, half an hour before departure. For overnight trips to Dhaka, you must reserve your ticket at the **BIWTC** (Band Rd) office, on the 2nd floor of an unmarked building across the main road from the ferry ghat.

Numerous other passenger ferries (cabin/2nd class Tk 1700/900), generally known as 'launches', drift slowly upriver from Barisal to Dhaka. Most leave a few hours after the Rocket, at around 8pm or 9pm, and use the main **Launch Ghat** (Band Rd), not the Rocket Ghat, which is a short walk away. From the Launch Ghat, there are also boats to Moju Chowdhury Hat (2nd/ deck class Tk 455/290, five hours).

Green Line (www.greenlinebd.com; Sadar Rd) operates a fast air-con catamaran service (1st/2nd class Tk 1000/700) between Barisal and Dhaka, departing the Launch Ghat at 2.30pm. The pricier seats come with a business-class-on-the-river feel, and allow you to savour the fleeting river scenery through the daylight hours, which is a definite bonus.

On the Rocket service, destinations include the following places. Fares were being reviewed at the time of research, and may rise marginally by the time you visit.

Chandpur 1st/2nd/deck class Tk 650/340/110, seven hours, 6.30pm, no service Sunday

Dhaka 1st/2nd/deck class Tk 1050/630/170, 12 hours, 6.30pm, no service Sunday

Hularhat 1st/2nd/deck class Tk 210/140/80, four hours, 6am, no service Saturday

BUS

The **main bus stand** (Dhaka–Barisal Hwy) is about 3km northwest from the town centre. A rickshaw from the main bus stand into town is Tk 30. From the main bus stand, buses go to Dhaka (Tk 410, seven to eight hours, 8am to 10pm). Buses for Kuakata (Tk 280, five hours, 6am to 4pm) leave from the **Kuakata bus stand** (Band Rd).

WORTH A TRIP

FLOATING RICE MARKET

Like the more famous floating markets in Southeast Asia, the small one at Banaripara – just an hour's bus ride from Barisal – is where locals who live in this river-laden part of Bangladesh come to buy and sell groceries without ever having to step off their boats. This particular market deals almost entirely in rice. It's not much use for the average tourist, but it does make a fascinating and undoubtedly unusual side trip on a foray into southern Bangladesh.

Trading takes place every day, but Saturday (locally known as the *haat* or market day) is the busiest here, when the river is full of bobbing 'shops', and the market stalls in the narrow lanes leading down to the river are at their most colourful.

Buses to Banaripara (Tk 40) leave all day from Barisal's main bus stand. To break the journey, you could stop at the large, modern and eye-catching Guthia Mosque (Tk 25, 40 minutes). Alternatively, if you're riding the Rocket from Barisal to Hularhat or Morrelganj, you will actually pass through the floating market, and can get a unique perspective of the goings on from the comfort of your boat deck.

Kuakata

☎ 04428 / POP 10,000

Located at the southern tip of the Bangladesh delta, this largely isolated beach was named by the original Mogh (Rakhine) Buddhist settlers, whose ancestors remain here today. *Kua* means 'well', and *kata* means 'dug'. Legend has it that the name originated from the early settlers' practice of digging wells in the area to harvest freshwater. You can see one of these *kuas* to your left as you walk up to the beach along the main Barisal–Patuakhali Rd.

The river mouths east and west of the beach ensure the sea is rather murky, and strong undercurrents make the sea unsafe for swimming. Also remember that Kuakata isn't the archetypal turquoise-coloured tropical ocean. The vibe is right, thanks to the long, palm-tree-lined beach that is largely deserted, but amenities are pricey (where available) and activities are scant.

A word of caution: some lone women travellers have complained about receiving excessive hassle from groups of local men in Kuakata.

🛏 Sleeping & Eating

The nicer hotels all have in-house restaurants, but many people eat at the roadside shacks on the approach road to the beach. Most are open from around 7am to 10pm. As you'd expect, fish and other marine goodies are the order of the day, with most places serving a selection of curried or fried catches of the day, usually dished up with rice and a vegetable curry. Expect to pay around Tk 120 for a meal. Breakfast (Tk 40) tends to be fresh paratha, dhal and vegetable curry.

Out on the beach, cart-pushing snack vendors serve *chaat* (spicy snacks) and freshly roasted nuts, along with tea in minuscule cups.

SEA CRUISE TO FATRA CHAR

For a great half-day trip, consider hopping aboard a boat to **Fatra Char**, a forested island about one hour's boat ride west of Kuakata, on the eastern edge of the Sundarbans.

A small clearing beside an oh-so-tempting freshwater lake makes the perfect picnic spot. The **Kuakata Tourist Centre** (☎ 01734-773580; Kuakata beachfront) – little more than a ticket counter on the beach at Kuakata – sells tickets to Fatra Char (Tk 500 return). The trip lasts for three to four hours, including about an hour on the island.

Banani Palace   HOTEL $$

(☎ 01713-674192; www.bananipalace.com; BP Rd; r without/with air-con from Tk 1650/3000; ❄ @) Set beside a small pond, Banani has clean, white-tiled rooms with TV, sofa, coffee table and a small attached bathroom with sit-down toilet. The cheapest rooms, on the ground floor, represent good value for Kuakata, although they aren't a patch on similarly priced hotels elsewhere. It's on the right as you walk away from the beach along the main Barisal–Patuakhali road.

Hotel Neelanjana   HOTEL $$

(☎ 01712-927904; Rakhine Market; r with/without air-con Tk 2800/1200; ❄ @) Painted in bold red and blue on the outside, this place has clean, comfortable rooms with private balconies and sit-down toilets in sparkling bathrooms. Service is quick and efficient, and the in-house food is recommended. From the beach, walk to the crossroads and then take the next right. Neelanjana will be on your left, after the playing field.

❶ Getting There & Away

Ramshackle buses to Barisal (Tk 280, five hours, 6am to 4pm) leave about once an hour from the crossroads just before the beach.

Rajshahi & Rangpur

Best Places to Eat

➡ RDRS Guesthouse (p96)

➡ Chili's (p86)

➡ Order's Up (p85)

Best Places to Sleep

➡ RDRS Guesthouse (p96)

➡ Chez Razzak (p84)

➡ Archaeological Rest House (p94)

Why Go?

The vast alluvial floodplains of northwest Bangladesh were a cradle of ancient Buddhist and Hindu kingdoms that held sway over the region for centuries, before eventually succumbing to Islamic conquerors. Modern-day Rajshahi and Rangpur divisions – which cover this heritage-strewn region – are thus rife with the tumbledown walls of many splendidly decaying ruins from these bygone eras. Needless to say, it's enough reason for history and archaeology buffs to visit.

In a nutshell, the area contains some of Bangladesh's finest rajbaris (Raj-era palaces), exquisitely decorated temples and the country's largest and most impressive Buddhist ruins. Small villages, colourful markets and remote communities living on fast-eroding sand islands all add to the allure of a trip to this part of the country. The idyllic rural landscape is stunning to boot, and lends a fantastic backdrop to the decaying, moss-hewn ancient architecture that steals the attention of your camera.

When to Go
Bogra

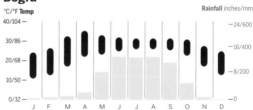

Oct–May Dry season; the best time to visit the flood-prone eastern regions.

May–Jun Mango season in the western areas between Rajshahi and Sona Masjid.

Nov–Dec Maha Raas Leela attracts pilgrims to Kantanagar Temple.

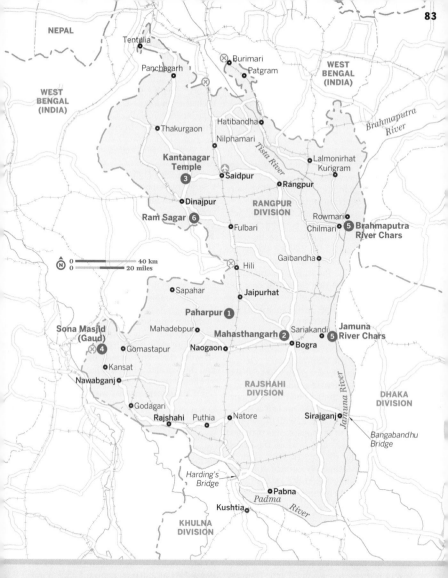

Rajshahi & Rangpur Highlights

1 **Paharpur** (p93) Exploring this ruined monastery, Bangladesh's standout archaeological site.

2 **Mahasthangarh** (p91) Wandering the ruined remains of the country's oldest known city.

3 **Kantanagar Temple** (p97) Walking through farming villages to this stunning temple, Bangladesh's finest example of Hindu architecture.

4 **Sona Masjid** (p88) Marvelling at the sublime architecture of this mosque, set amid the scattered ruins of the lost Islamic city of Gaud.

5 **River Chars** (p89) Discovering how a million Bangladeshis live on shifting river islands by visiting one of the islands of the Jamuna or the Brahmaputra rivers.

6 **Ram Sagar** (p97) Picnicking on the banks of this serene lake on the outskirts of Dinajpur.

Rajshahi

☏ 0721 / POP 470,000

Built on the northern bank of the Padma River, Rajshahi is a fun university town with enough colour and attractions to keep you occupied for a short visit. It also makes a sensible base from which to dig through the layers of history in Sona Masjid, Puthia and Natore.

The Padma's riverbank affords pleasant views. In the late afternoon, a carnival-like atmosphere pervades with people strolling and chatting, children playing and vendors selling tea, ice cream and other snacks.

Looking across the vast flood plain, you will see India (the border is about 2km beyond the opposite bank), where the river is called the Ganges. In the dry season, it's sometimes possible to walk across the riverbed, which aids the thriving smuggling trade along the border. Boats will take you for a river ride (Tk 20), but it's advisable not to set foot on the other bank (Sona Masjid is the nearest official border crossing).

◉ Sights

★ **Varendra Research Museum**   MUSEUM
(Saheb Bazar Rd; Tk 50; ⊙10am-5pm Sat-Wed, 2.30-5pm Fri) This gem of a museum is tucked away in an unassuming building on a quiet street, but can easily take up half a day of your time. Founded in 1910 with the support of the maharaja of Dighapatia, it is managed by Rajshahi University and is the oldest museum in the country. Housed within is a fantastic and superbly curated collection of relics spanning the entire subcontinent, from the earliest civilisation of Mohenjodaro in Pakistan to local archaeological excavation sites.

Keep enough time in hand to view the wonderful sculpture galleries, with exquisite figurines of Hindu gods, goddesses and mythical figures. The collection of Islamic artefacts from the medieval era, comprising weapons, ensembles, daily objects and a number of ornate hand-written copies of the Quran, is simply stunning. The building itself is a curious mix of British and Hindu architectural styles.

Raj Historic Buildings   BUILDINGS
Thrown around the central zone of Rajshahi (to the west of the junction known as Zero Point) are some interesting Raj-era

buildings, which you can view on a stroll around the area. **Rajshahi Government College**, which dates back to 1873 when several maharajas donated money to its establishment, is an elegant two-storey edifice with beautiful semi-circular arched windows. Other elegant buildings nearby include **Collegiate School**, which was built in 1836 and comprises two single-storey structures east of the college with verandahs along the facades.

There's also **Fuller House**, built in 1909, a large two-storey red brick building that is similar in appearance to the government college.

🛏 Sleeping

Hotel Dalas International   HOTEL $$
(☏0721-773839; off Station Rd; s/d incl breakfast from Tk 1500/2000; ❄ @) This is the best mid-range option in town by some distance, and the just-completed renovation job makes it an even better choice. The colourfully themed rooms are universally spacious and well equipped with TV, chairs and big beds. Toilets are clean and tiled with 24-hour hot showers. It's handy for both the town centre and the bus and train stations.

There's no wi-fi yet (and that's a shame), but management says it's working on it.

Hotel Nice   HOTEL $$
(☏0721-776188; www.hotelniceraj.com; Saheb Bazar Rd; d incl breakfast from Tk 1400; ❄ @ 🛜) Among the more comfortable places to stay in the city centre, the well-maintained Nice has reasonably smart, colourful rooms with TV, air-con and clean attached bathrooms with sit-down toilets. Staff members speak English, and the in-house Ohona Restaurant on the 1st floor does some mean beef, fish and poultry dishes.

Chez Razzak   GUESTHOUSE $$$
(☏01711-958708; www.chezrazzakservice.com; House 310, Rd 2, Padma Housing Estate; r incl breakfast from Tk 3500; ❄ @ 🛜) Preferred by foreign NGO staff and aid agency officials, this 'guesthouse' is a seven-storey affair with state-of-the-art rooms that pack in large comfy beds, pearly white linen, elegant drapes and smart loos. It's a bit out of the way, located in an upscale residential area, but it's a quiet and welcome escape from the city-centre chaos. The food is delicious.

Rajshahi

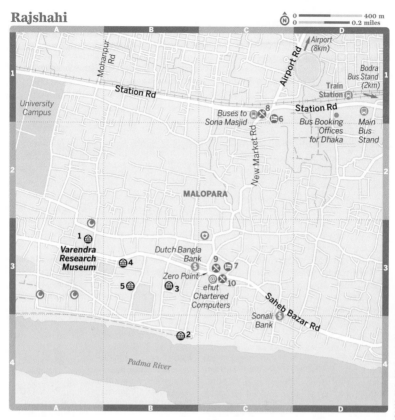

0 — 400 m
0 — 0.2 miles

Rajshahi

◎ Top Sights
1 Varendra Research Museum A3

◎ Sights
2 Bodo Kuthi B4
3 Collegiate School B3
4 Fuller House B3
5 Rajshahi Government College B3

🛏 Sleeping
6 Hotel Dalas International C1
7 Hotel Nice C3

✕ Eating
8 Bindu Restaurant C1
9 Chili's C3
10 Order's Up C3

The place is a Tk 30 rickshaw ride from the city centre, but only a short walk from Vodra bus stand. The management speaks very good English.

✕ Eating

Bindu Restaurant BANGLADESHI $
(Station Rd; mains from Tk 80; ⊗7am-10pm) Located on a busy road crossing just opposite Hotel Dalas International, this proletarian eatery is popular for dhal-roti breakfasts and set Bangladeshi meals that can be paired with a wide choice of fish and meat curries. There's very little English spoken; even the signage is in Bengali. But ask anyone and you'll be pointed in the right direction.

Order's Up CAFE $$
(Saheb Bazar Rd; snacks from Tk 100; ⊗11.30am-10pm) This stylish eatery on the 2nd floor of a shopping complex attracts college kids who file into its wood- and glass-panelled interiors to while away time over umpteen servings of frappe-style coffee and snacks such as barbecued chicken wings and nuggets. A few big steak meals are also available, along with hamburgers and sandwiches. There's an English menu.

THE INFAMOUS INDIGO KUTHIS

In the 18th and early 19th centuries, the trade in indigo – the plant that yields the indigo hue for dyeing – was the rage in Bengal. By the mid-1800s, the Rajshahi region alone had more than 150 indigo *kuthis* (factories), and the local zamindars (landowners) even loaned money to peasants so that they could plant more indigo. Indeed, trade was so lucrative and the *kuthis* so numerous that labourers had to be imported to keep up production and meet market demands.

The farmers, however, didn't profit much from the trade. Interest rates on loans were high, and peasants were paid a pittance for their crops compared to the rates commanded in the European market. When they tried to change crops, angry zamindars used torture and oppression, and sometimes went as far as committing murder and burning whole villages, to terrorise them into continuing with indigo production. An adage at the time held that 'no indigo box was dispatched to England without being smeared in human blood'.

In 1859, the peasants revolted. The Indigo Revolt lasted two years and brought the cultivation of indigo to a halt. Eventually, the government had no choice but to decree that the peasants could no longer be forced to plant indigo. As a result, by the end of the century, the indigo trade had completely disappeared. Some of the *kuthis* were converted into silk factories, but most simply fell into ruin.

High on the riverbank in Rajshahi, although locked away behind gates and walls, **Bodo Kuthi** is one of the last remaining examples of the indigo *kuthis* in this region. Originally built by the Dutch as a silk factory in the early 19th century, Bodo Kuthi also served as a fort in times of emergency before being converted into an indigo *kuthi* by the British East India Company. It was in operation for around 25 years before being abandoned and subsequently falling into disrepair.

Chili's
BANGLADESHI $$

(Saheb Bazar Rd; mains Tk 100-200; ⊙11.30am-10pm) Chili's runs a food empire of sorts, with three restaurants located on both sides of the main drag. While the cafe and the Chinese eateries both come highly recommended, this flagship Bangladeshi restaurant is clearly the best of its kind in town. Try the *kachchi* biryani; the aroma will linger in your mind long after you've left town.

ⓘ Information

Dutch Bangla Bank (Saheb Bazar Rd) One of several ATMs that accept foreign cards.

ehut Chartered Computers (Saheb Bazar Rd; internet per hour Tk 50; ⊙9am-9pm) This 2nd-floor place has fast connections, but you can expect a crowd of students to be there most of the time.

ⓘ Getting There & Away

AIR

US Bangla Airlines (☑01777-777788; www.us-banglaairlines.com) currently operates three flights a week (Tk 3000) from Rajshahi to Dhaka, on Sunday, Wednesday and Friday.

BUS

Many of the main bus stand services stop at Vodra bus stand on the way out of town. For Sona Masjid (Tk 140, three hours, hourly 7.30am to 4pm), head to the **stop** (cnr New Market & Station Rds) at the crossroads of New Market Rd and Station Rd. For non-air-con (Tk 450) or air-con (Tk 1000) coaches to Dhaka (six hours, 6am to midnight), go to the ticket booking **offices** (Station Rd) just west of the main bus stand.

It's Tk 10 per person in a shared CNG from the main bus stand, also known as 'Terminal', to Vodra bus stand, from where buses go to Kushtia (Tk 180, two hours, 6am to 4pm).

From the **main bus stand** (Station Rd), buses also leave for the following destinations:
Bogra Tk 160, 2½ hours, 6.30am to 4.30pm
Natore Tk 70, one hour, 6.30am to 6.30pm
Puthia Tk 40, 30 minutes, 6.30am to 6.30pm
Rangpur Tk 270, 4½ hours, 6am to 4pm

TRAIN

From Rajshahi's central **station** (☑0721-774040; Station Rd), three trains go to Dhaka (AC berth/AC seat/shuvon Tk 1080/725/315, six hours, 7.30am daily except Sunday, 4pm daily except Tuesday and 11.20pm daily except Friday). One train also runs to Khulna (1st seat/shuvon Tk 400/190, seven hours, 2pm daily except Monday).

Puthia

📞 0721 / POP 20,000

The delightful little village of Puthia (*poo-tee-yah*) is home to a handful of dilapidated palaces and bewitching temples, and is one of the shining highlights of this part of Bangladesh. If Puthia were in almost any other country, the ruins would be seething with camera-snapping tourists, but lost as it is in the remote paddy fields of Bangladesh, you'll have it all to yourself (barring the odd bus-full of school kids who turn up from time to time).

The vegetation-draped village is centred on a cheerful bazaar and a number of lily-covered ponds in which people fish, swim and wash themselves, their clothes and their buffalo. It's wonderful to explore the surrounds on foot, but remember to ask for permission before you take photos of people engaged in their daily chores (they'll always agree with a smile).

◉ Sights

In addition to Govinda and Shiva temples and the main palace, there are plenty of other temples and rajbaris, in various states of decay, scattered among the tree-shaded villages and surrounding banana plantations. It's a beautiful place to walk around.

Note that some of the temples and monuments are under the supervision of the Archaeology Department and remain locked for security reasons. Ask around the main palace or the Shiva Temple for the person with the key.

Govinda Temple   HINDU TEMPLE
(⊘ dawn-dusk) Arguably the most startling monument in Puthia village is the Govinda Temple, located inside the palace, on the left-hand side of the inner courtyard. Erected between 1823 and 1895 by one of the maharanis of the Puthia estate, it's a large, square structure with intricate terracotta designs embellishing the surface. Most of the terracotta panels depict scenes from the love affair between Radha and Krishna as told in the Hindu epics.

The temple now contains a Krishna shrine and is visited by many of the local Hindu population. There is a second, smaller temple complex on the other side of the pond, which is off to the left as you exit the palace. It contains three beautifully renovated temples – Govinda, Gopala and Anika –

with domed, egg-shell roofs and carvings that come close to rivalling that of the main Govinda Temple.

Shiva Temple   HINDU TEMPLE
(⊘ dawn-dusk) Built in 1823, the towering Shiva Temple sits at the entrance to Puthia village, overlooking a pond. It's an excellent example of the *pancha-ratna* (five-spire) Hindu style common in northern India. Unfortunately, many of the stone carvings and sculptures were disfigured during the 1971 Liberation War. The inside contains a huge black-stone phallic representation of Shiva. The arched corridors of the temple looking out to the pond can provide some interesting photo-ops, notwithstanding the reservoir's limpid and polluted waters.

Many Hindus come here to offer puja early in the morning or in the early evening and, with the mist rising off the pond and the light setting everything aflame, this is a beautiful time to visit. An even more rewarding time to visit is during one of the two major pilgrimages that take place here – one in March/April and the other during the final week of August.

Puthia Palace   PALACE
This stately, multi-columned, two-storey palace was built in 1895 by Rani Hemanta Kumari Devi in honour of her illustrious mother-in-law, Maharani Sharat Sundari Devi. She was a major benefactor in the Rajshahi region, having built a boarding house for students and a Sanskrit college, for which she was given the title 'maharani' in 1877. Though access to the palace's interior is restricted, it's enough just to marvel at the grand exterior and perfect setting, with its large grassy playground and frog-filled pond.

The building is in just passable condition to serve as a college today, but its walls are crumbling and are direly in need of restoration work.

Facing Puthia Palace across the maidan is **Dol Mondir**, a white pyramid-shaped temple with four tiers, built in 1875. The imposing Govinda Temple can be accessed through a side door to the left of the facade, which is open to visitors all day.

ℹ Getting There & Away

There are numerous buses from Rajshahi to Natore and they all stop at Puthia (Tk 30, 30 minutes, 6.30am to 6.30pm). From the main road, follow the sign for 'Puthia Temple' going right, and keep walking for about 500m.

It's easy to pick up buses on the side of the main road here to either Rajshahi or Natore (Tk 20, 30 minutes), from where you can also catch buses to Dhaka and Bogra.

Sona Masjid (Gaud)

A site of great historical importance, Gaud (pronounced gour, but better known on this side of the international border as Sona Masjid, the name of the main mosque here) was a medieval kingdom that reached great heights in the pre-Mughal and Mughal eras. The Hindu Senas established their capital here, after which the Khiljis from Turkistan took control for three centuries, to be followed in the late 15th century by the Afghans. Under the Afghans, Gaud became a prosperous city, surrounded by fortified ramparts and a moat, and spread over 32 sq km. Replete with temples, mosques and palaces, the city was visited by traders and merchants from all over Central Asia, Arabia, Persia and China.

◉ Sights

Gaud is like an architectural park where ruins and relics lie scattered amid fields, orchards and public areas on both sides of the border, with many ancient monuments in India as well. The Bangladeshi side has a number of splendid mosques dating back to the region's glory days, several of which are still standing today. Some have been restored, although none of the buildings from the earlier Hindu kingdoms remain. Most prominent buildings are well signposted for you to discover along foot trails.

Chhoto Sona Masjid   MOSQUE
(◷ dawn-dusk) Built between 1493 and 1526, the well-preserved 'Small Golden Mosque' is oddly named, given that it's actually jet black with just patches of terracotta brickwork. It's a fine specimen of pre-Mughal architecture, the chief attraction being the superb decoration carved on the black-stone walls. On both the inner and outer walls, ornate stonework in shallow relief covers the surface. It also features an ornate women's gallery, arched gateways and lavishly decorated mihrabs (niches facing Mecca). Buses from Rajshahi stop beside it.

This living mosque draws in large crowds for Friday prayers, but outside prayer time

it's fine for non-Muslims to enter. This mosque is usually just referred to as 'Sona Masjid' – the Chhoto (small) prefix is in context to a Bodo (big) Sona Masjid that stands on the other side of the nearby international border, in the Indian part of Gaud.

Tahkhana Palace Ruins   RUIN
About 100m beyond Sona Masjid, turn left down a signposted lane and keep walking for about 250m until you reach this small complex of ruins overlooking a small pond. The principal building is the Tahkhana Palace, built by Shah Shuja in the early 17th century and the area's major Mughal-era building. A large two-storey brick edifice, it once contained more than two-dozen rooms as well as a *hammam* (bathhouse) served by terracotta water pipes.

Just beyond this is the attractive **Shah Niamatullah Mosque**, a three-domed mosque built in 1560. Close by is the **Mausoleum of Shah Niamatullah Wali**, with one dome and four squat towers.

Khania Dighi Mosque   MOSQUE
(◷ dawn-dusk) About 750m beyond the turn-off for Darasbari Mosque, turn right at the bus stand and keep walking for around 250m until you see a sign directing you off to the right to this gorgeous single-domed mosque. Also known as Rajbibi Mosque, it was built in 1490 and is in excellent condition. It has some ornately decorated walls, embellished primarily with terracotta floral designs. The dome is particularly fascinating, and is in perfect architectural unison with the gracefully proportioned building.

Built of thousands of minuscule bricks, Khania Dighi is one of the more arresting mosques in the country. Like Chhoto Sona Masjid, it's a working mosque, in which Friday prayers are especially animated. It's fine for women to enter outside prayer time but they must be respectfully dressed. The mosque's position, crouching under huge stumpy mango trees (May to June is mango season) beside a large lily- and duck-covered pond, only helps to enhance its beauty, and it's a perfect spot for a picnic.

Darasbari Mosque   RUIN
About 1km north of Sona Masjid along the main road, turn left down a lane signposted 'Darasbari Mosque'. About 500m along this lane you'll come to this palace-like mosque built in 1470. It's no longer an active mosque, and is largely in ruins – the domed roof col-

lapsed some time ago – but its red-brick archways are highly attractive, as is the secluded grassy location.

🛏 Sleeping & Eating

Gaud does not have hotels. However, that's not a problem, considering you can get buses back to Rajshahi until 4.30pm and can thus easily visit the place on a day trip.

Bring a packed lunch with you; there are few restaurants here that serve decent food. Bottled water can be bought everywhere.

❶ Getting There & Away

Direct buses from Rajshahi to Sona Masjid run from a crossroads near the train station roughly every hour (Tk 150, three hours, 7.30am to 4pm). Not all buses are direct, and you may end up having to change at Nawabganj en route.

The first place your bus will come to as it enters the area is Sona Masjid. It makes sense to get off there, then walk to the other sights before catching a return bus from the bus stand. The stand is about 2km down the road, further towards the border post, at a point where the road bears round to the right towards Khania Dighi Mosque.

There are a few rickshaws knocking about if you don't fancy walking. Shared CNGs (per person Tk 20) ply the main road between Sona Masjid and the border.

Buses from Gaud to Rajshahi run from 7.30am to 4.30pm and leave roughly every hour from the bus stand. Buses stop to pick up passengers at Sona Masjid as they leave the area.

Bogra

📞 051 / POP 260,000

A sprawling town centred around the hectic Shat Matha (seven-road) junction, Bogra acts primarily as a transport hub for travellers. This is the best place to base yourself for trips to Bangladesh's most famous and impressive archaeological sites – Mahasthangarh and Paharpur. It's also the closest major town to the Indian border at Hili.

For those interested in experiencing life on Bangladesh's chars (islands made of silt and sand deposit), a few mid-river settlements on the Jamuna River can be explored on a half-day trip from Bogra, via Sariakandi Ghat.

WORTH A TRIP

CHARS OF THE JAMUNA

A short bus ride from Bogra brings you to Sariakandi Ghat on the banks of the Jamuna River. From here you can catch boats to any one of a number of **chars**.

Chars (pronounced 'chawrs') are large sandbank islands, created from silt deposits caused by ongoing river erosion. They are forever being extended and reduced in size by the waters of Bangladesh's largest rivers, and can be found in many parts of the northwest, as well as in Barisal in the south.

An estimated one million Bangladeshi people live on chars. These are among the poorest and most vulnerable people in the country. The chars they live on are very fertile strips of land, but are extremely susceptible to flooding and further river erosion. They also have no electricity, no running water and no transport systems (apart from country-made boats).

Chars are not tourist attractions, but visiting them is a fascinating opportunity to learn more about the unusual livelihoods of the people who reside on them. To find out more, visit the website of the Chars Livelihoods Programme (www.clp-bangladesh.org).

To get to the chars in this area, take a bus from Bogra's Sariakandi Ghat bus stand to Sariakandi (Tk 30, one hour) then take a rickshaw (Tk 20) to the ghat, from where you can rent boats. Local boathands will know what you want to see, so not speaking Bengali won't prevent you from visiting one of the chars. However, if you're able to bring a Bengali-speaking friend or guide with you, then it'll obviously increase your chances of being able to have some sort of meaningful interaction with the people who live on these islands.

Rates for a one-hour boat trip, including a stop at a char, hovers around Tk 200, but can rise and fall depending on demand.

Bogra

◉ Sights

1 Mohammed Ali Palace Museum
  & Park...B2

⬛ Sleeping

2 Red Chillies Guest House A4

⊗ Eating

3 Akboria Restaurant A1
4 Cozy Café...A3
  Red Chillies....................................(see 2)
5 Rofat Doi Ghar..A2

🛏 Sleeping

YMCA Guesthouse   GUESTHOUSE **$**
(☏ 01713-368354; Bhai Pagla Masjid Rd; d without/with air-con 700/900; ❋) For a pleasant hostel-like experience in Bogra, head south of town to this simple guesthouse, which has clean and tidy rooms managed by very welcoming staff. It's on the 3rd floor of a YMCA-run school, so it's very lively in the daytime. A rickshaw from Shat Matha costs about Tk 30. Food can be arranged from outside by hotel staff.

The building is down the lane beside a mosque called Bhai Pagla Masjid, which is on the left-hand side of Sherpur Rd as you come from Shat Matha.

Hotel Naz Garden   HOTEL **$$**
(☏ 01755-661199; www.hotelnazgarden.com; Bogra Bypass Rd, Silimpur; d incl breakfast from Tk 2600; ❋ @ 🛜 🏊) Catering largely to foreign business travellers and aid agency officials, this upscale place offers good-value rooms with requisite creature comforts and very clean loos. Around 4.5km from the centre, the surroundings are quiet, and the swimming pool really ups the game by several notches, giving you an option to unwind in style after long day trips. A rickshaw from Shat Matha costs Tk 30.

Red Chillies Guest House   HOTEL **$$**
(☏ 051-69777; www.redchilliesbg.com; Sherpur Rd; d incl breakfast from Tk 1650; ❋ @ 🛜) This well-run place probably has the most comfortable beds in town. The rooms are smallish but impeccably appointed, with floral printed linen, faux-cedar furniture and good loos. It's associated with a popular restaurant of the same name, so there's good in-house food available on the other end of an intercom call.

◉ Sights

**Mohammed Ali Palace
Museum & Park**   MUSEUM
(Nawab Bari Rd; grounds Tk 20, museum Tk 50; ⏱ 11am-7pm Sat-Thu) This museum is housed inside one of only a handful of furnished rajbaris in Bangladesh. This one is the former home of a line of influential nawabs, which included former foreign minister Mohammed Ali Bogra. The mosaic ceiling of the audience hall is impressive, and the rooms have mannequins dressed to impress in both Bengali and British fashions. The last room is dedicated to modern art – it's a compelling display, but the lack of English explanation makes it somewhat obscure.

The grounds of the museum have been turned into a mildly pleasant garden and a rundown amusement park with rickety fairground rides. In the far corner is a small row of cages containing monkeys clearly affected by their captivity.

Parjatan Motel   HOTEL **$$**
(📞051-67024; Dhaka–Rangpur Hwy; r without/
with air-con Tk 1400/2000; ❄ @) This colour-
fully tiled government place is a little out of
town, but offers clean and spacious rooms
with balconies and large bathrooms. The
restaurant does average Bangladeshi and
Chinese dishes. If you want some respite
from traffic noise, this is probably the place
to stay. It's a Tk 40 rickshaw ride from Shat
Matha heading south along Sherpur Rd, or
Tk 20 in a shared CNG.

✖ Eating

Not every restaurant in town opens for
breakfast. For some early morning dhal and
roti, try the roadside eateries around Shat
Matha.

Akboria Restaurant   BANGLADESHI **$**
(Kazi Nazrul Islam Ave; mains Tk 60-120; ⊘7am-
11pm) This is by far the most popular res-
taurant in town. Come at any time of the
day, and you'll have to jostle for a table with
local diners digging into their platters of
tasty *bhajis*, *bhortas*, curries, biryanis and
kebabs. There's no English menu, but the
place has an open kitchen so you can actual-
ly walk up and choose.

Rofat Doi Ghar   SWEETS **$**
(Shat Matha; mishti doi per plate Tk 100;
⊘7am-midnight) Bogra's best-known *mish-
ti doi* (sweetened yogurt) stall, this place
serves up clay plates of the yummy dessert
for you to take away and devour back in
your hotel room. There are loads of similar
places across town, but locals say this is the
best of the lot.

Red Chillies   CHINESE **$$**
(Sherpur Rd; mains Tk 150-320; ⊘11am-10pm)
This upstairs place overlooking Bogra's
main thoroughfare is a smart and popular address where you'll see entire families
happily gobbling up huge spreads of tasty
Chinese dishes. The Indian-style naan and
chicken tikka meals also seem to strike a
chord with diners. There's an English menu.

Cozy Café   CAFE **$$**
(Sherpur Rd; mains Tk 140-200, coffee Tk 50;
⊘11am-10pm) This is a good place to stop for
a quick bite in between bus rides. Located
on the main drag, it does tasty fried chicken,
a few jumbled Chinese dishes and instant
coffee. Thanks to its floor-to-ceiling glass-
work out front, you can also watch the world

go by as you nibble on your food. There's an
English menu.

❶ Information

Internet Zone (Kazi Nazrul Islam Ave; internet
per hour Tk 50; ⊘10am-10pm) This is a con-
venient place to check email and browse the
internet.

Standard Chartered Bank (Sherpur Rd) Has
an ATM that accepts foreign cards.

❶ Getting There & Away

BUS

The main bus stand is a Tk 20 rickshaw ride from
Shat Matha, or Tk 10 in a shared tempo (note:
the tempos take you only as far as the railway
crossing, just north of Shat Matha, from where
you'll have to walk it). From here, numerous
services run.

Dhaka Tk 360, five hours, 5am to midnight
Dinajpur Tk 220, four hours, 10.30am to
3.30pm
Jaipurhat Tk 60, 1½ hours, 6am to 8pm
Mahasthangarh Tk 10, 30 minutes, all day
Natore Tk 90, 2½ hours, 6.30am to 4pm
Rajshahi Tk 140, three hours, 6am to 8pm
Rangpur Tk 120, 2½ hours, 7am to 9pm

For Paharpur, you will have to go to Jaipurhat
and change from there.

Green Line (📞01730-060004; www.green
linebd.com; Sherpur Rd) runs two daily air-con
coaches to Dhaka (Tk 560, five hours, 10.30am
and 1am). The morning coach leaves from the
office; the night coach from the Parjatan Motel
(p91).

The Sariakandi Ghat bus stand is a Tk 20 rick-
shaw ride from Shat Matha, or a 20-minute walk,
and has regular buses all day to Sariakandi (Tk
30, one hour).

TRAIN

Rail connections are poor, but two trains run
direct to Dhaka. The *Rangpur Express* (1st
berth/1st seat/shuvon Tk 730/485/365, eight
hours, 11pm) runs every day except Sunday. The
Lalmoni Express (1st berth/1st seat/shuvon Tk
730/485/365, 7½ hours, 1.30pm) runs every
day except Friday.

Mahasthangarh

Considered the oldest city in Bangladesh,
Mahasthangarh dates back to at least the
3rd century BC, and is an easy half-day
trip from Bogra. Very few ancient struc-
tures remain within this walled complex
(*garh* literally means fortification), so what

you'll see is essentially an archaeological site consisting of foundations and hillocks, which merely hint at past riches. Over the centuries, the site was home to Muslims, Hindus and most importantly Buddhists. The Buddhist Pala emperors of North Bengal ruled over this region from the 8th to the 11th centuries and it is from this period that most of the visible remains belong. Amongst the ruins, a few relics still stand tall and command attention, and the rural setting is incredibly peaceful. All in all, it's a very pleasant excursion.

⊙ Sights

Sights in Mahasthangarh are scattered and can be best accessed on foot. The principal site, the Citadel, contains traces of the ancient city around it. The other major structure, called Bashor Ghar, stands to the southern end of the complex, about 3km away from the Citadel. Many other sites in between are lumped together under the generic name Mahasthangarh.

You'll simply have to ask people for directions along the way, and pass through villages, vegetable fields and orchards to get to the different points of interest.

Citadel   RUIN
(⊙dawn-dusk) Running along the left of the road as you walk from Mahasthangarh town towards the museum, the Citadel – or what's left of it – forms a rough rectangle covering more than 2 sq km. It was once surrounded on three sides by the then-mighty Karatoya River, which still flows but has been reduced to a trickle. Hindus make an annual pilgrimage to the river in mid-April. The site shows evidence of various Hindu empires, as well as Buddhist and Muslim occupations.

Probably first constructed under the Mauryan empire in the 3rd century BC, the Citadel fell into disuse around the time of the Mughal invasions. Most of the visible brickwork dates from the 8th century, apart from what was added during phases of restoration. Nowadays, there isn't a lot left to see aside from the edge of the exterior walls – some of which rise three or four metres above the ground level – and various unidentifiable grassy mounds.

Not far inside the first entranceway you come to if you walk from town, you'll see **Jiyat Kunda** (Well of Life), an 18th-century well, the waters of which were said to have supernatural healing powers. Only a few paces ahead is the plinth work of the

Parshuram Palace, the residence of one of the Hindu kings of yore. You can walk the length of the citadel from here, roughly following the line of the main road, to the museum, which is located just outside the far entrance to the site. The Citadel's interior is now used mostly as farmland and is fabulous picnic territory.

Bashor Ghar   HISTORIC SITE
(Gokul; Tk 100; ⊙10am-1pm & 2.30-5pm Tue-Sun, 2.30-5pm Mon) Possibly the grandest of Mahasthangarh's historic sites, this lofty and multi-tiered red-brick pavilion dates back to around the 7th century, although it was excavated only about 80 years ago. Local legend describes it as the *bashor ghar* or wedding pavilion of Behula, the daughter of a rich Bengali trader, whose husband was tragically bitten by a snake on the very night of her wedding (presumably in this very pavilion) but later brought back to life by the goddess Manasa.

The main entrance to the pavilion is still buried under the earth, but you can climb up a ragged staircase to the top of the building, stepping around grass-covered, pit-like cells along the way. The ramparts provide some good photo-ops, and the gardens and village areas around the structure are also worth a wander. The complex is located in Gokul village, which is a short walk from the Gokul turn-off on the main road to Bogra, about 1.5km south of Mahasthangarh.

Mahasthangarh Museum   MUSEUM
(Tk 100; ⊙10am-1pm & 2.30-5pm Tue-Sun, 2.30-5pm Mon) This small but well-maintained museum has a lively set of objects discovered in the antique-rich surroundings, and is a good place to familiarise yourself with local history. The highlights are the statues of Hindu gods, terracotta plaques depicting scenes from daily life, and some well-preserved bronze images found in nearby monastery ruins, which date from the Pala period. Other notable objects are the necklaces and the fragments of ancient toilet seats. The gardens are an attraction in their own right.

Mazhar of Shah Sultan Balkhi   TOMB
(⊙dawn-dusk) In the heart of Mahasthangarh town, near the bus stop, is the mausoleum of Shah Sultan Balkhi, a 14th-century Afghan warrior who – according to legend – came and defeated the Hindu king Parshuram and ruled the region for many years. It's a serene complex where you can immerse

yourself in a few minutes of soul searching, before moving on to check out the small but colourful market adjoining the mausoleum, selling everything from tinsel-lined fabric to tasty local sweetmeats.

Govinda Bhita Hindu Temple   RUIN

(Tk 20; ⊙10am-1pm & 2.30-5pm Tue-Sun, 2.30-5pm Mon) Opposite the Mahasthangarh Museum, the remains of a 6th-century Hindu temple dedicated to Lord Krishna overlook a picturesque bend in the river. The temple looks like a broken-down step pyramid and is another peaceful spot to spend a few quiet moments, either in silent contemplation or taking photos of the pretty surrounds.

🅸 Getting There & Away

Buses run all day from Bogra to Mahasthangarh (Tk 20, 30 minutes). From the main drop-off point, you can take a CNG (Tk 20) or walk the 1.7km to the museum, located at the far end of the Citadel. There's a smaller side entrance to the Citadel, which you'll soon see on your left as you walk along the road towards the museum. If you're walking, take the first left after the point where the bus drops you off, and just keep going while staying to the left. For Bashor Ghar, you'll have to either take a CNG (Tk 20) or walk 1.5km along the highway back towards Bogra. Turn right at the Gokul bus stop and follow the village road for about a kilometre.

Paharpur

One of only two historic sites in Bangladesh that have been given Unesco World Heritage status (the other being Bagerhat), the Somapuri Vihara at Paharpur was once the biggest Buddhist monastery south of the Himalaya. It dates from the 8th century AD and, despite being in complete ruin, is still the most impressive archaeological site in the country.

🅾 Sights

All of Paharpur's major sights are clustered together within the Somapuri Vihara complex. Entry to the complex is from the eastern periphery; you'll find the gate after passing through a mud-hut village and a string of stalls.

★Somapuri Vihara   RUIN

(Tk 100; ⊙10am-1.30pm & 2.30-5pm Tue-Sun, 2.30-5pm Mon) The hulking 20m-high remains of a 1300-year-old red-brick stupa form the central attraction of the vast monastery complex at Somapuri Vihara. Shaped like a quadrangle covering 11 hectares, the complex has monastic cells that line its outer walls and enclose an enormous open-air courtyard with the stupa at its centre. The stupa's floor plan is cruciform, topped by a three-tier superstructure. Look out for clay tiles lining its base, which depict various people and creatures in a variety of postures.

Apart from the walls of the central stupa (now undergoing careful restoration), pretty much every other structure within the complex has been reduced to its plinths and base walls over time. Lining the outer perimeter are 177 small monastic cells – once living quarters for monks, and later used as meditation rooms. Ninety-two of these house ornamental pedestals, the purpose of which still eludes archaeologists. It is possible they contained the remains of saintly monks who had once resided here.

On the eastern wing of the south side is an elevated brick base with an eight-pointed star-shaped structure that is thought to have been a shrine. To the west lie the remains of what appears to have been the refectory and kitchen of the complex.

Except for the guardhouse to the north, most of the remains outside the courtyard lie to the south. They include an oblong building, linked to the monastery by a causeway, which may have been the wash house and latrines. In the same area is a bathing ghat, probably of Hindu origin. Close to the ghat is the rectangular ruin of a Hindu temple, with an octagonal pillar base in the centre and a circular platform to the front.

The monastery is thought to have been successively occupied by Buddhists, Jains and Hindus, which explains the curious mixture of artwork. The Jains would have constructed a *chaturmukhar* (a structure with all four walls decorated with stone bas-reliefs of deities). The Hindus replaced Buddhist terracotta artwork with sculptural stonework of their own deities, and terracotta artwork representing themes from the Mahabharata and the Ramayana. Artefacts discovered at the site range from bronze statues and bas-reliefs of the elephant-headed Hindu god Ganesh, to statues of the Jain god Manzuri, bronze images of the Buddha and statues of the infant Krishna.

Halud Vihara   RUIN

(Dwipganj; ⊙dawn-dusk) About 15km southwest of Somapuri Vihara, in the small village of Dwipganj, is the impressive and underrated Halud Vihara. The central mound, akin to Somapuri, is about 30m wide and 7m high but is badly damaged, with bricks strewn across the village. Nevertheless, it's an interesting place to explore. Expect to pay at least Tk 200 in a CNG from Somapuri.

Paharpur Museum MUSEUM
(Tk 100; ⏱10am-1.30pm & 2.30-5pm Tue-Sun, 2.30-5pm Mon) The small but well-kept museum gives a good idea of the range of cultures that have used this site. Stucco Buddha heads unearthed here are similar to the Gandhara style of Indo-Hellenic sculpture from what is now northwestern Pakistan. Sculptural work includes sandstone and basalt sculptures, but the stonework of Hevagara in passionate embrace with Shakti is the collection's finest item. The most important find, a large bronze Buddha, is usually away wooing fans on a seemingly endless world tour.

🛏 Sleeping & Eating

There are a few stalls near the entrance to the Somapuri Vihara complex serving basic Bangladeshi food (biryani Tk 140). An under-construction tourist complex, scheduled to open in 2017, promises to introduce better options and amenities in the area.

Archaeological Rest House GUESTHOUSE $
(📞01718-653708; Somapuri Vihara complex; per person Tk 500) For an off-beat experience, you could try negotiating with officials at the Somapuri Vihara complex to open one of the two rooms at the adjoining resthouse for you. The good-value rooms are large, clean and have attached bathrooms, but are available only if official guests aren't scheduled to visit. Simple home-style meals (Tk 150) are served upon prior notice.

You can view the stupa from one of the bedroom windows and, as the resthouse is inside the grounds of the ruins, you can even go for a night-time stroll around the complex once the rest of the tourists have left.

ℹ Getting There & Away

From Bogra, take a local bus to Jaipurhat (Tk 70, 1½ hours, 6am to 6pm). From there, buses leave regularly for Paharpur (Tk 20, 30 minutes, 7am to 4pm). To get to the sights from Paharpur village, take a rickshaw (Tk 50). Don't count on getting a bus from Jaipurhat back to Bogra after 6pm.

Rangpur

📞0521 / POP 250,000

Far from the chaos and commotion of southern Bangladesh, Rangpur in the north is a small divisional headquarter town with tree-lined streets, Raj-era bungalows, the splendid Carmichael College and the majestic Tajhat Palace – arguably one of the country's most imposing rajbaris. It's also possible to visit some fascinating river chars (sandbanks that double as residential or agricultural land) from here. The beautiful Kantanagar Temple and the town of Dinajpur are also within range, and make a good local itinerary in conjunction with Rangpur.

◉ Sights

Tajhat Palace PALACE
(Tajhat Rd; Tk 100; ⏱10am-5pm Tue-Sat & 2.30-5pm Mon) The flamboyant and delightfully maintained Tajhat Palace is arguably one of the finest rajbaris in Bangladesh. The palace was constructed in the 19th century by Manna Lal Ray, a Hindu trader who was forced to emigrate from Punjab and found his way to Rangpur. He eventually became a successful jeweller, acquired a lot of land, subsequently won the title of raja (landlord or ruler) and built this huge mansion. Local villagers believe there is treasure hidden in its walls.

Structurally, the palace is similar to Dhaka's Ahsan Manzil (Pink Palace), and has a frontage of about 80m. The main building is crowned by a ribbed conical dome, and features an imposing central staircase made of imported white marble. The balustrade originally featured marble sculptures of classical Roman figures, but these have long since disappeared. During the regime of General Ershad (1982–91), the mansion was used as the divisional High Court, but today it houses a small museum stuffed with old manuscripts and bits and bobs excavated from the archaeological sites of Paharpur and Mahasthangarh.

A rickshaw from the town centre to the palace costs around Tk 70.

Kali Temple HINDU TEMPLE
(Tajhat) Used actively for worship, this interesting architectural folly with red Corinthian pillars is modelled on a Florentine dome (or at least a Bengali vision of an English adaptation of a Florentine dome) and is topped with statuettes of Hindu gods. The

Rangpur

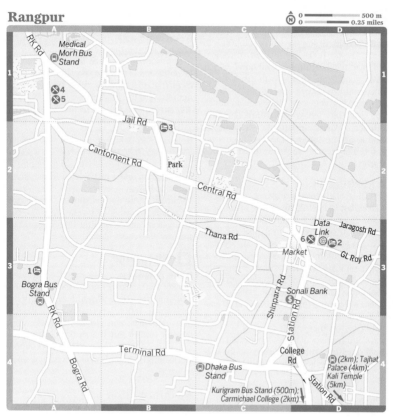

Rangpur

courtyard also doubles as a village school. The temple lies about 1km south of Tajhat Palace. A rickshaw from the palace (ask for *kali mondir*) costs Tk 20. Dress modestly and remove your shoes before entering the temple compound.

Carmichael College   ARCHITECTURE
(কারমাইকেল কলেজ; College Rd; ⊙8am-4pm Sat-Thu) This splendid heritage structure dating from 1916 is one of Bangladesh's largest colleges in terms of area and enrolment. Its architectural grandeur derives from a splendid fusion of classical British and Mughal architecture. Situated on the outskirts of town, the college – with a grand frontage of over 100m – is similar in inspiration to Curzon Hall in Dhaka. Its domes rest on slender columns, and a series of arched openings add to its mosque-like appearance.

The college campus – located roughly 3km from the town centre – is spacious and rural, with cows grazing on the main lawn and students keen to talk of the wider world while resting in the shade. A rickshaw ride to the college is around Tk 100 (from Tajhat Palace, it's Tk 30).

🛏 Sleeping

Park Hotel
HOTEL $

(☑0521-66718; GL Roy Rd; s/d Tk 500/700, with air-con Tk 900/1100; ❄) Budget travellers will love this delightful central hotel, which offers good-value rooms with fresh linen, functional woodwork and clean sit-down loos with hot showers. There's no in-house food available, but you're within shouting distance of Mitali Restaurant, which serves good local fare through the day. There's no wi-fi available, but you'll find internet cafes nearby.

★ RDRS Guesthouse
GUESTHOUSE $$

(☑0521-66492; www.rdrsbangla.net; Jail Rd; s/d incl breakfast Tk 1500/2000; ❄@⊚) Run by a highly deserving NGO that works on health, educational and agricultural projects, this fabulous guesthouse housed in an ivy-clad red-brick building has polished, spacious rooms, piping-hot showers in modern bathrooms, satellite TV, internet access, a pool table and a team of wonderful chefs.

Its **restaurant** (meals Tk 375; ⊘12.30-2pm & 7.30-9pm) offers delicious set-meal platters that bring together a wide range of local flavours and ingredients (the *bhorta* and *bhaji* offerings are truly delightful). Sadly, it is open only to guests staying within the RDRS premises.

Now the caveat: the guesthouse is perpetually booked out, so get your room well in advance.

Parjatan Motel
HOTEL $$

(☑0521-63681; RK Rd; d from Tk 1900; ❄@⊚) Located on the main road to Bogra, this excellent government lodge stands amid pleasant flower gardens and offers a string of universally clean and comfortable rooms with balconies and large bathrooms. The in-house restaurant does a good-value fixed Bangladeshi meal (Tk 200) along with some Chinese and Indian usuals. A rickshaw from the town centre costs Tk 30.

✕ Eating

Kosturi
BANGLADESHI $

(RK Rd; main Tk 80-140; ⊘7am-11pm) Possibly the best among equals in Rangpur, this eatery serves a good collection of local fish and meat staples. There's no English menu, but just say 'fish' and the waiters will blurt out all the catches available for the day – feel free to choose. The fluffy and aromatic mutton biryani is also worth a try.

Mitali Restaurant
BANGLADESHI $

(GL Roy Rd; mains from Tk 80; ⊘9am-10pm) Accessed down a narrow dingy alley, with an English sign on the main road, this charmingly disorganised place has been a locals' favourite for years. The specialty is the *aloo chop* (potato croquette filled with minced mutton) and the fried chicken. There's biryani, curries and kebabs in the evening. No menu but some English spoken by the staff.

Boishakhi Restaurant
INDIAN $

(RK Rd; mains Tk 80-100; ⊘7am-1am) Very popular with locals, Boishakhi does a decent biryani for lunch and a tasty North Indian-style grilled chicken (served with mint-and-cucumber-chutney) for dinner. There are a few kebabs available on the side, too. No menu here, and very little English spoken. Just say your order aloud.

🛍 Shopping

RDRS Enterprise
CLOTHING

(Jail Rd; ⊘10am-8pm) Run by the same NGO that runs the RDRS Guesthouse next door, this small outlet specialises in *satranji* mats and rugs, and also stocks some very tasteful cotton and silk saris. All products are sourced from empowerment-oriented workshops that employ women from nearby villages.

ⓘ Information

Data Link (GL Roy Rd; internet per hour Tk 50; ⊘10am-10pm) Data Link has good connections, and also burns photos on CDs (Tk 100).
Sonali Bank (Station Rd; ⊘10am-4pm Sat-Thu) Changes cash and travellers cheques. If you're exiting to India via the checkposts at Burimari or Hili, pay your Tk 500 departure tax here.

ⓘ Getting There & Away

BUS

Buses to Dhaka (without/with air-con Tk 450/650, seven hours, 7am to 10pm) depart from the **Dhaka bus stand** (Terminal Rd). The **Bogra bus stand** (Bogra Rd) serves Bogra (Tk 120, 2½ hours, 7am to 9pm) as well as a number of other destinations. The **Medical Morh bus stand** (RK Rd) serves Dinajpur (Tk 80, two hours, 6am to 8pm), where you can change for Hili on the Indian border to the southwest. Medical Morh bus stand also has connections to Burimari (Tk 160, four hours, 7am to 3pm) on the Indian border to the north. For visiting the chars near Chilmari, take a bus to Kurigram (Tk 70, 90 minutes, 7am to 6pm) from the **Kurigram bus stand** (College Rd).

TRAIN

Rangpur train station is poorly connected; there is only one direct train to Dhaka called *Rangpur Exp* (8pm, 11 hours, 1st berth/1st seat/shuvon Tk 930/620/390) every day except Sunday. The equivalent train coming to Rangpur leaves Dhaka at 9am daily except Sunday.

Dinajpur

✐ 0531 / POP 160,000

Outlying Dinajpur serves as a good access point for the magnificent Kantanagar Temple, which is the main reason why tourists traipse all the way to this northwestern town. That said, it has a handful of quaint and rural sights, some very colourful street markets packed with sari shops and a number of serene lakes hemmed with greenery.

Security has been a growing concern in and around Dinajpur following a bomb blast in November 2015 and deadly communal violence in early 2016. Be sure to check the latest travel advisories for the area before visiting.

◉ Sights

Hiring a dedicated CNG is the best way to see all of Dinajpur's sights, including Kantanagar Temple, within one day. It'll cost you about Tk 1500, but will save you a lot of time and transport hassles.

Ram Sagar LAKE

(Tk 100; ◷10am-4pm) Commissioned in 1750 by Raja Ramnath, a local landlord, this placid and expansive reservoir is nearly a kilometre long and sits at the heart of the **Ramsagar National Park**, a beautiful patch of forest on the outskirts of Dinajpur. Its banks are a perfect place for a daytime

---

DON'T MISS

KANTANAGAR TEMPLE

Set amid gorgeous countryside, the vault-roofed rouge sandcastle of **Kantanagar Temple** (Tk 20; ◷dawn-dusk), also known locally as Kantaji, is a stunning piece of religious artwork, and one of the most impressive Hindu monuments in Bangladesh.

Built in 1752 by Pran Nath, a renowned maharaja from Dinajpur, it is the country's finest example of brick and terracotta style temple architecture. Its most remarkable feature, typical of mid-18th-century Hindu temples, is its superb surface decoration, with infinite panels of sculpted terracotta plaques depicting both figurative and floral motifs.

The folk artists who lent their masterful touches to the temple were superb storytellers. In one panel, a demon is depicted swallowing monkeys, which promptly reappear from his ear. Other scenes are more domestic, such as a wife massaging her husband's legs and a lady combing lice from another woman's hair. Amorous scenes are often placed in obscure corners. These intricate, harmonious scenes are like a richly embroidered patchwork of Bangladeshi society, culture and mythology.

The 15-sq-m, three-storey edifice was originally crowned with nine ornamental two-storey towers, which collapsed during the great earthquake of 1897 and were never replaced. The building sits in a courtyard surrounded by offices and pilgrims' quarters, all protected by a stout wall. Visitors can no longer go inside the inner sanctum of the temple, which houses a Krishna shrine, but the intricate detail of its exterior will keep you engaged.

The centuries-old Hindu festival of **Maha Raas Leela** – which celebrates the life of a young Lord Krishna – takes place here around full moon in late November or early December, attracting up to 200,000 pilgrims. This is also when a rural fair takes place around the temple complex, marked by stalls selling objects of daily village life and folk artists engaging in music and dance performances.

Buses run regularly all day from Dinajpur's main bus stand to the village of Kantanagar (Tk 30, 30 minutes, 7am to 7pm). A more comfortable and efficient alternative is to grab a return CNG ride from Dinajpur (Tk 1000 including waiting time). From the main road where the bus drops you, it's a lovely 10-minute walk to the temple past stretches of lush farmland, over a concrete river bridge and through a couple of mud-hut villages. En route, you can also stroll down to the river where, in the dry season, the sandbanks exposed by the dropping water levels make a handy cricket pitch for local kids.

Dinajpur

Dinajpur

⊙ Sights
1 Dinajpur Rajbari D1

🛏 Sleeping
2 Hotel Al-Rashid B2
3 Hotel Diamond B2
4 Hotel Unique...B3

✕ Eating
5 Food Garden...A3
6 New Hotel A4
7 Purnima..A4

picnic – snack stalls by the lake whip up basic eats and stock soft drinks. Fishing permits (per day Tk 4000) are available on site, but you'll have to bring your own gear.

While the permits are expensive, the deal is that you can take home whatever you catch. The still waters of the lake are home

to some big fish: the largest catch was reportedly an 80kg carp that was hooked a few years ago.

There's a menagerie of sorts on the premises, with a few enclosures housing monkeys, spotted deer and two lazy rock pythons.

To get here, follow the Pirganj Rd for about 14km, travelling south from Dinajpur. A CNG will cost you Tk 200.

Dinajpur Rajbari   HISTORIC BUILDING
(Rajbari Rd) Mostly in ruins now, the 100-plus-years-old Dinajpur Rajbari still pulls in the crowds not because of its crumbling walls and moss-hewn pillars, but because of the two Hindu temples standing within its grounds. The one on the right as you enter – **Durga Temple** – has a large peaceful courtyard, but is, like the rest of the rajbari, largely in ruins. To the left, though, is the still-active **Krishna Temple**, slapped in bright bold paint, and full of columns and statues.

Thanks to Dinajpur's Hindu population of around 38% (one of the highest in the country), this place is often heaving with devotees, making it an extremely lively place to visit. Some Hindu families live permanently in the yellow-wash houses built into the walls of the temple enclosure.

Directly behind the complex, a 10-minute walk first through the market area and then an embankment, is the **Sukh Sagar** lake, once the private reservoir of the rajbari but now open to the public.

🛏 Sleeping

Following a few communally charged incidents in the area in 2015 (including an explosion during a fair at the Kantanagar Temple), authorities were advising against foreigners staying overnight in Dinajpur. It's eminently possible to cover Dinajpur as a day trip from Rangpur instead.

Should things improve, the **Hotel Al-Rashid** (📞01716-535956, 0531-65658; Nimtola More, Nimtola), **Hotel Diamond** (📞0531-64629; Nimtola-Maldhapatty Rd) and **Hotel Unique** (📞0531-52203, 01736-335264; www.hoteluniquebd.com; Nimtola Rd; ❄) may reopen to foreign guests.

Parjatan Hotel   HOTEL **$$**
(📞0531-64718; Fulbari Rd; s/d Tk 1700/2200; ❄ @) Three kilometres out of town, this is one of the few hotels in Dinajpur that was willing to accept foreign guests at the time of writing. The overall staying experience is bland, with lacklustre housekeeping and an air of smugness, and rooms are a tad overpriced. Even so, it's the best and safest place to sleep in Dinajpur, if you must.

🍴 Eating

New Hotel   BANGLADESHI **$**
(Station Rd; meals Tk 80; ⊙7am-11pm) One of the better Bangladeshi restaurants in the town centre, this eatery draws locals and is usually always full, except during the leaner late-afternoon hours. You can get some vegetarian fare here, in the form of dhal and *shobji* (vegetable curry) dishes. Most people settle for a set-meal that comprises the day's offerings from the kitchen.

Food Garden   CHINESE **$$**
(Station Rd; mains Tk 140-200; ⊙11am-10pm) This is a cheerful Chinese restaurant that is popular at both lunch and dinnertime, and serves full and half portions of food depending on your appetite. The usual noodle dishes and chicken in myriad gravies move the quickest. There's an English menu.

Purnima   BANGLADESHI **$$**
(TNT Rd; meals Tk 120-160; ⊙9am-10pm) This cafe-like eatery has a reputation for preparing the best *kachchi* biryani in town, which is clearly in greater demand than its other offerings. Wash it all down with a cup of instant coffee (Tk 40). No English menu, no English spoken, but the staff are eager to help.

ℹ Information

AB Bank ATM (Station Rd) This ATM accepts foreign cards.
Galaxy Computers (off Station Rd; per hour Tk 60; ⊙10.30am-9pm) This is a central place to go online.

ℹ Getting There & Away

BUS

Dinajpur's main **bus stand** (Bypass Rd) is on Bypass Rd and is a Tk 20 rickshaw ride from town. Destinations include Kantanagar Temple (Kantaji; Tk 30, 30 minutes, 7am to 7pm) and Rangpur (Tk 120, two hours, 7am to 6pm).

A short stretch of Station Rd known as **Kalitola** (Station Rd) contains a cluster of offices for coach companies, which run services to Dhaka (Tk 650, 10 hours, 7am to 11pm).

The **BRTC bus stand** (Bypass Rd) is close to the main bus stand, on a lane that runs parallel to and west of Bypass Rd. Destinations include Dhaka (Tk 650, 10 hours, 7am to 11pm), Rajshahi (Tk 280, six hours, 7am to 4pm) and Bogra (Tk 180, four hours, 7am to 3pm).

TRAIN

While it's quicker to catch buses for destinations within Rajshahi division, you might want to consider the two trains for Dhaka (1st berth/1st seat/shuvon Tk 855/570/360, 10 hours), called *Drutojan Exp* (7.40am daily except Wednesday) and *Ekota Exp* (9.20pm daily except Monday).

Chittagong Division

Includes ➡

Best Places to Eat

➡ Handi (p105)

➡ Tohzah Restaurant (p114)

➡ Mermaid Café (p119)

Best Places to Sleep

➡ Radisson Blu Bay View (p103)

➡ Hillside Resort (p113)

➡ Mermaid Eco-Resort (p120)

Why Go?

The most diverse region of Bangladesh, Chittagong is a land that stretches from forested hills and scenic lakes to sandy beaches and coral islands. It's a land of off-the-beaten-track adventure, with great hiking and remote boat trips, but also one of cultural contrasts – around a dozen Adivasi groups live here.

Home to Bangladesh's largest port, Chittagong is a place where you can see wooden fishing boats being pieced together on one beach, while disused ocean liners are picked apart on the next. You can trek through forests where elephants roam wild, or walk along the world's longest natural beach before retreating to your hotel's rooftop pool.

Some travellers are put off by the hassles of permits (actually very easy to arrange) or the dangers of social unrest (check the latest before you come). But those who persist are rewarded with experiences you simply can't find in any other region of Bangladesh.

When to Go
Chittagong

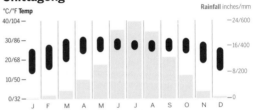

Oct–Feb Best time for hiking the Hill Tracts.

Oct–March Best time for St Martin's Island, before tropical storms start.

Jun–Sep Rainy season. Quietest and cheapest time to visit Cox's Bazar.

DHAKA
DIVISION

SYLHET
DIVISION

Brahmaputra River

Jamuna River

Bhairab
Chandura
Brahmanbaria
Akhaura
Agartala
DHAKA
Meghna River
Sonargaon
Daudkandi
Comilla
Chandpur
Lakshmipur
Feni
Noakhali
Moju Chowdhury Hat

TRIPURA
(INDIA)

Khagrachhari

MIZORAM
(INDIA)

CHITTAGONG

Kaptai
Lake **④**

Sitakunda
Rangamati

Sandwip
Sandwip Island
Kaptai

BARISAL
DIVISION

Meghna River

Shahbazpur Channel

Hatia

Chittagong

Nijum Dwip

Bandarban **②**
Khokhongjiri
Boga Lake
Sangu River **③**
Ruma Bazar
Keokradong (986m)
Thanchi Bazar
Chittagong Hill Tracts **①**
Ramakri Bazar
Mowdok Taung (1064m)
Tazingdong (830m)

Kutubdia

Maheskhali Island

BAY OF BENGAL

Cox's Bazar **⑤**
Ramu
Himachari Beach **🏄**

Inani Beach **🏄**

MYANMAR
(BURMA)

Teknaf Wildlife Sanctuary
Teknaf

Shah Porir Dwip
St Martin's Island **⑥**

Chittagong Division Highlights

① **Chittagong Hill Tracts** (p107) Teaming up with a trusted guide and hiking your way into the depths of the hills.

② **Bandarban** (p111) Learning about Adivasi culture by visiting some of the tribal villages around this forested hillside town.

③ **Sangu River** (p111) Enjoying what's arguably the most scenic river trip in Bangladesh by taking a boat ride along the serene Sangu.

④ **Kaptai Lake** (p114) Spending a day floating across this enormous lake at Rangamati.

⑤ **Cox's Bazar** (p117) Checking out the surf at this epically long beach.

⑥ **St Martin's Island** (p120) Enjoying the tropical beach vibe at Bangladesh's only coral island.

Chittagong

⏺ 031 / POP 5.2 MILLION

Chittagong is Bangladesh's second-largest city and the country's largest port. It's a gritty, polluted and congested place, but as the gateway to the Chittagong Hill Tracts – one of the most beautiful and fascinating corners of the country – it's somewhere that many visitors pass through at some point. As well as a place to sort your travel permits for the Hill Tracts, it also makes sense to rest up here for at least one night if you're planning to hit the beaches of Cox's Bazar or St Martin's Island.

History

Locals say the word 'Chittagong' originated from *chattagram* (small village), though it more likely comes from the Rakhaing (Arakanese) phrase *tsi-tsi-gong* ('war should never be fought'), inscribed on a tablet brought by an invading Buddhist army.

Despite its name, Chittagong has been consistently fought over. In 1299 Muslims occupied the city, until Rakhaing Buddhists retook it and retained it until 1660. The Mughals took possession next, only to be expelled by the Rakhaing in 1715. Finally, in 1766, the British raised their flag.

The evolution of the city followed a similar pattern to Dhaka, except that the oldest parts (where the city of Sadarghat now stands) were wiped out during the British and post-Independence periods. The Pakistani navy shelled the city heavily during the Liberation War.

◉ Sights

◉ Old City

Sadarghat   AREA

As in Dhaka, the city's oldest area is the waterfront part called Sadarghat, and as in Dhaka, it's a cacophony of sensual assaults. The early arrival of the Portuguese is evinced by the proximity of the Paterghatta District, just next to Sadarghat, which remains a Christian area and a quiet, clean place to walk around.

For a fun, albeit perhaps slightly scary side-trip, hop on a wooden rowboat (per person Tk5) from Sadarghat and cross the ship-laden river to the **fish harbour and market**.

If you're walking to Sadarghat from Station Rd, notice the **rickshaw makers**, with their tiny streetside workshops, hammering away on Sadarghat Rd.

Central Bazar   MARKET

(cnr Jubilee & Station Rds; ⊙ closed Fri morning) The Central Bazar is a warren of alleyways between the lower ends of Jubilee and Station Rds. It's almost impossible not to lose your way among the densely packed rows of clothing shops, but it's a lot of fun trying to find your way out again.

◉ British City

Zia Memorial Museum   MUSEUM

(SS Khaled Rd; admission local/foreigner Tk 10/100; ⊙10.30am-4.30pm Sat-Wed, 3.30-7.30pm Fri) This museum is rather unexpectedly housed in a mock-Tudor mansion. Among its much-revered collection is the microphone and transmitter with which President Zia proclaimed the country's independence in 1971.

WWII Memorial Cemetery   CEMETERY

(ওয়ার সিমেট্রি; Badsha Mia Rd; ⊙8am-noon & 2-5pm) This sombre cemetery contains the graves of hundreds of soldiers from both Allied and Japanese forces who died on the Burma front. Many are inscribed with simple and powerful epitaphs of loss and love. The cemetery is maintained by the Commonwealth War Graves Commission.

◉ Agrabad

Ethnological Museum   MUSEUM

(জাতিতাত্ত্বিক জাদুঘর, Jatitantik Jadhughar; Agrabad; admission Tk 20; ⊙9am-5pm Tue-Sat & 1.30-5pm Mon Oct-Mar, 10am-6pm Tue-Sat & 1.30-6pm Mon Apr-Sep) The interesting Ethnological Museum has displays on Bangladesh's tribal people. Unfortunately, it isn't always open when it should be. Some of the exhibits are looking a bit tattered, but it covers all the major tribal groups of the nearby Chittagong Hill Tracts.

🏃 Activities

Bangladesh Ecotours   TOUR

(⏺ 031-257 3257, 01819-318345; www.bangladesh ecotours.com; Riad Center, 4th fl, 4508A Arakan Rd) Chittagong-based local tour company specialising in the Hill Tracts.

Fairy Hill   HIKING
For some fresh air and great views across the city, ascend Fairy Hill by climbing the path leading off Jubilee Rd just north of the pedestrian bridge. If you get lost, ask for the High Court, which sits on top of it.

DC Hill   HIKING
DC Hill offers more good views over Chittagong if you feel the need to climb above the traffic haze.

🛏 Sleeping

Asian SR Hotel   HOTEL **$$**
(☑031-285 0346; www.asiansrhotel.com; 291 Station Rd; s/d from Tk 1000/1870, with air-con Tk 1600/2800; ❄@🛜) Very smart and well run, this is probably the best hotel on Station Rd. Rooms are slick and clean, though it's worth noting that the singles don't have external windows. There's a decent restaurant, but room rates don't include breakfast.

Hotel Sylhet Super   HOTEL **$$**
(☑031-632265; 16 Station Rd; s/d from Tk 820/1250, with air-con Tk 1600/2300; ❄) A good choice among the large number of budget offerings on Station Rd, Sylhet Super has cool-blue tiling and small but clean-enough rooms. Staff members are welcoming and speak a bit of English.

Hotel Golden Inn   HOTEL **$$**
(☑031-611004; 336 Station Rd; s/d/t/q Tk 900/1350/1700/2200, with air-con Tk 1500/2100/2800/3200; ❄@) Golden Inn has long been a favourite for budget travellers, though prices are hardly budget these days. It's a vast, echoing place with enough rooms to ensure it's rarely full, and the triples and quads are handy for groups of friends. The

restaurant is decent (if poorly lit) and there's a rooftop courtyard with city views.

Hotel al-Faisal International   HOTEL **$$**
(☑031-619000; www.hotelalfaisal.com; 1050 Nur Ahmed Rd; s from Tk 800, d with/without air-con Tk 1800/1200; ❄) A good option, the large rooms here have heat-repelling tiled floors and crispy clean bed sheets. The manager is chatty and it's not far from the stadium, so you can catch cricket-match-day enthusiasm, plus there are some decent places to eat within walking distance.

Hilltop Inn   GUESTHOUSE **$$$**
(☑031-655762; htopinn@yahoo.com; House 6, Rd 2, Khulshi; r from TK 3500; ❄@🛜) Housed in the very peaceful upmarket residential area of Khulshi, this guesthouse has rooms which are like those you'd expect to find in a decent city-centre apartment: bright, clean and spacious, with TV and wi-fi. Expect a homey atmosphere and helpful staff.

Peninsula Chittagong   HOTEL **$$$**
(☑031-285 0860, 031-285 0869; www.peninsula ctg.com; 486 CDA Ave; r from Tk 17,000; ❄@🛜❄) The Peninsula ruled the roost as Chittagong's flashest hotel for quite some time, although recent competing developments have threatened its status. Rooms are very smart, with super-shiny wood flooring and decent wood furniture. There's free wi-fi, coffee and breakfast, and a rooftop pool, plus a choice of restaurants, a bar serving alcohol and one of the few spas in the city.

Radisson Blu Bay View   HOTEL **$$$**
(☑031-619800; www.radissonblu.com/hotel-chit tagong; SS Khaled Rd, Lalkhan Bazar; r from Tk 13,000; ❄🛜❄) This freshly minted hotel is Chittagong's first international five-star

---

SHIP-BREAKING YARDS

Chittagong's controversial industry of ship breaking takes place along the coast northwest of the city at Bhatiary. Here, beached along the shore, you can find every kind of ocean-going vessel, from tugboat to super tanker, each one lying stranded as an army of workers dismantles it, section by section, piece by piece. The whole operation is done by hand by workers who, according to both the EU and local watchdog groups, are ill-equipped, under-trained and, in many cases, under age. Because of the high injury rate the average working life is short, but the work is relatively well paid, so the ship-breaking yards have little difficulty recruiting.

The yards have received bad press in recent years, and when we visited, owners were not allowing foreigners with cameras (even on their phones) to stroll along the beach taking photos of workers tearing apart the giant hulls of rusting ships. It is, nevertheless, an incredible sight. Stranded on land as they are, some of the super tankers seem impossibly large. It is recycling writ-large, and most of the steel is reused within Bangladesh.

Chittagong

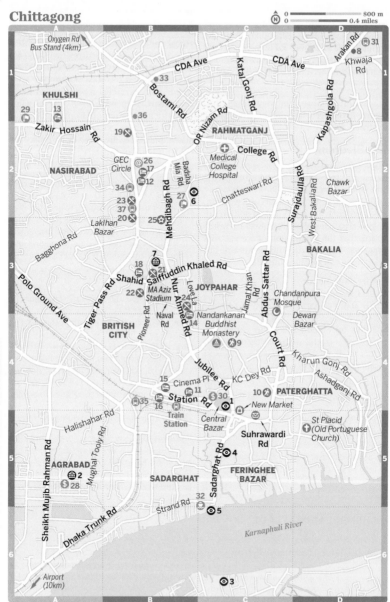

offering. As you'd expect, it's a lovely place, with delightful starlight effect lighting on each floor rising over the central atrium. Tune up your serve on the tennis court, or lounge in the doughnut-shaped infinity pool. There's a superb restaurant, a bar with lighter bites and a coffee shop, too.

The president of Bangladesh was staying when we visited, which gives you an idea of the service on offer.

Chittagong

⦿ Sights

1 Central Bazar	C4
2 Ethnological Museum	A5
3 Fish Harbour & Market	C6
4 Rickshaw Workshops	C5
5 Sadarghat	C6
6 WWII Memorial Cemetery	B2
7 Zia Memorial Museum	B3

⊕ Activities, Courses & Tours

8 Bangladesh Ecotours	D1
9 DC Hill	C4
10 Fairy Hill	C4

🛌 Sleeping

11 Asian SR Hotel	B4
12 Grand Park Hotel	B2
13 Hilltop Inn	A1
14 Hotel al-Faisal International	B4
15 Hotel Golden Inn	B4
16 Hotel Sylhet Super	B4
17 Peninsula Chittagong	B2
18 Radisson Blu Bay View	B3

🍴 Eating

19 Bonanza Food Plus	B2
20 Dhaba	B3
21 Fushka Stalls	B3
22 Greedy Guts	B3
23 Handi	B2
Hotel ABP	(see 1)
Rio Coffee Corner	(see 22)
24 Tai Wah Restaurant	B3

⊕ Entertainment

25 Bistaar Chittagong Arts Complex	B3

ⓘ Information

26 Cyber World	B2
27 Divisional Commissioner's Office	B2
28 HSBC	A5
29 Indian High Commission	A1
30 Standard Chartered Bank	C4

ⓘ Transport

31 Bahaddarhat Bus Stand	D1
32 Bangladesh Inland Waterway Transport Corporation Office	C5
33 Biman Bangladesh	B1
34 Green Line	B2
35 Kadamtali Bus Stand	B4
36 Regent Airways	B1
37 Soudia Air-Con	B2

Grand Park Hotel   HOTEL $$$

(☏ 031-620044; www.pavilliongrandpark.com; 787 CDA Ave; s/d from Tk 3415/4045; ❄ @ 🛜) This is a pretty smart place to stay, and puts you very close to GEC Circle. Some of the rooms are absolutely huge. As well as breakfast, the rates include laundry and a complementary transfer from the train station or airport. The hotel has its own restaurant.

✖ Eating

Fushka Stalls   BANGLADESHI $

(SS Khaled Rd; plate of fushka Tk 30) If you're after cheap street eats, this series of daytime stands in front of a small park will sell you a hearty plate of filling *fushka* for pennies. Fill up on the pastry shells stuffed with chickpeas, onion, tomato and chilli – they're delicious.

Hotel ABP   BENGALI $

(Jubilee Rd; meals TK 150-200; ⊘ 6am-midnight) Tuck into tandoori masala-spiced chicken, grilled by the entrance, and mop up some dhal or curried vegetables with freshly baked paratha. You'll have to bluff your way through ordering as there's no English menu, but at least one member of staff speaks a little English.

Handi   INDIAN $$

(CDA Ave; mains Tk 160-440, set lunch from Tk 170; ⊘ 1pm-11pm) This is a handy choice if you want to match good-value Bangladeshi and Indian meals with classy surroundings and good service. The competitively priced set lunches (available 1pm to 4pm) deservedly draw a good crowd, but if it's South Indian dhosas you're after, they aren't served until after 4pm.

Dhaba   INDIAN $$

(CDA Ave; mains Tk 150-250; ⊘ 1.30-10.30pm) Part of the ever-popular Bangladeshi chain, Dhaba knocks out some tasty curries, kebabs, paratha rolls and *chaat* (spicy snacks). It's basically Indian street food in a clean restaurant environment. Wash it down with a *lassi* (yogurt drink).

Rio Coffee Corner   CAFE $$

(Naval Ave; ⊘ 10am-11pm; 🛜) Housed in a corner of the 2nd floor of a clean, multi-level fast-food complex, Rio is one of the few places in Chittagong (outside the top-notch hotels) that does proper fresh coffee (from Tk 80). As if that wasn't enticing enough, there's free wi-fi along with the usual coffee-shop sweets and an ice-cream counter next door.

ⓘ CHITTAGONG BY BOAT

There are no direct boats to Chittagong from Dhaka but that doesn't mean that you can't make an adventure out of a trip to either.

From Dhaka, you need to head to the fishing town of Chandpur and then connect by bus or train. Boats leave from Sadarghat in Dhaka roughly every hour from 6.30am until midnight, and take around four hours to reach Chandpur (1st/2nd/chair class Tk400/240/150).

Once you get to Chandpur, you can continue to Chittagong by bus (Tk 200, four hours) or train (1st seat/shuvon Tk 240/150, five hours, 5am and 3pm).

In the other direction, regular boat services from Chandpur to Dhaka start drying up at around 4.30pm, although there is usually a late-evening boat at around 11.30pm.

★**Bonanza Food Plus** ASIAN $$$
(✆031-652079; 1692 CDA Ave; mains TK 200-400; ☺noon-3.30pm & 6-11pm) One of Chittagong's best dining options, this swish, air-conditioned restaurant has an excellent pan-Asian menu, including Chinese, Indian, Thai and Korean. The Indian dishes are particularly good. You can also eat in between the official lunch and dinner times, but from the Chinese menu only.

Tai Wah Restaurant CHINESE $$$
(1052 Nur Ahmed Rd; mains TK 250-650; ☺noon-3pm & 6-10pm) With soups, noodles, rice dishes and dumplings, this is probably the most authentic Chinese in Chittagong. The atmosphere is pleasant, with red lanterns creating just the right level of lighting, and walls adorned with giant Chinese knots and decorative fans.

Greedy Guts INTERNATIONAL $$$
(✆031-285 0147; www.greedygutsbd.com; Pioneer Rd; mains from Tk 375) If you feel the need to take a break from your daily Bangladeshi rice quota, Greedy Guts will see you right with its well-presented menu of pasta and continental dishes. There's good Indian food as well, but the place really attracts customers for its steaks and seafood. Watch for the tax upping the bills by 25%.

☆ Entertainment

Bistaar Chittagong Arts Complex ARTS VENUE
(✆031-285 4595; www.bistaar.org; 688/C Mehedibagh Rd) Chittagong's home of the arts. Come here for regular film screenings, art exhibitions, talks and live music performances.

ⓘ Information

Cyber World (3rd fl, 650 OR Nizam Rd; per hour Tk 25; ☺10am-10pm) Above Niribilee restaurant.

Divisional Commissioner's Office (✆01734-859390, 031-634022; samiul_masud@yahoo.com; 1st fl, 718 Chatteshwari Rd; ☺9am-5pm Sun-Thu) Come here for Chittagong Hill Tract permits. It's housed in old colonial building on the corner of Badsha Mia Rd and Chatteswari Rd, but not signed in English.

HSBC (Sabdar Ali Rd; ☺10am-4pm Sun-Thu)

Indian High Commission (✆031-654201; www.ahcictg.net; Zakir Hossain Rd; ☺9am-4pm Sun-Thu) Can issue Indian visas. See website for application details.

Medical College Hospital (✆031-619400; www.cmc.edu.bd; Nasirabad)

Standard Chartered Bank (Station Rd; ☺10am-4pm Sun-Thu)

ⓘ Getting There & Away

The Dhaka–Chittagong Hwy is the most dangerous stretch of road in Bangladesh and catching a bus between the two cities is a heart-in-mouth experience for much of the way. If you can, take the train or a boat, or fly.

AIR

Dhaka is a 30-minute flight from Chittagong. Tickets cost around Tk 4000 one way. **Regent Airways** (✆02-5566 9911; www.flyregent.com; Plot 1634, Asian Hwy, East Nasirabad, Panchlaish) and **Biman Bangladesh** (✆031-650671; www.biman-airlines.com; CDA Ave) both have flights. It's also possible to fly via Dhaka to Kolkata in India.

BOAT

There's a weekly service departing Mondays to Barisal (cabin with attached/share bathroom Tk 2140/1260, 3rd class chair Tk 365, 20 hours), but to get Dhaka by boat, you have to leave from Chandpur.

If you miss the Barisal boat, you can also catch a ferry to Hatiya Island (1st/2nd/chair class Tk 910/640/395, seven hours, departs 9am daily except Friday and Sunday), via Sandwip Island (four hours), and catch a direct ferry from there.

Buy tickets from the **Bangladesh Inland Waterway Transport Corporation office** (BIWTC; ☏ 031-613358; www.biwtc.gov.bd; Sadarghat Rd; ⊘ Sun-Thu), located near the waterfront end of Sadarghat Rd, about 100m to the west.

BUS

Destinations from **Bahaddarhat bus stand** (Map p104) include Cox's Bazar (Tk 240, five hours, 6am to 9pm) and Bandarban (Tk 110, three hours, 6am to 6pm).

Oxygen Rd bus stand serves Rangamati (Tk 120, 2½ hours) and Kadamtali bus stand serves Chandpur (Tk 200, four hours).

As well as the public bus services, a number of private coach companies run from Chittagong, with offices just south of GEC Circle. **Green Line** (☏ 031-630551; www.greenlinebd.com; CDA Ave) has air-con coaches to Dhaka (Tk 1000, seven to eight hours, 10 daily), Cox's Bazar (Tk 650, five hours, 9am) and Sylhet (Tk 1000, eight hours, 9pm). Nearby **Soudia** (☏ 031-9701 5610; CDA Ave) has a very similar timetable with slightly cheaper prices.

TRAIN

Note that most Dhaka and all Sylhet trains go through Comilla (1st/shuvon Tk 210/135, three hours) and, for the Indian border, Akhaura (1st/shuvon Tk 265/165, four to five hours).

ⓘ Getting Around

There isn't always a bus to meet incoming flights and the airport is a long way out from town – CNGs (auto-rickshaws) cost at least Tk 200. You could try catching a bus to New Market (Tk 10) at the T-junction, 500m from the airport.

A rickshaw between Station Rd and GEC Circle is about Tk 70. Further afield you'll have to take a CNG: from Station Rd to Bahaddarhat bus stand

and Oxygen Rd bus stand cost Tk 100 and Tk 70 respectively.

Chittagong Hill Tracts

Decidedly untypical of Bangladesh, both in topography and culture, this largely Buddhist Adivasi (tribal) stronghold is the homeland of the Jumma people. It's a stunning region of hills, ravines and cliffs covered with dense jungles of bamboo, creepers and shrubs, and dotted with tall, slender waterfalls.

The whole region is full of the flavours of neighbouring Myanmar (Burma). It's utterly fascinating and exceedingly beautiful. It also offers a chance to stretch the legs with some of the country's best hiking on offer, though access is often limited for foreigners.

There are three districts: Khagrachari, Rangamati and Bandarban. Most tourists visit only the latter two, which are the more scenic, and are the two we cover here. While it's generally safe to visit, all foreign visitors require a special permit, and the whims of officialdom can sometimes put a frustrating brake on which parts of the Hill Tracts are accessible to travellers.

History

Under the British, the Hill Tracts gained special status and only Adivasis could own land here, but the Pakistani government abolished the special status of the Hill Tracts as a 'tribal area' in 1964. The construction of Kaptai Lake (in Rangamati) for hydroelectricity in 1960 was an earlier

SELECTED TRAINS FROM CHITTAGONG

DESTINATION	TRAIN NAME	DEPARTS	ARRIVES	FARE (1ST/SHUVON)	OFF DAY
Chandpur	Sagharika Ex	7.40am	4.15pm	Tk 240/150	none
Chandpur	Meghna Ex	5pm	10.45pm	Tk 240/150	none
Dhaka	Subarna Ex	6.40am	1.20pm	Tk 425/265	Fri
Dhaka	Mohanagar Provati	7am	2.50pm	Tk 425/265	Sun
Dhaka	Mohanagar Godhuli	3pm	10.30pm	Tk 425/265	none
Dhaka	Dhaka Mail	10.30pm	8am	Tk 635/425/265*	none
Dhaka	Turna Ex	11pm	6.40am	Tk 635/425/265*	none
Sylhet	Paharika	8.15am	6pm	Tk 460/290	Mon
Sylhet	Udayan Ex	9.45pm	7.25am	Tk 690/460/290*	Sat

* 1st berth/1st seat/shuvon

CHITTAGONG DIVISION CHITTAGONG HILL TRACTS

HILL TRACTS TREKS

The Chittagong Hill Tracts offer some great opportunities to really get off the beaten track. If the District Commissioner's office smiles on your permit application, here are a few of the treks with the best potential.

Moderate

MT KEOKRADONG

This has traditionally been referred to as the tallest peak in Bangladesh, although at 986m above sea level, it is in fact lower than Mowdok Taung. Keokradong is one of the most-climbed peaks in the country, and the trail is wonderfully scenic. You need to climb various hillocks and cross a number of streams en route. You will also pass Chingri Jhiri waterfall.

Duration Three days, two nights from Bandarban.

How To On day one, head from Bandarban to Ruma Bazar by local bus or jeep (three to four hours). Trek from Ruma Bazar to Boga Lake (four to six hours), and overnight in an Adivasi guesthouse at Boga Lake. On day two, hike to Keokradong via Chingri Jhiri waterfall, and return to Boga Lake for the second night. On day three, hike back to Ruma Bazar then bus back to Bandarban. Note that in winter some jeeps will take you all the way from Bandarban to Boga Lake.

NAFAKHUM FALLS

Located at a picturesque river spot in Thanchi, in Bandarban district, this is one of the most beautiful waterfalls in the country.

Duration Three days, two nights from Bandarban.

How to Day one takes you from Bandarban to Thanchi Bazar by local bus or jeep (four to five hours) then to Ramakri Bazar by private wooden boat. Overnight at Ramakri guesthouse. On day two, hike to Nafakhum Falls and back to Ramakri Bazar. Stay in the same guesthouse. On day three, return to Thanchi Bazar then Bandarban.

Hard

THANCHI TO RUMA CIRCUIT

This circular trail will allow you to summit two of the Hill Tracts' most popular peaks (Tazingdong and Keokradong).

Duration Five days, four nights from Bandarban.

How To On day one, go from Bandarban to Thanchi Bazar by bus jeep (four to five hours) then trek up to Boarding Headman Para village (four to five hours) to stay the night. On day

blow, submerging 40% of the land used by the Adivasis for cultivation, and displacing 100,000 people. The land provided for resettlement was not sufficient and many Adivasis became refugees in neighbouring northeastern India.

During the 1971 Liberation War, the then Chakma king sided with the Pakistanis, so when independence came the Adivasis' plea for special status fell on deaf ears. The Chakma king left for Pakistan and later became that country's ambassador to Argentina.

Meanwhile, more and more Bengalis were migrating into the area, taking the land. In 1973 the Adivasis initiated an insurgency. To counter it, the government, in 1979, started issuing permits to landless Bengalis to settle here, with titles to Adivasi land. This practice continued for six years and resulted in a mass migration of approximately 400,000 people into the area – almost as many as all the Adivasi groups combined. Countless human-rights abuses occurred as the army tried to put down the revolt.

From 1973 until 1997 the Hill Tracts area was the scene of a guerrilla war between the Bangladeshi army and the Shanti Bahini rebels. The troubles stemmed from the cultural clash between the Adivasi groups and the plains people.

Sheikh Hasina's government cemented an internationally acclaimed peace accord in December 1997 with Adivasi leader Jyotirindra Bodhipriya (Santu) Larma. Rebel fight-

two, hike to Prata Para village, summiting Tazingdong en route. Day three is a hike to Thaikhong Para village, including a 20-minute detour to Baklai Falls. Overnight in Thaikhong Para. On day four, hike to Boga Lake Para, summiting Keokradong en route. On day five, hike to Ruma Bazar from where you can catch a bus or jeep back to Bandarban.

MOWDOK TAUNG

Situated in Mowdok Mual range, and now largely recognised as the highest peak in Bangladesh, having been measured at 1064m, this peak is also known as Shaka Haphong/Tlangmoy. The last leg of the trail is inside dense forest and bamboo bush, while the peak is on the Bangladesh–Myanmar border.

Duration Seven days, six nights from Bandarban.

How To Day one starts from Bandarban to Thanchi Bazar by bus or jeep (four to five hours), then hike to Boarding Headman Para (four to five hours) where you overnight. Day two, hike to Siplampi Para village (five to six hours) and overnight. You can detour (about one hour) to summit Mt Tazingdong (830m) en route. Day three, hike to Nefew Para village (seven to eight hours), including wading through a stream called Ramakri Khal. On day four, hike to Mowdok Taung peak then back to Nefew Para, and on day five hike to Serkor Para village for an overnight stay (this is a very long day, so start early). Day six: hike back to Thanchi Bazar for an overnight stay, and on day seven take a bus or jeep back to Bandarban.

Need to Know

Permits At the time of research, foreigners needed permits to visit anywhere in Bandarban District. Permits were tricky to get for Mt Tazingdong and Mowdok Taung. Your chances will improve if you get an established tour operator to apply for you, but you will then have an obligation to use their guides (you may want to, of course).

Police All visitors should report to the local police upon arrival in Bandarban, Ruma and Thanchi.

Guides Unless you've brought your own guide from Bandarban, Chittagong or Dhaka, you will need to hire a local guide (per day Tk 500) in Thanchi Bazar or Ruma Bazar before you continue towards the peaks mentioned above. Don't worry about finding them. They'll find you.

Malaria Malaria is a genuine threat in the Chittagong Hill Tracts. If you haven't brought your own malaria drugs, you can buy doxycycline at **Lazz Pharma** (Map p40; ☑ 02-911 7839; www.lazzpharma.com; 64/3 Lake Circus, Zubida Super Market, Kalabagan, Dhanmondi), a 24-hour pharmacy in Dhaka.

ers were given land, Tk 50,000 and a range of other benefits in return for handing in their weapons. The peace deal handed much of the administration of Khagrachhari, Rangamati and Bandarban districts to a regional council. The struggle to have the accord fully honoured continues today.

Hill Tribes

A dozen or so different Adivasi groups live in the Chittagong Hill Tracts, and make up about half the total population. Major groups include the Chakma, the Marma and the Tripuri. Collectively, they are known as the Jumma people.

About half of Bangladesh's Adivasi population is Chakma (roughly 240,000 people), while roughly one-third is Marma. Among the many much smaller groups, the Mru (called Murung by Bangladeshis) stand out as the most ancient inhabitants of the area.

The culture and lifestyle of the Adivasis are very different from that of the Bangladeshi farmers of the plains. Some tribes are matriarchal, for example, and most make their homes from bamboo, covered by thatched roofs of dried leaves. Most Jumma are Buddhist or Hindu, though small numbers have converted to Islam or Christianity.

Adivasi groups are quite different from each other, each having their own distinctive

TRAVEL WARNING: SECURITY IN THE HILL TRACTS

The Chittagong Hill Tracts is the most restive part of the country, with Hindu and Buddhist groups claiming neglect and persecution by the national government. Tens of thousands of people are still internally displaced after the government suppressed a tribal insurgency in the 1990s, and resentment periodically erupts into violence. Because of the security concerns, the government mandates that tourists obtain a permit before travelling to the Hill Tracts, and the conditions for this change regularly. Always check the security situation and the latest permit rules before you visit.

rites, rituals, dialect and dress. Chakma women, for example, wear indigo-and-red-striped sarongs. Adivasi women are particularly skilled in making handicrafts, while some of the men take pride in hunting with bows and arrows.

Adivasi people you're mostly likely to meet in this region are the Chakma, in Rangamati, and the Marma, Tripuri and Bawm in and around Bandarban. Most of the Bawm people have converted to Christianity and you'll find a handful who speak decent English in Bandarban. The last time we visited, all of the guides at Hillside Resort in Bandarban were Bawm.

 Activities

Hiking

There are some fantastic hikes in this part of Bangladesh. None is technically challenging, but some are multiday trips, which require hikers to be fit and adventurous. It's not unusual, for example, to find yourself having to wade through rivers en route to your ultimate destination, and hikers to more remote areas will have to be prepared to rough it. Accommodation will either be in tents (if you bring your own) or in small villages with almost no facilities.

Also bear in mind that many of the more remote areas are often off-limits to foreigners. If you apply for permits to climb some of the peaks in these areas, you may be denied them. That doesn't stop some foreigners having a go, though.

Blazing a trail through previously unhiked areas of the Hill Tracts is the community-run hiking group, Bangla Trek (www.banglatrek.org). It's a very welcoming group of amateur hikers, most of whom are based in Dhaka, and many of them speak good English. If you're looking for ideas for places to hike to, or just want to hook up with like-minded walking enthusiasts, try contacting them through their website.

Guides & Permits

The permit situation for the hill tracts region is in a constant state of flux. At the time of research it was necessary to be accompanied by a local guide in the Hill Tracts – the ripples of security incidents in Dhaka can reach this far, and authorities may even decide that your vehicle needs a police escort. In previous years you could arrange your own Hill Tracts permit and then explore much of the region on your own. Hopefully this will return in time, but it's essential to check the latest information before you leave.

Permits currently cost Tk 1200 for Rangamati and Tk 1500 for Bandarban. Apply seven days in advance of travel, with a copy of your passport and visa. If private permit applications are being allowed, you'll need to go to the Divisional Commissioner's Office (p106) in Chittagong. Take plenty of patience as well as an itinerary covering everywhere you want to go.

Make multiple copies of your permit, which you should keep handy to dish out to any checkpoint police on the road, and hotel receptionists at check in.

The following companies are recommended for handling permit applications, and can also arrange guides and transport:

Bangladesh Ecotours (p102) Based in Chittagong, this operator specialises in the Hill Tracts.

Guide Tours (p42) Long-established tour operator, and owner of the Hillside Resort (p113) in Bandarban.

Guides typically cost around Tk 2000 per day, with vehicle hire around Tk 5500.

Because of the frequent changes in permit regulations, we advise you get on the Bangladesh branch of Lonely Planet's Thorn Tree forum (https://www.lonelyplanet.com/thorntree/forums/asia-indian-subcontinent/bangladesh) before you leave for Chittagong division, just to double-check the latest.

Bandarban

📞 0361 / POP 30,000

There is no better place in which to experience the magic of the Hill Tracts than in the lively small town of Bandarban, which lies on the Sangu River, 92km from Chittagong. The river is the centre of local life: epically long bamboo rafts, steered by a solitary boatman, drift leisurely downstream, while country boats make slow trips to neighbouring villages.

Frustratingly, Bandarban also tends to be the place where officialdom is at its most restrictive. As elsewhere in the Chittagong Hill Tracts, all foreigners need a permit to visit. However, at times the authorities may choose to restrict where you can go in or outside the town – talk to a guide company before planning your trip to get an idea of where you'll be allowed to visit.

◉ Sights

The town itself, which has a couple of interesting sights, isn't overly attractive, but the surrounding countryside is some of the finest in Bangladesh and offers one of the few opportunities to really escape the masses. Many of the inhabitants belong to the Buddhist Marma tribe, and there are villages in the hills which you can easily hike to.

Tribal Bazar   MARKET
(⊘ Wed & Sun) Bandarban has a small street market most days, but the place really throngs on Sunday and Wednesday when traders come in from across the district to buy and sell produce. Trading is conduct-

---

ADIVASI CUISINE

A visit to the Hill Tracts offers a chance to broaden your palate beyond Bangladeshi cuisine. You'll find Adivasi restaurants in Bandarban and Rangamati, featuring the cuisine of the Marma and Chakma tribes respectively. Food here frequently uses a fish paste as a base (like Thai fish sauce), and is heavy on the ginger and fresh chilli. Buddhist practices place no prohibition on pigs, so you'll also find pork on the menu – and sometimes a very potent local rice wine.

---

ed in Marma rather than Bengali, and it's quite unlike anything you'll see elsewhere in Bangladesh. Expect piles of gorgeous fruit and vegetables, sticky mounds of fish paste (a base for much local cooking), buckets of crabs, frogs and fish and lots of old women smoking hand-rolled cheroots.

Dhatu Jadi   BUDDHIST MONASTERY
(Golden Temple; Tk 10) Perched on a hilltop about three kilometres north of town in Bala Gata village is the large glowing Dhatu Jadi, also known as the Golden Temple (Shorna Mondir) because of its beautiful golden stupa, one of the most impressive in the country. The Arakanese-style monastery complex, housing the second-largest Buddha in Bangladesh, was only built in 2000, but visiting it is a Burmese blast through and through.

It's a one-hour uphill walk from Sangu Bridge, or Tk 150 in a CNG.

Bandarban Museum   MUSEUM
This small museum offers some interesting insights into the traditional cultures of the Hill Tracts. There are displays of tribal dress, jewellery, basketwork and so on. There's not much interpretation to the exhibits, so you'll get more out of it if you have a guide. It's not signed in English (ask for *kudro ni gusti*), and you might need to ask for it to be opened up.

🏃 Activities

There are a number of short, half-day and full-day walks and hikes you can take in and around Bandarban. The forested scenery is beautiful and is dotted with small Adivasi villages.

Hillside Resort (p113), the excellent guesthouse run by Guide Tours (www.guidetours.com), is the best place to enquire about possible places to visit. They also have guides (per hour/day Tk 100/1000). Otherwise, try to get in touch with the amateur hikers who run Bangla Trek (www.banglatrek.org).

Sangu River Boating   BOAT TOUR
The boat trip along the Sangu River, upstream from Bandarban, is about as exquisitely picturesque and fabulously peaceful as you can possibly get in Bangladesh. Rustic river boats drift down the river to Bandarban from **Ruma Bazar** (Tk 100, three hours, once every two hours from 8am), accessible

Bandarban

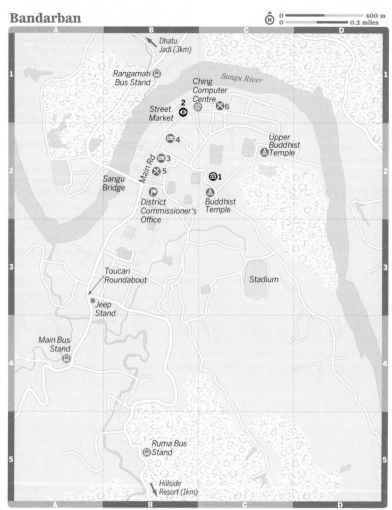

0 | 400 m
0 | 0.2 miles

Dhatu Jadi (3km)

Rangamati Bus Stand

Sangu River

Ching Computer Centre

Street Market

2

@

6

Upper Buddhist Temple

4

Main Rd

3

5

1

Sangu Bridge

Buddhist Temple

District Commissioner's Office

Toucan Roundabout

Stadium

Jeep Stand

Main Bus Stand

Ruma Bus Stand

Hillside Resort (1km)

from Bandarban's Ruma bus stand. The trip is easier with a guide, but possible (if difficult) independently.

Depending on the condition of the road, buses to Ruma Bazar may terminate at **Khokhongjiri** (two hours from Bandarban). If this happens, just clamber down to the river past a cluster of tea stalls and small restaurants. At the riverbank, you can either catch a wooden ferry (known as a 'service boat') upstream to Ruma Bazar (per person Tk 30, two hours), or downstream back to Bandarban (per person Tk 120, 3½ hours).

From either Ruma Bazar or Khokhongjiri, the lazy ride back to Bandarban is magical, as you pass villages only accessible by boat and enjoy some mesmerising scenery; sometimes rugged, sometimes rural, but always stunning. There may be no service boats, in which case you'll have to try to pay for your own 'reserved boat'. Expect to pay at least Tk 3000 from Khokhongjiri, and more from Ruma Bazar. Either way, it's worth every penny. Note that boats all the way from Ruma Bazar may only operate when the water is at its highest levels, between May and November.

Bandarban

⊙ Sights
1 Bandarban Museum.............................C2
2 Tribal Bazar B1

🛏 Sleeping
3 Hotel Purbani...B2
4 Hotel Royal B2

⊗ Eating
5 Hotel Amiribad & Biryani House.........B2
6 Tohzah Restaurant................................C1

Boga Lake   HIKING

Hillside Resort organises a trip to the beautiful, tree-lined Boga Lake, which is very popular, although depending on the current permit situation you can usually reach the lake on your own via Ruma Bazar. It takes around four hours to hike to the lake from Ruma. There is basic accommodation by the lake.

Haatibandha & Sangiya Villages   HIKING

These two villages are a short walk through the forest from Hillside Resort. Follow the road uphill leading away from the guesthouse then take the first track on your right. Follow a narrow brick path downhill. The first path on your left crisscrosses a small stream, leading to Sangiya Village, where around a dozen families live – some Tripuri, some Marma – in bamboo huts on stilts.

Back up on the brick path, continue straight past the turn to Sangiya and take the first right, again down a part-brick pathway. You'll notice a green-painted church on your right as you enter the pretty village of Haatibandha, home to 28 Marma families. The people here are very Burmese-looking, and some of the elder women are decked out in hundreds of bead necklaces, bangles that coil serpent-like around their arms, and strange earrings that look more like bolts and which stretch out the wearer's ear lobes. Always ask before taking photos. You'll need around two or three hours to see both villages from Hillside Resort.

If you go straight rather than turning left to Sangiya Village, or right to Haatibandha, the track from the main road takes you all the way up to Tiger Hill, a popular viewpoint in this area.

Sangu River Walk   HIKING

A steep but easy-to-follow pathway snakes its way down from the dormitory building at Hillside Resort all the way to the Sangu River below. It takes about half an hour to climb down to the river. From there, you can either walk, or try to catch a wooden rowboat on towards Bandarban town centre.

You may catch sight of one of the incredible bamboo rafts, which float their way down river to Bandarban. Some are literally dozens of metres long!

Shailapropat Falls   HIKING

This easy walk follows the quiet road that leads uphill away from Hillside Resort. It takes about an hour to reach Shailapropat Falls, a small waterfall, which trickles from the roadside down into a ravine below. It's popular with local tourists, so there are tea and snack stalls set up. The falls are virtually dry in the winter months.

Close to the falls is the Bawm village of **Faruk Para**, where you can buy handwoven baskets, fish traps and rugs.

🛏 Sleeping

Hotel Royal   HOTEL $

(☎ 0361-62926; Main Rd; s/d Tk 525/900, with air-con Tk 1050/1350; ❄) The best-value accommodation in Bandarban, the Royal is a simple, friendly hotel that gets the small things right. The rooms are modest but cosy and kept very clean, and the wood/bamboo wall panels add a little local character. The air-con is only needed in the hottest months.

Hotel Purbani   HOTEL $

(☎ 0361-63424; Main Rd; s/d/tr Tk 400/700/1150; ❄) Very clean tiled rooms with TV and attached bathroom (squat loo) run by friendly staff members who, unlike staff at some other hotels in town, are happy to welcome foreign guests.

★**Hillside Resort**   GUESTHOUSE $$$

(Milonchhori;   ☎ 01730-045083;   www.guidetoursbd.com;   Chimbuk Rd;   dm Tk 900, s Tk 2500-3355, d Tk 3000-3660, tr Tk 3700-4270; ❄) Thrown haphazardly across a steep jungle-smothered hillside, this wonderful guesthouse, run by Guide Tours, is a treat. Cottages are fun and comfortable, and the dorm allows for budget travellers to enjoy its choice location, perched up in the forested hills, 4km from the town centre. Showers are cold water only, although the cottages have hot-water taps.

The food is excellent (mains Tk 180 to Tk 400), as are the views. There are guides available, plus great travel advice about the area should you want it. It costs Tk 150 to get here from town in a CNG. The walk is a 45-minute uphill slog, but you pass a number of interesting villages (with excited-to-see-you children) en route.

✖ Eating

★**Tohzah Restaurant**   MARMA $
(Main Rd; mains Tk 80-150; ☺8am-10pm) This modest restaurant is the best place in town to sample Marma cuisine. The main themes are a mountain of ginger and a volcano of chillies, plus the novelty of finding pork on the menu. There's no English menu, but the staff seem happy to help with orders, offering up some tasty greens as side dishes plus rice and soup.

If you're lucky (and brave) you might even find lizard on the menu; those of a more hesitant disposition might prefer to opt for bamboo chicken.

Hotel Amiribad &
Biryani House   BANGLADESHI $
(off Main Rd; mains Tk 50-100; ☺5am-11pm) This popular no-frills restaurant knocks up reliable Bengali dishes including fish, chicken, mutton and beef curries, plus biryanis, of course. It's also a great spot for huge dhal-and-paratha breakfasts. No English menu, but some staff members speak a little English.

❶ Information

Ching Computer Centre (Main Rd; internet per hour Tk 30; ☺3-8pm)

District Commissioner's Office At the time of research, Hill Tracts permits were most easily obtained through a tour operator, but the District Commissioner's Office can help in a last resort – if you're persistent.

❶ Getting There & Away

There's a **jeep stand** just down from the main bus stand where you can hire jeeps, known here as *chander gari*, to places such as Ruma Bazar (return/overnight Tk 3000/4500, two hours each way).

From **Ruma bus stand** buses go to Ruma Bazar (Tk 100, three hours, every two hours from 8am). Rangamati (Tk 110, four hours, 8am and 2pm) buses leave from the **Rangamati bus stand**. From the **main bus stand**, destinations include the following:

Chittagong Tk 110, three hours, 5.45am to 6pm

Cox's Bazar Tk 170, three hours, 7.30am to 5pm

Dhaka Tk 620/950 (non-AC/AC), nine hours, 10am, 9.30pm and 10pm

Rangamati

☑ 0351 / POP 65,000

Rangamati is the most popular destination in the Chittagong Hill Tracts for Bangladeshi visitors, who come to enjoy the scenic splendour of Kaptai Lake, the country's largest artificial lake, which was created in 1960 for hydroelectricity. The lake, dotted with islands, is unquestionably beautiful, and a boat trip across it is a fantastic way to spend a day out here, but it's worth knowing that approximately 100,000 Adivasis – mostly Chakma – were displaced when it was created, and around 40% of the land they previously cultivated was submerged forever.

◉ Sights

Most of the sights around Rangamati are out on the lake.

Kaptai Lake   LAKE
Dotted with islands, Kaptai is Bangladesh's largest artificial lake, created in 1960 for a hydroelectric project. It's a beautiful spot, and very popular with Bengali sightseers, but because of permit restrictions, the number of places foreigners can visit on the lake is constrained.

The most popular trip is **Shuvalong Falls** (90 minutes one way). This modest waterfall is little more than a trickle for most of the year, but the boat trip out to it is fabulous; first crossing the vast expanse of the main lake, then entering an area of islands covered with banana plants, and finally a dramatic pass through a steep-sided gorge.

The **Hanging Bridge**, a low suspension bridge, not far from the Parjatan Holiday Complex, is another popular boat-trip destination.

The small Chakma islands at the other end of Rangamati are another popular boat stop, although, like the Hanging Bridge, they can also be reached by land.

Another popular trip with local tourists is the two-hour ride to **Kaptai Town**, but the town itself is a bit of a dump.

There are small boat ghats all around the lake, but the main two are Reserve-Bazar Ghat and Tobolchuri Ghat. Passenger ferries shuttle locals from Reserve-Bazar to places such as Kaptai Town. They're sometimes reluctant to take foreigners, but you can get to Shuvalong Falls for Tk 50 if they let you

Rangamati

Rangamati

◉ Sights

1 Bana Vihara Monastery	B1
2 Chakma King's Modern Palace	A1
3 Hanging Bridge	C4
4 Tribal Cultural Institute Museum	A1

🛏 Sleeping

5 Hotel Golden Hill	C2
Hotel Nadisa International	(see 5)
6 Hotel Sufia	B2
7 Parjatan Holiday Complex	C4

✕ Eating

8 Biryani House	C2
9 Thai Mart	A1

on. Otherwise, you'll have to hire your own boat. Prices depend largely on your bargaining skills. At the time of research, Tk 600 per boat per hour was the going rate.

Bana Vihara Monastery BUDDHIST MONASTERY
Bana Vihara, which can be reached, either via Rajbari Ghat, or via a bridge slightly further west, houses a large Buddhist monastery, constructed by Chakma Buddhist monks in 1972. You can wander the grounds, peek inside the temples (ask first) and see monks making wooden boats by the water's edge on the eastern side of the island.

Chakma Islands ISLAND
This whole area is a Chakma stronghold, but two islands in particular are interesting to visit. **Rajbari** (which means palace) is where the Chakma king has his rather unimpressive, recently rebuilt palace. You can't enter the **palace**, but you can peek inside the nearby Buddhist temple. There are stalls set up here selling brightly coloured handmade Chakma fabrics. A rowboat (Tk 2) brings people across to Rajbari from Rajbari Ghat.

Tribal Cultural Institute Museum
MUSEUM

(Manik Charri Rd; Tk 20; ⊙ 9.30am-4.30pm, closed Sat) This museum has well-thought-out displays on the Adivasis of the Hill Tracts, including costumes, bamboo flutes, coins, silver-and-ivory necklaces and animal traps. There is also a map showing where the different people of the region live. Look out for the Marma and Chakma 'books' carved onto palm leaves, which date from the 1860s.

🛏 Sleeping

Hotel Golden Hill
HOTEL $

(☑ 01820-304714; Reserve Bazar; s/d from Tk 350/600) A very basic option for those on a tight budget. All rooms have attached bathroom with cold-water shower and squat toilet. Check a few first though, as they come in various shapes and sizes (and degrees of cleanliness). Those with the shared balconies are the best value.

Hotel Nadisa International
HOTEL $$

(☑ 0351-63269; www.hotelnadisa.com; Reserve Bazar; s/d Tk 1400/2550; ❄ 🤶) This new and fresh-looking hotel, with a distinctive green-glass front, is excellent value. While the rooms are spacious and clean, a few at the back struggle with tiny windows. Others at the front are a lot brighter and even offer balconies.

Hotel Sufia
HOTEL $$

(☑ 0351-62145; Kathaltoli; s/d from Tk 600/1800, with air-con Tk 1250/2850; ❄) Rooms are clean and well looked after here, with sit-down toilets but cold-water showers, and the location in the busiest part of town is handy for food, internet access and finding CNGs. Rooms at the back have balconies and small lake view. There's also a reasonable restaurant.

Parjatan Holiday Complex
HOTEL $$$

(☑ 0351-63126; Deer Park; d without/with air-con Tk 2900/3200, cottages Tk 3800-6800; ❄) It's a bit out of the way but this is the best accommodation in Rangamati. The location, overlooking a quiet hyacinth-clogged backwater of the lake, is a lovely spot. Service is good and rooms are quaint and clean and some come with balconies overlooking the lake. The complex also has hot water, a decent restaurant and private boat rental (per hour Tk 600).

🍴 Eating

Biryani House
BANGLADESHI $

(Hotel Shundarban, Reserve Bazar; mains Tk 80-240; ⊙ 5am-11pm) Pocket-sized locals' favourite with no English menu but a manager who can talk you through which curries and biryanis are on offer that day. Great fun, good value, and also a good bet for dhal-and-roti breakfasts.

Peda Ting Ting
ADIVASI $$

(Kaptai Lake; mains from Tk 180; ⊙ 9am-5pm) A popular stop on boat trips to Shuvalong Falls, this shanty-looking restaurant, on a small low-lying island, does good-quality indigenous food in an unmatched location. Has an English menu. Expect a round trip from Reserve Bazar, including eating time, to take at least two hours.

Thai Mart
ADIVASI $$

(Stadium; mains from Tk 150; ⊙ 8am-11pm) Run by a young and friendly group of Chakma staff and cooks, this relaxed restaurant with bamboo roofing does a mix of Chakma and Bengali dishes. There's an English menu, but despite the name, Thai food doesn't appear on it.

🛍 Shopping

Rangamati is a good place to buy hand-woven textiles and clothing. There's a cluster of shops close to Hotel Sufia on Kathaltoli, towards the Trust Bank ATM. You can also buy textiles from stalls on the Chakma island of Rajbari.

ℹ Information

A couple of ATMs accept foreign cards – one ATM (Reserve Bazar) is next to Hotel Green Castle on Reserve Bazar, the other ATM (Kathaltoli) is a short walk from Hotel Sufia on Kathaltoli – but there's nowhere to change money.

Ehut (Kathaltoli; internet per hour Tk 25; ⊙ 10am-9pm) offers net access.

ℹ Getting There & Away

Buses leave regularly for **Chittagong** (Tk 120, 2½ hours, 7am to 4pm) from outside Hotel Green Castle on Reserve Bazar. Some buses from Chittagong will drive all the way to Reserve Bazar Ghat. You can also catch some buses from here.

Two buses a day leave for **Bandarban** (Tk 130, four hours, 7.30am and 2pm) from the bus stand near Hotel Sufia on Kathaltoli.

ⓘ Getting Around

The area's two main ghats are **Reserve Bazar Ghat** and **Tobolchuri Ghat**. While passenger ferries shuttle locals to various locations, they won't always permit foreigners onboard; if not, you'll have to hire your own boat. You can also sometimes hire boats from **Rajbari Ghat**. Rates will vary according to your haggling skills; at the time of research, Tk 600 per boat per hour was the going rate.

Cox's Bazar

📞 0341 / POP 52,000

Cox's Bazar – named for an 18th-century British East India Company captain – is a place dear to most Bangladeshis' hearts. As everyone you meet will tell you, it's the longest continual natural beach on the planet (a whopping 125km), and the place where the country likes to come to relax.

You'll find tourist facilities here that are better than most places outside Dhaka, but don't expect a slice of southern Thailand. In fairness, the beach isn't a world wonder, but swapping the pollution of the cities for the fresh breeze off the Bay of Bengal is still invigorating, and the chance to see Bangladesh at play will give you a fun lesson in how the country likes to see itself.

Surfing is a possibility on the city's famous beach strip.

◉ Sights

Beach BEACH

The main reason to come to Cox's Bazar is for the beach. It's a very long, very exposed stretch of sand, rather than a picturesque tropical-island type of affair. It's fun for a quick paddle, though, and there are sun loungers and umbrellas you can rent (from Tk 10). The main attraction, though, is being able to take lazy sunset walks along the sand. There is also a handful of decent beach cafes.

If you want more secluded spots for either sunbathing or swimming, try heading about 10km south to **Himachari Beach** (Tk 200 in a CNG from Kolatoli Circle) or, better still, a further 15km to **Inani Beach** (Tk 300).

Aggameda Khyang BUDDHIST MONASTERY

(off Ramu Rd) Founded in 1812, the current structure of this monastery – Burmese in style – was built in 1898. The main sanctuary is built around massive timber columns, with polished teak flooring. Hidden among the trees behind is **Maha Thin Daw Gree**, a

shrine housing a number of Buddhist effigies – including one (called Cathat Ashun) which is dedicated to Captain Hiram Cox, the British East India Company representative who endeared himself to the indigenous Arakanese and after whom Cox's Bazar is now named.

🏃 Activities

Bangladesh Surfing School SURFING

(📞 01715-729777; www.surfingbangladesh.com; 1-day lesson Tk 1500, daily board hire TK 1000) Run by the exuberant Jafar Alam, self-styled 'first surfer in Bangladesh', this surfing school offers a unique and fun way to experience the country through its waves and breaks. Head out from Green Beach, just north of Cox's Bazar, for a day in the sea.

The surf is year-round, though beginners will learn better on the smaller waves between October to April, while the experienced will get a kick from the livelier surf between May to September.

🛌 Sleeping

It's not super pretty, but the rapid (over) development in the Kolatoli area means you can find better hotel and tourist facilities in Cox's Bazar than in most places outside Dhaka. Expect spotless rooms and bathrooms (with hot-water showers), free wi-fi in some places, good hotel restaurants, decent English-language skills, and swimming pools in the more expensive hotels. A long-awaited **Radisson** is finally due to open in 2016. Budget hotels are tough to find, although there are a few in Laldighi, but if you're looking for a clean, comfortable, midrange hotel, there are literally dozens.

Hotel Panowa HOTEL $

(📞 0341-63282; Laldighi Par; s/d from Tk 400/650) Down a lane beside Laldighi Lake, Panowa is a choice for those more concerned with budget than comfort. It's as basic as the prices suggest, and the cheapest rooms have common bathrooms only, but it seems well-run and often full.

Hotel Silver Shine HOTEL $$

(📞 0341-64610; www.hotelsilvershine.com; 26 Motel Rd; r from Tk 1750; ✹ @ 🛜 🛄) Closer to Laldighi than the beach, but better value because of it, Silver Shine has very clean, spacious rooms, a good restaurant and a rooftop pool (guests/nonguests Tk 100/150). It wins no prizes for excitement, but you'll probably get a decent sleep here.

Cox's Bazar

N
0 _____ 400 m
0 _____ 0.2 miles

Bakhali River

Airport Rd

Kastura Ghat (for
Maheskhali Island)

Airport

Fish
Market

Hanif
Coaches

Sky Lark
Cyber Café
@ Laldighi
Lake

Bazar
Area

Soudia
Coaches

3

Zinuk
Tourist
Market

District
Forestry
Office

Green Line
Coaches

Burmese
Market

Ramu Rd

Bus
Terminal
(2km)

LALDIGHI

4

1

Hotel Sayeman Rd

Motel Rd

New Circuit House Rd

Biman
Bangladesh

Buddhist
Stupas

Lighthouse

Regent
Airways

Beach

Radisson
(Under
Construction)

AB Bank
ATM

Hotel Motel Zone Rd

9

Green Line
Coaches

8

Hanif Coaches

2

Soudia
Coaches

KOLATOLI

Bay of
Bengal

7

Bus
Terminal
(2km)

Kolatoli Rd

5

Kolatoli Circle

Himachari
Beach (10km);
Mermaid Eco-Resort
(18km); Inani Beach
(25km)

6

Cox's Bazar

Ocean Paradise   HOTEL **$$$**

(✆ 0341-52370; www.oceanparadisehotel.com; Kolatoli Rd; r from Tk 7200; ✴@ 🗐 🗑) Easily one of the best hotels in town, offering both excellent service and facilities. Rooms are immaculate and there's a good choice of restaurants. The pool is free for guests, and a spa was due to open when we were here. Package deals and discounts are frequently on offer.

Hotel Coral Reef   HOTEL **$$$**

(✆ 0341-64469; www.coralreefbd.com; Kolatoli Rd; r without/with air-con from Tk 3250/3700, ste k 6000-7500; ✴) Of Cox's Bazar's many mega-hotels, this is one of the more charming (and smaller). The immaculate rooms make you feel too dirty to be in them. The staff are helpful and the restaurant receives good reviews. In cooler months, the non-air-con rooms are great value.

✖ Eating

Most hotels have their own restaurants, and there's a cluster of cheap roadside restaurants by Kolatoli Circle. Dry fish is a local speciality of the area, used as a base for lots of meals. Your nose will very quickly tell you where it's sold.

★**Devine Sea Stone Café** INTERNATIONAL **$$**

(Cox's Bazar beachfront; mains from Tk 350; ⊙11am-midnight) Right by the beach and on the 1st floor of a wooden building to give it extra sea views, this cafe-restaurant is great for seafood. The service is good, and if you don't want a full meal, the waiters can ply you with coffee and delicious fresh juices and shakes.

Taranga   BARBECUE **$$**

(Hotel-Motel Zone Rd; mains from Tk 300; ⊙7am-midnight) Taranga has a fairly standard menu of Bengali and Chinese dishes, but the added attraction of garden seating. Evening is the time to come, because from 5pm onwards they stoke up the barbecue and dish out a range of very tasty kebabs and fresh bread from their tandoor.

★**Mermaid Café** INTERNATIONAL **$$$**

(✆ 01713-160029; Cox's Bazar beachfront; mains from Tk 600; ⊙noon-midnight) This sprawling, shaded, Goa-style beach shack serves such tasty food in such cool surroundings that you probably won't eat anywhere else once you've tried it. The fish dishes are sumptuous, but everything is top-notch, including the delicious desserts and fresh juices. The only downside: it's just a bit too far back for sea views.

🍷 Drinking & Nightlife

Cox's Bazar is pretty dry for a holiday resort, even in Bangladesh. Ocean Paradise has a bar.

Cafe 14   CAFE

(Kolatoli Rd; ⊙10am-2am) The only cafe with real fresh coffee (from Tk 150), this Western-style coffee shop, attached to Long Beach Hotel, also serves up ice cream, cakes and sandwiches.

ℹ Information

AB Bank ATM.

Sky Lark Cyber Café (Ramu Rd, Laldighi; internet per hour Tk 30; ⊙9am-midnight) Local cybercafe.

ℹ Getting There & Away

AIR

There are several flights a day direct between Cox's Bazar and Dhaka with **Biman Bangladesh** (✆ 0341-63461; www.biman-airlines.com; Motel Rd) and **Regent Airways** (✆ 02-5566 9911; www.flyregent.com; Hotel Kollol, Hotel-Motel Zone Rd). Tickets usually start at around Tk 8000. Biman Bangladesh flights are via Chittagong.

BOAT

Boats to Maheskhali Island depart from Kastura Ghat.

BUS

Various coach companies, including Green Line, Hanif and Soudia, have offices clustered on

WORTH A TRIP

MERMAID RESORTS

If you want to get away from the Bangladeshi bustle, there are two resorts about 15km south of Cox's Bazar when you can chill and watch the waves lap in from the Bay of Bengal.

Unlike most of the accommodation in town, **Mermaid Eco-Resort** (☑ 01841-416464; www.mermaidecoresort.com; bungalows Tk 4400-5000, villas Tk 6250-8750; ◙ ☎) ⬗ is very low impact, with comfortable wooden huts that are raised on stilts above the swampland they're dotted around. They're connected to each other by wooden walkways. The resort is peaceful and environmentally friendly, the bungalows all offer a good level of comfort and the setting is magical, with a private beach just a short boat trip away.

At the more luxurious end of the spectrum, **Mermaid Beach Resort** (☑ 01841-416468; www.mermaidbeachresort.net; villas Tk 13,750-18,750; ✳ ☎) has stylish thatched bungalows secluded among the trees along the property's private beach. There are two restaurants, one of which is open to catch the sea breeze at dinner. Meals abide by a slow food ethic, but the service itself is anything but plodding.

Both resorts offer spa facilities and activities from fishing and boat trips to surfing, beach volleyball and guided hikes in the nearby hills.

Both resorts can arrange transfers from Cox's Bazar. Otherwise, catch a CNG (Tk 200, 30 minutes) from Kolatoli Circle. You'll see the sign for the eco-resort on your right, about 7km after Himachari Beach. Coming back from the eco-resort, staff will help you nab a seat in a shared auto (Tk 50).

Kolatoli Rd; Green Line, Hanif and Soudia also have offices on Beach Rd in Laldighi. Each has three or four daily air-con services to Dhaka (Tk 1300 to Tk 1800) and Chittagong (Tk 450 to Tk 650), which tend to leave either mid-morning or mid-evening. Green Line also runs to Teknaf (Tk 400), with the service meeting their ferry to St Martin's Island.

The main bus stand, a few kilometres from town, is known as Bus Terminal. From here to either Laldighi or Kolatoli Circle, a rickshaw costs Tk 30 to Tk 40. A shared auto is Tk 10.

Chittagong Tk 240, five hours, 6am to 3.30pm

Dhaka Tk 700, nine to 10 hours, 10pm

Teknaf Tk 200, two hours, 6.30am to 8pm

St Martin's Island

South along the coast from Cox's Bazar, St Martin's Island is Bangladesh's only coral island, and for once the beaches actually match the hype. The island is fairly small – about 8km in length and rarely more than 1km wide – so it's easy to navigate. Rickshaws are available, but you can also just walk around it from beach to beach. The population lives primarily off fishing, but increasingly from the domestic tourism industry. As unregulated tourism booms, St Martin's is becoming an increasingly stressed environment.

The area around the jetty, on the northeast tip of the island, is called Narikeldia, where you'll find a few hotels and restaurants. From here you'll pass through the small village of Uttarpara en route to West Beach, which is the nicest place to stay. The southern part of the island is called Dakshinpara. Even further south is Cherradhip, a thin strip of untouched land which is cut off from the rest of the island at high tide.

◉ Sights

The main attraction is, of course, the beach. Most people head to **West Beach** (walk straight on from the ferry jetty for 20 minutes, or take a Tk 20 rickshaw), as there's some decent accommodation there, but all the beaches are nice, and you can walk along the beach around the whole island in just a few hours. Boats from the main jetty can take you south to **Cherradhip** (Tk 150 return), which is the most remote and undeveloped part of St Martin's. It takes around two hours to walk there.

You can dive and snorkel between November and March with the dive group Oceanic, based on **East Beach**, which stretches away to your left as you step off the ferry.

🏃 Activities

Oceanic   DIVING
(☑ 01711-867991;   www.bddiver.com;   East Beach; single dive for beginner/qualified diver Tk 2000/3000, snorkelling Tk 600) A small diving centre run by ex-navy divers. Can offer four-day qualifications for Tk 18,000.

🛏 Sleeping & Eating

Beachside restaurants or cafes are sadly lacking on St Martin's. There are snack and drinks stalls, but if you want a meal, you'll have to eat at one of the hotels or guesthouses, or in Narikeldia by the jetty.

Abakash Parjatan HOTEL $$
(☑ 01713-145584; r Tk 1800-2200, cottages Tk 1200; ❄) Popular with domestic tourists, this three-storey building has ordinary hotel rooms as well as a handful of good-value concrete cottages in the garden. The restaurant here is decent (mains from Tk 100), and you can eat your meals in the garden.

The road from the jetty ends at the back gate to this place, so to access West Beach – and the other accommodation options – you need to walk through its garden.

Shemana Pereye BUNGALOW $$
(☑ 01819-018027, 01911-121292; cottage Tk 2200-2800, villa Tk 3000; ❄) Eight cottages dotted around a well-tended, tree-shaded garden, beside West Beach. Food is available. Walk through Abakash Parjatan to West Beach, turn left and it's just past Panna Resort.

Blue Marine Resort HOTEL $$
(☑ 01817-060065; s/d Tk 1200/1500) Probably the best place to stay on the island, even though it has looked to Cox's Bazar for architectural inspiration. It has rooms that gleam, a generator guaranteeing 24-hour power and a couple of self-catering 'cottages' (Tk 2000) that are more block houses than quaint cottages.

Hotel Prashad Paradise HOTEL $$
(☑ 01815-152740; r Tk 1200) The first hotel you'll see immediately as you step onto the island, Hotel Prashad Paradise has clean rooms, some with balcony. This is a good example of the type of hotel under construction, and some would say demonstrative of the (over) developed direction the island is taking.

❶ Getting There & Away

Agencies along Kolatoli Rd (and many hotels) in Cox's Bazar offer packages to St Martin's Island, including joint bus and ferry tickets. A day trip, leaving around 6am costs as little as Tk 1200, but the transport used isn't always the best. Buses from Cox's Bazar cost around Tk 150.

Three or four large passenger ferries (lower deck/upper deck/lounge Tk 500/700/900) leave for St Martin's (two hours) at 9.30am daily from a ferry ghat on the main road between Cox's Bazar and Teknaf. The ghat is about 5km before Teknaf. Tell your bus driver you want 'St Martin's launch' or just 'St Martin's' and he'll know where you want to be dropped.

The ferry ticket counters open at around 7am. The best-value ticket is the upper-deck one. The closed lower deck is a bit stuffy, but there's no need for the air-conditioned lounge because the sea breeze on the open deck keeps everyone cool.

The smaller, more expensive **Green Line Ferry** (www.greenlinebd.com; Tk 1200) leaves from a ghat a few hundred metres further towards Teknaf. Green Line operate a coach from Cox's Bazar (TK 400) to meet the ferry. During monsoon season, this may be the only boat available, but is still sometimes cancelled. If you're still really intent on reaching St Martin's at this time of year, some local wooden boat operators offer trips to St Martin's from **Shah Porir Dwip**, a totally undeveloped beach used by fishermen, 13km south of Teknaf.

Maheskhali Island

With its small-village atmosphere and collection of serene Hindu and Buddhist temples, the island of Maheskhali (Moshkhal-ee) makes a peaceful escape from Cox's Bazar, and getting here by boat from Cox's Bazar is half the fun.

When you get to Maheskhali, you'll probably be collared by English-speaking touts. Unless you want a guided tour of the island, ignore them, and walk the 500m or so to Goroghata, the island's main town, from where you can pick up an ordinary tout-less rickshaw.

◉ Sights

The impressive **Adinath Temple** (New Jetty Rd) is the most famous sight on the island. On the way there, look for the boat-builders working largely by hand beside the river. You can also take a rickshaw to Maheskhali Beach (Tk 30), a completely deserted beach on the south of the island.

🛏 Sleeping

Maheskhali Island only has a couple of extremely basic accommodation options, and is better as a day-trip from Cox's Bazar.

❶ Getting There & Away

Around 500m north of the Laldighi area in Cox's Bazar, you'll find a ricketty jetty (Tk 2) that leads to Kastura Ghat, from where speedboats (Tk 70, 15 minutes) or large traditional wooden ferries (Tk 25, 45 minutes) wait to take passengers to Maheskhali. Watch for the many traditional wooden fishing boats. Also notice to the east the huge fish market that services all those hotels in Cox's Bazar, and the unusual ice-making houses shooting oversized blocks of ice down runners and into waiting boats.

The last boats back to Cox's Bazar leave at around 6pm.

Teknaf Wildlife Sanctuary

Teknaf, a scruffy border town wedged into a peninsula facing Myanmar, is home to some of Bangladesh's few remaining wild elephants, in the Teknaf Wildlife Sanctuary (confusingly also sometimes called Chokoria Game Reserve). The town itself has a large bazaar with goods smuggled from across the border.

◉ Sights

Teknaf Wildlife Sanctuary   PARK
(টেকনাফ গেম রিজার্ভ; entrance Tk 200; ☺ dawn-dusk) This rarely visited wildlife reserve is home to some of the country's few remaining wild elephants. Your chances of seeing one of them are slim (the best chance is in the evening), but hiking into the hilly forest is an adventure in itself. The **Nishorgo Network** (www.nishorgo.org) keeps a list of local guides, although few speak English. The trails, though, are marked on wooden signboards (albeit in Bengali only), so it's reasonably easy to find your way around.

The chances be you'll be the only tourist walking the forest trails, although you may bump into local villagers as they venture into the hills to collect firewood. Deforestation caused by a growing but poor population has meant that the area has lost 90% of its forest cover in the last four decades.

Technically there's an Interpretation Centre by the entrance and some basic accommodation, but both were shut when we visited.

🛏 Sleeping

Hotel Dwip Plaza   HOTEL $
(Chittagong Rd; d Tk 400) This hotel is pretty basic, with squat toilets only, but is a cheap option in Teknaf centre.

Hotel Ne-Taung   HOTEL $$
(☏01712-449553; r without/with air-con Tk 1200/1800; ▣) Close to the ferry, this ramshackle Parjatan-run hotel is the normal lacklustre government offering. However it's

the best option near to both Teknaf and the St Martin's Island ferry, has hot water and some rather nice gardens. Its restaurant serves reasonably priced Bangladeshi food.

❶ Getting There & Away

Take a Teknaf-bound bus from Cox's Bazar (Tk 200, two hours, 6.30am to 8pm) or an air-conditioned coach (Tk 400). The reserve is about 8km before Teknaf proper – look for the elephant sign on the right-hand side of the road. A shared auto-rickshaw from the bus station costs Tk30 to the reserve or Tk 20 to the St Martin's ferry ghat (4km before Teknaf).

Comilla

📞 081 / POP 346,000

The only reason for tourists to visit the boisterous and bustling market town of Comilla is to see the Buddhist ruins of Mainimati. Sadly, most of them are located within a military camp on the outskirts of town, and so are off-limits to the general public. Salban Vihara, the most impressive of them all, is just outside the military boundary and can be visited.

◉ Sights

Hidden away for years in the low Mainimati-Lalmai ridge of hills are the remains of the bygone Buddhist splendour of **Mainimati**. Between the 6th and 13th centuries, Mainimati was famous as an important centre of Buddhist culture and today the scattered ruins count as some of the most impressive in Bangladesh. The three most important of the 50-odd Buddhist sites are Salban Vihara, Kotila Mura and Charpatra Mura, although only Salban Vihara can be visited.

Salban Vihara   RUIN
(Admission local/foreigner Tk 10/100; ☺ 9am-5pm Oct-Mar, 10am-6pm Apr-Sep) This ruined 170-sq-m monastery has 115 cells for monks, facing a temple in the centre of the courtyard. The royal copper plates of Deva kings and a terracotta seal bearing a royal inscription found here indicate that the monastery was built by Sri Bhava Deva in the first half of the 8th century. The entire basement wall was heavily embellished with decorative elements such as terracotta plaques and ornamental bricks.

To get here, take a shared auto from Kandirpar Circle to Kotbari (Tk 40), a small

Comilla

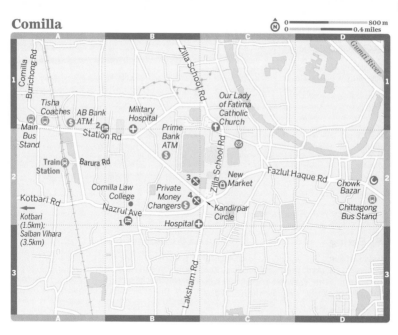

Comilla

🛏 Sleeping
1 Ashik Residential Resthouse	B2
2 Red Roof Inn	A1

🍴 Eating
3 Khaja Garden	B2
4 Midpoint Restaurant	B2
Red Roof Inn	(see 2)

village just across the Dhaka–Chittagong Hwy and a couple of kilometres from the ruins. Then either walk or take another shared auto (Tk 10) the rest of the way. Your best bet for shared autos is the road leading south off Kandirpar Circle, as that's the way they go to Kotbari. A private CNG will cost around Tk 150 each way.

Mainimati Museum   MUSEUM
(Salban Vihara; local/foreigner Tk 10/100; ⊙ 9am-5pm Oct-Mar, 10am-6pm Apr-Sep) The small Mainimati Museum, adjacent to Salban Vihara, is worth a diversion. The collection includes terracotta plaques, bronze statues, 4th-century silver and gold coins, jewellery, kitchen utensils and votive stupas embossed with Buddhist inscriptions. The marvellous terracotta plaques reveal a rural Buddhist art alive with animation and vivid natural realism.

Also on display is an unusually large bronze bell from one of the Buddhist temples and some 1000-year-old large, well-preserved black-stone carvings of Hindu gods and goddesses, including Vishnu, Ganesh and Parvati.

🛏 Sleeping

Ashik Residential Resthouse   HOTEL $
(🖉 081-68781; 186 Nazrul Ave; s/d Tk 600/800, with air-con Tk 1000/1500; 🌞) Old-school hotel with huge, well-furnished rooms. Slightly run-down, and far from spotless, but the space makes up for the tattiness. No hot-water showers, but hot water can be provided. Some English spoken.

Red Roof Inn   HOTEL $$
(🖉 081-306091; red.roof_inn@yahoo.com; Station Rd; s/d Tk 1500/2500, with air-con Tk 2000/2500; 🌞🛜) This tall modern hotel is Comilla's best sleeping option. Rooms are well turned out and comfortable, and a few even have small balconies. There's a good restaurant with Bangladeshi cuisine.

SELECTED TRAINS FROM COMILLA

DESTINATION	TRAIN NAME	DEPARTS	ARRIVES	FARE (1ST/ SHUVON)	OFF DAY
Akhaura	Samatat Ex	10.10am	12.15pm	Tk 80/45	none
Chittagong	Jalalabad Ex	7.25am	1.15pm	Tk 210/135	none
Chittagong	Mohanagar Provati	11.50am	3.40pm	Tk 210/135	none
Chittagong	Paharika Ex	6.50pm	10.20pm	Tk 210/135	Sat
Dhaka	Dhaka Ex	2.45am	7.30am	Tk 375/250/160*	none
Dhaka	Upaban Ex	12.15pm	5.25am	Tk 250/160	Wed
Dhaka	Mohanagar Provati	6pm	10.30pm	Tk 250/160	none

* Air-con berth/1st seat/shuvon

Eating

Khaja Garden　　　　　　　　　　BANGLADESHI **$**
(Kandirpar Circle; mains Tk 140; ⊙5am-11pm) Kebab heaven, with charcoal-grilled chicken and mutton *sheekh* topping the list. Also does excellent naan bread. There's no menu, and only limited English is spoken, but pointing at the food on other tables tends to do the trick.

Midpoint Restaurant　　　　　　BANGLADESHI **$**
(Kandirpar Circle; mains Tk 120; ⊙7am-11pm) This heaving locals' favourite serves up spot-on Bengali dishes (curries, biryanis). There's no English sign or menu, but some English is spoken.

Red Roof Inn　　　　　　　　　　BANGLADESHI **$$**
(SEL Nisa Tower, Station Rd; mains from Tk 180; ⊙7am-10pm) This tidy restaurant of the Red Roof Inn (p123) is on the first floor before reception. It serves up delicious and very generously portioned Bangladeshi and Indian curries, with a few Chinese dishes thrown in for good measure.

ⓘ Information

Comilla has a couple of foreign-friendly ATMs, including Prime Bank and AB Bank. There are private **moneychangers** (Nazrul Ave) on Nazrul Ave.

ⓘ Getting There & Away

BUS

Tisha Coaches runs comfortable, good-value coaches to Dhaka (Tk 160, two to three hours, 5am to 9pm) and Chittagong (Tk 160, four hours, 6am to 6pm). The Dhaka ones leave from the Tisha office by the main bus stand. The Chittagong ones leave from the office at the Chittagong bus stand.

It costs Tk 10 in a rickshaw to get from Kandirpar Circle to either the Main Bus Stand or the Chittagong Bus Stand.

The main bus stand serves Shaista Ganj (for Srimangal; Tk 200, 4½ hours, 6am to 5pm) and Sylhet (Tk 340, seven hours, 6am to 5pm). Go to the Chittagong bus stand for Chittagong (Tk 140, four hours, 6am to 6pm).

TRAIN

Trains to Dhaka all pass through Akhaura (for the Indian border, 1st/shuvon Tk 80/45, one hour).

Sylhet Division

Best Places to Sleep

➜ Nishorgo Nirob Ecoresort (p136)

➜ Nazimgarh Garden Resort (p127)

➜ Grand Sultan Tea Resort (p137)

Best Places to Eat

➜ Panshi Restaurant (p129)

➜ Woondaal (p129)

➜ Kutum Bari (p137)

Why Go?

Pastoral Sylhet packs in more shades of green than you'll possibly find on a graphic designer's shade card. Blessed with glistening rice paddies, the wetland marshes of Ratargul and Sunamganj, the forested nature reserves of Lowacherra, and Srimangal's rolling hills blanketed in waist-high tea bushes, Sylhet boasts a mind-blowing array of landscapes and sanctuaries that call out to nature lovers from around the world.

Even while offering plenty of rural adventures for those willing to go the extra mile, Sylhet scores over several other divisions in terms of its easy accessibility. Good transport links mean Sylhet's famous tea estates, its smattering of Adivasi mud-hut villages, its thick forests and its serene bayous are all just a few hours' drive or train journey from Dhaka.

Given its relaxed grain, Sylhet is best enjoyed at leisure. Schedule a week at least for your trip here, especially if you love outdoor activities.

When to Go
Sylhet

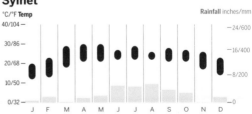

Mar–Nov
Tea-picking season. Time for those classic teapicker photos.

Oct–Mar Dry season; time for hiking, boat trips and birdwatching.

Mar–May If Dhaka is too hot, Sylhet provides a relatively cooler escape.

0   20 km
0   10 miles

MEGHALAYA
(INDIA)

Shillong

Cherrapunji   Dawki   Tamabil
              Jaflong
                    Jaintiapur

Tahirpur   Sunamganj
                    3 Ratargul

Jamalganj
Dharmapasha   4 Sylhet

                              Beani
                              Bazar
Derai   Jagannathpur
                                        Madhabkunda
SYLHET   Fenchuganj
DIVISION

DHAKA
DIVISION

              Nabiganj

                    Moulvi
                    Bazar
              Lowacherra
              National
Habiganj   Park 2 Upazilla
Shaista   Srimangal 1
Ganj   Kulmaghat
              Madhabpur   Kolobagan
Satchari   Lake   5 Hum Hum
National   Falls
Park
                    Rajkandi
                    Forest
                    Reserve
Chandura   TRIPURA
                  (INDIA)

CHITTAGONG
DIVISION

Sylhet Division Highlights

1 Srimangal (p131)
Ambling through expansive
tea estates and sip on quirky,
multicoloured seven-layered
tea.

**2 Lowacherra National
Park** (p133) Keeping an eye

out for rare hoolock gibbons
while strolling the walking
trails of this semi-evergreen
forest.

3 Ratargul (p130) Rowing
a skiff under a canopied forest
while exploring this swampy
wilderness.

4 Sylhet (p127) Tucking
in at some of the country's
best curry houses in the
region's capital city.

5 Hum Hum Falls (p136)
Getting off the beaten track
with a daylong hike to these
remote falls.

Sylhet

📞 0821 / POP 480,000

Friendly Sylhet is a divisional capital with a pronounced small-town feel, its congested streets and bustling roadside markets chipping in with requisite measures of sights, sounds and smells. The town, however, also gives off a strong underlying sense of economic prosperity. The majority of British Bangladeshis hail from here, and those with stronger ties to the homeland continue to visit their families regularly and pour money back into the local economy. This has helped create a city that is more modern than other comparable urban centres in Bangladesh. For tourists, it also means the availability of better hotels and restaurants, easier access to creature comforts and a disproportionately large local population that speaks good English.

Sylhet, of course, is best known for its tea. This is where the country's commercial tea production first began, and a few of the region's 130-odd tea estates are walking distance from the city centre.

◉ Sights

Shrine of Hazrat Shah Jalal   MAUSOLEUM

This fascinating and atmospheric shrine of the revered 14th-century Sufi saint Shah Jalal is one of Bangladesh's biggest pilgrimage sites. Housing a mosque *(masjid)* and the main tomb *(mazar)*, the complex is accessed via an open staircase from the East Darga Gate entrance. Shah Jalal's tomb is covered with rich brocade, and the space around it is illuminated with candles in the evenings, lending a magical feel. Non-Muslims can enter (dress conservatively). Shoes have to be removed at the steps.

The saint's sword and robes are preserved within the mosque, but aren't on display. You can also walk around the hillside graveyard behind the shrine, dotted with tombs. Being buried near the saint is considered a great honour. Women can enter the complex – there is even a special prayer hall for women here – but are not usually allowed to enter the shrine itself (doing so would mean passing through part of the mosque, which is out of bounds to women).

The pond at the northern end of the complex is filled with sacred catfish that are fed by pilgrims and are, according to legend, metamorphosed black magicians of the Hindu raja Gour Govinda, who was defeated by Shah Jalal in 1303.

Kean Bridge   BRIDGE

(Dhaka–Sylhet Hwy) The more central of the two bridges spanning the Surma River, Kean Bridge hails from the British era and was repaired after being damaged by Pakistani bombers during the Liberation War. It's no architectural wonder, but crossing it is a unique experience that can roughly be summarised as being immersed in a seething mass of humanity either driving, cycling, walking or simply running its way in and out of the city.

🛏 Sleeping

Hotel Golden City   HOTEL $

(📞 0821-726379; www.hotelgoldencitybd.com; East Zinda Bazar Rd; s/d incl breakfast Tk 600/850, with air-con Tk 1200/1700; ❄) Sandwiched between two of Sylhet's most popular restaurants, this good-value hotel has simple but comfortable rooms appointed with cane and faux-cedar furnishings. Floors are tiled, and the bathrooms have sit-down toilets and hot-water showers. Some staff members speak English, and the service is both prompt and friendly.

Surma Valley Rest House   HOTEL $$

(📞 0821-712680; Shah Jalal Rd; d incl breakfast from Tk 1400, with air-con from Tk 1750; ❄ @) Once a preferred address for state VIPs visiting Sylhet, this guesthouse-like oldie tucked away in the chaos of Bandar Bazar offers fantastic home-style lodging at unbelievable prices. Located in the upper floors of a commercial building, it comes with sparkling clean rooms full of light, air, leafy views and little homey touches. The service is prompt, English-friendly and polite.

★ Nazimgarh Garden Resort   RESORT $$$

(📞 0821-287 0338; www.nazimgarh.com; Khadimnagar; d incl breakfast from Tk 11,000; ❄ @ 🛜 ☷) Built on six acres of impeccably landscaped greens and located about 6km east of town amid bucolic surroundings, Nazimgarh is a superb getaway that offers luxury and serenity in equal measures. Rooms are stylish affairs with huge balconies overlooking paddies, the bathrooms come fitted with Jacuzzis and rain showers, and the restaurant serves a limited but delectable range of dishes.

Cooperative kitchen staff can arrange for a greater variety of local dishes with advance notice, and the swimming pool

Sylhet

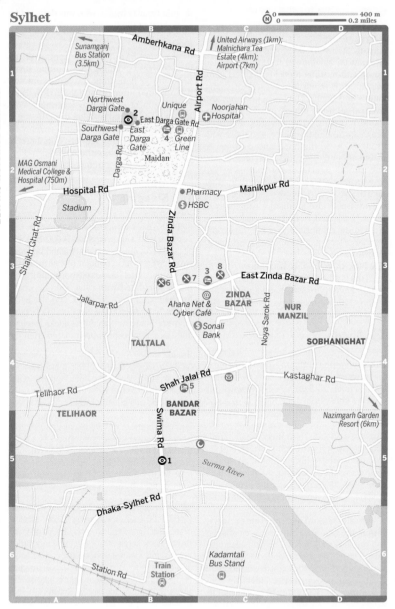

N 0   400 m
0   0.2 miles

Amberhkana Rd

Sunamganj
Bus Station
(3.5km)

United Airways (1km);
Malnichara Tea
Estate (4km);
Airport (7km)

Airport Rd

Northwest
Darga Gate

Unique

Noorjahan
Hospital

East Darga Gate Rd

Southwest
Darga Gate

East
Darga
Gate

Green
Line

Darga Rd

Maidan

MAG Osmani
Medical College &
Hospital (750m)

Hospital Rd

Manikpur Rd

Stadium

Pharmacy

HSBC

Shaikh Ghat Rd

Zinda Bazar Rd

East Zinda Bazar Rd

Jallarpar Rd

ZINDA
BAZAR

NUR
MANZIL

Ahana Net &
Cyber Café

Noya Sarok Rd

TALTALA

Sonali
Bank

SOBHANIGHAT

Shah Jalal Rd

Kastaghar Rd

Telihaor Rd

BANDAR
BAZAR

Swima Rd

Nazimgarh Garden
Resort (6km)

TELIHAOR

Surma River

Dhaka-Sylhet Rd

Station Rd

Train
Station

Kadamtali
Bus Stand

located in the upper reaches of the complex is perfect for flopping about in the evenings. The property can also arrange for bicycles if you want to explore the rural landscape on your own. A CNG to the resort from Sylhet costs Tk 100.

Hotel Star Pacific   HOTEL **$$$**
(☏ 01937-776644, 0821-727945; www.hotelstar pacific.com; East Darga Gate Rd; d incl breakfast from Tk 6500; ❄ @ 🛜 ☒) Central Sylhet's flagship hotel is sharp, modern and stylish, its comfortable rooms boasting a smattering

Sylhet

◉ Sights
1 Kean Bridge	B5
2 Shrine of Hazrat Shah Jalal	B1

🛏 Sleeping
3 Hotel Golden City	C3
4 Hotel Star Pacific	B2
5 Surma Valley Rest House	B4

✕ Eating
6 Panshi Restaurant	B3
7 Pritiraj	B3
8 Woondaal	C3

of luxe creature comforts. The atmospheric precinct of the shrine of Hazrat Shah Jalal is just across the road, but the soundproof windows keep outdoor noise to a minimum. Service is excellent, and in-house facilities include a good restaurant, rooftop pool plus a small gym.

✕ Eating

Local food in Sylhet is among the yummiest in Bangladesh. The best curry houses outside of Dhaka are located here, along with some eateries in the style of London's Brick Lane, specialising in robust North Indian flavours.

Pritiraj   BANGLADESHI $
(East Zinda Bazar Rd; mains Tk 80-100; ⊙7am-11pm) A friendly neighbourhood restaurant where filling biryanis, tasty grilled chicken and fish dishes as well as a range of mouth-watering curries fly thick and fast during mealtimes, centrally located Pritiraj is a great place for a cheap yet memorable meal. Try the *kachchi* biryani, in which the rice and mutton chunks are slow cooked together from start to finish.

★Panshi Restaurant   BANGLADESHI $$
(Jallarpar Rd; meals Tk 200; ⊙6am-10.30pm) At this iconic and wildly popular proletarian restaurant, the grade of cooking is nothing short of culinary wizardry. Bringing every possible permutation of local ingredients and flavours to your table, the al fresco eatery is perpetually thronged by locals, and you might have to share tables at peak hours. Skip the menu and simply ask the friendly waiters to surprise you.

★Woondaal   INDIAN $$
(East Zinda Bazar Rd; mains Tk 140-220; ⊙11am-11pm) If you've ever been to a Bangladeshi-run Indian restaurant on London's Brick Lane – where many of the restaurants are run by expats from Sylhet – then you'll recognise all your curry favourites on the menu here (you'll sorely miss the beer, though). The service is slick, the decor is modern and the food is simply superb.

The (English) menu here is really more North Indian than Bangladeshi, so feel free to order yourself an assorted platter of kebabs served with pickled onions and mint chutney, followed by the signature mutton biryani or one of the many yummy curried or chargrilled chicken dishes, best polished off with naan. Very often, there's live sporting action on TV to go with your meal.

ℹ Information

Ahana Net & Cyber Café (East Zinda Bazar Rd; per hour Tk 50; ⊙10am-8pm) Sylhet's most central internet cafe. Connections are fast, but expect a queue.

HSBC (Zinda Bazar Rd; ⊙10am-4pm Sat-Thu) This is the best place to change money or use an ATM for foreign cardholders.

MAG Osmani Medical College & Hospital (☑0821-714368; Medical College Rd) This is a state-run institution that packs in both basic and advanced healthcare and has a well-stocked pharmacy on site.

Sonali Bank (www.sonalibank.com.bd; Zinda Bazar Rd; ⊙10am-4pm Sat-Thu) If you're crossing over to India, you can pay your Tk 500 'travel tax' at this bank before heading to the Indian border at Tamabil.

ℹ Getting There & Away

BUS

Sylhet's main bus stand is **Kadamtali bus stand** (Zakiganj Rd). It's a sprawling collection of roadside bus stands with buses to pretty much anywhere. Most run from around 6am up until around 8pm. Services include several buses departing through the day for Dhaka (from Tk 370, five hours), Srimangal (Tk 160, two hours) and Tamabil for the Indian border (Tk 90, two hours).

Sunamganj bus stand (Amberkhana Rd), also known as Kumargaon bus terminal, is a few kilometres northwest of town, along Amberkhana Rd (which intersects Airport Rd) with buses running to Sunamganj (Tk 130, two hours, every hour 6am to 8pm). A CNG to this bus stand costs about Tk 150.

Green Line (www.greenlinebd.com; East Darga Gate Rd) is a private operator and has air-con coaches to Dhaka (Tk 900, five daily, 6.45am to 5.30pm), while **Unique** (☑01190-806447; East

Darga Gate Rd) is one of a number of companies in town with non-air-con coaches departing through the day for Dhaka (Tk 450).

TRAIN

All the trains listed stop at Srimangal (1st seat/shuvon Tk 200/135, about two hours). The Chittagong trains also stop at Comilla (1st seat/shuvon Tk 295/190, about six hours).

AIR

Novoair (☑01755-656660; www.flynovoair.com) and **US Bangla Airlines** (☑01777-777788; www.us-banglaairlines.com) both have modern fleets, are efficiently run and operate daily flights to and from Dhaka (from Tk 3200).

❶ Getting Around

Expect to pay around Tk 300 for the 30-minute CNG ride to the airport. Taxis for the same journey usually cost about Tk 900. Within town, rickshaws and CNGs are your best options for going about. Fares for both start at Tk 20.

Ratargul

☑0821 / POP 6000

About 35km northwest of Sylhet lies Ratargul, Bangladesh's only freshwater swamp forest, formed by the spilling over of the Gowain River into a 200-hectare jungle basin shaded by innumerable evergreens. The water level in this 'Amazonian' swamp peaks at about 7.5m in the rainy season, dropping to about 3m during winter. A variety of trees, including the readily recognisable millettia or *koroch*, stand with their trunks immersed in water and provide refuge to bird species such as kingfishers, cormorants, cranes and herons, as well as a large assortment of snakes.

🏃 Activities

Exploring Ratargul's swamps on a skiff-like country boat can be an experience straight out of a Lara Croft movie. Winding in and out of several meandering water channels, rowing around trees and ducking to avoid creepers that hang low from the branches above, you can navigate these silent and still marshes and spot resident wildlife through the better part of a day. If you keep your eyes trained, you might even see a surefooted fishing cat go about preying on the fish in the water. However, stay on board your boat at all times. Stepping into the water is not advised. Boatmen don't speak English, but can point you in the direction of interesting sights.

Being a relatively new place on the region's tourist map, Ratargul has scant infrastructure. You will see quite a few tourist groups here in the winter months, but the place remains virtually deserted (or flooded over) through the rest of the year.

Amir Ali   BOAT TOUR
(☑01720-184847; Chowmohani Bazar) Amir Ali, with his associates Sona Mian and Fazlu Mian, manage a community development project in Ratargul offering boating and guiding services, as well as lunch for guests prepared upon advance notice (per person Tk 200). Their homestay project may also see the light of day in 2017.

🛏 Sleeping & Eating

There are currently no hotels in Ratargul. A few villagers have plans for extending homestay facilities to tourists, but that won't happen until 2017 at the earliest.

Carry dry food and water from Sylhet, as Ratargul offers little in terms of provisions. Amir Ali, a local boatman, guide and

SELECTED TRAINS FROM SYLHET

DESTINATION	TRAIN NAME	DEPARTS	ARRIVES	FARE *	OFF DAY
Chittagong	Paharika Ex	10.15am	8.05pm	Tk 690/460/345	Sat
Chittagong	Udayan Ex	9.20pm	6.35am	Tk 690/460/345	Sun
Chittagong	Jalalabad Ex	10.50pm	12.40pm	Tk 690/460/345	none
Dhaka	Joyantika Ex	8.40am	4.20pm	Tk 595/395/295	Thu
Dhaka	Parabat Ex	3pm	10.35pm	Tk 595/395/295	Tue
Dhaka	Surma Mail	8pm	9.45am	Tk 595/395/295	none
Dhaka	Upaban Ex	10pm	5.25am	Tk 595/395/295	none

* 1st berth/1st seat/shuvon

proprietor, can prepare home-style lunch (per person Tk 200) comprising rice, vegetables, duck meat and fish from the swamps if notified in advance.

🛈 Getting There & Away

Ratargul is best visited on a day trip from Sylhet, so hire a taxi for the day (Tk 3000). The rural dirt road to Ratargul is among the prettiest in the country, cutting through bamboo forests, tea plantations and lush paddies, offering plenty of photo-ops along the way. From the pier at Ratargul, you can hire a boat (Tk 1000) for a three-hour safari. Each boat seats up to four people (excluding boatmen).

Sunamganj

📞 0871 / POP 50,000

Approximately 70km west of Sylhet, this small town acts as a gateway to the *haors* (wetlands) of the region, which are rife with bird life. From midwinter through the end of March (and sometimes April), migrant winter birds and the region's resident avian fauna all get together for a big bird party. Varieties of rails, raptors, ducks, sandpipers and other species congregate on these wetlands, which are worth a day's birdwatching trip from Sylhet.

🏃 Activities

Birdwatching

Of the 170-odd bird species, the endangered Baer's pochard (a diving duck native to Russia and China) is the rarest bird you're likely to see on an outing to the *haors*. Other pochards include the white-eyed and red-crested varieties. The Baikal teal and the falcated teal are both impressive winter guests, along with an assortment of crakes. You'll also see the spotted redshank and the blue-bearded bee-eater, plus various sandpipers and lapwings. A number of raptors are found here as well, including several fishing eagles, such as the grey-headed and spotted Pallas' eagles.

The three *haors* that seem to be best for bird-watching – Aila Haor, Pasua Haor and the most accessible Tanguar Haor – are several hours upstream from Sunamganj. Visiting all of them is a four-day affair, which (except for hardcore bird enthusiasts) is more than most travellers can digest. If a lovely day out in the wilds is all you want, a simple day trip from Sylhet will suffice.

🛏 Sleeping & Eating

Sunamganj has few hotels that meet acceptable standards. Furthermore, due to prevailing security alerts at the time of research, tourists were being advised not to spend nights here, and return to Sylhet instead. Intrepid adventurers may be able to arrange overnight stays on one of the boats in the *haors*, but with the current security situation, this is not recommended.

Stock up on dry food and water in Sunamganj, as there's little opportunity to buy things on a trip to the *haors*.

🛈 Getting There & Away

Buses to Sunamganj leave regularly from the Sunamganj bus station in Sylhet (Tk 130, two hours, every hour 6am to 8pm). For day trips, make sure you set out at first light. From Sunamganj's old bus stand, it's a five-minute walk to Gudara Ghat. If your bus pulls in at the new bus stand, you'll have to take a shared CNG (per person Tk 10) to the old bus terminal. To speed up this journey considerably, consider hiring a taxi from Sylhet for the day (Tk 3500).

If local guides don't find you at Gudara Ghat already, step on to a boat and cross the Surma River (Tk 10). The other side is called Olir Bazar. From here you can hire a two-pillion motorcycle taxi (Tk 300, 90 minutes) to Solemanpur Bazar, from where you can hire boats (Tk 1200) for a three-hour round trip around Tanguar Haor, before returning the way you came.

Several hotels in Sylhet can arrange private transport (and possibly an English-speaking driver) for you if informed a day in advance.

Srimangal & Around

📞 08626 / POP 21,500

Sylhet may be the primary city in the eponymous division, but sylvan Srimangal is the undoubted star of this region. Blessed with rolling hills carpeted with endless tea plantations, dense forest sanctuaries and a sprinkling of tribal villages, this place is bound to rank among your most treasured experiences in Bangladesh. The town itself is small, friendly and easy to manage, but it's the surrounding countryside that's the real draw, with hiking, wildlife-watching and, of course, tea-drinking all high on the agenda.

In the wake of travel advisories pertaining to the safety of foreigners at the time of

Srimangal

research, cycling (once the most popular activity among tourists) was suspended in the region until further notice. This has somewhat dampened the experience for a lot of outdoorsy travellers, but most areas still remain open to hiking and general ambling.

⊙ Sights

The outlying region around Srimangal is covered with lush tea estates as far as the eyes can see. The closest ones of significance are Zareen Tea Estate and the British-owned Finlays Tea Estate, both of which you can walk or take a CNG to. Of academic and scientific importance is the **Bangladesh Tea Research Institute** (☑ 08626-71225; BTRI Rd), also within walking distance, where you could get up close and personal with the many nitty gritties of tea production.

The estates are somewhat informal affairs, although wandering in is not welcomed. It's polite to go to the main entrance, knock on the door of the manager's office and ask if it's OK to look round. They will almost always say yes, and will sometimes throw in a free tour of the tea factory if you ask sweetly.

Finlays Tea Estate TEA ESTATE
(Srimangal–Bhanugach Rd) The sprawling Finlays Tea Estate, just on the edge of Srimangal, is easily accessible, and you can step into the bushes and interact with tea pickers once you have taken prior permission from the estate office by the Srimangal-Bhanugach road. The gardens also spill over to the other side of the road from the estate office.

Zareen Tea Estate TEA ESTATE
(Radhanagar Village) Zareen Tea Estate is home to the renowned Ispahani tea that is loved and consumed in copious quantities across Bangladesh. The glistening plantations lie about 1.5km beyond Radhanagar village,

Lowacherra National Park 1st Gate (2km);
Lowacherra National Park Main Gate (4km);
Upazilla (10km)

RADHANAGAR
VILLAGE

temple symbol of the Manipuri, which is often woven into the fabrics they sell.

Lowacherra National Park   WILDLIFE RESERVE
(Srimangal–Bhanugach Rd; local/foreigner Tk 20/400; ☺9am-5pm) This wonderful patch of tropical semi-evergreen forest, around 8km east of Srimangal, provides some lovely forest walks and also your best chance of seeing the endangered hoolock gibbons in the wild. These are the only apes in Bangladesh and there are only around 200 left in the country, some 60 of which live here. Protected as part of the government-run **Nishorgo Network** (www.nishorgo.org), the park now has walking trails as well as knowledgeable eco-guides who charge Tk 400 an hour.

Apart from the hoolocks, a further 19 mammal species have been identified here including capped langur, macaques, the delightful slow loris, orange-bellied Himalayan squirrel and barking deer. There are also some 246 bird species and 20 varieties of orchid.

Remember this is a dense forest, so sightings are not guaranteed and are completely contingent on luck. One thing you won't miss, though, are the enormous orb spiders – black, red and yellow monsters that hang

past some beautiful farmland, extending over rolling hillocks that are so typical of the region.

Ramnagar   VILLAGE
The closest Manipuri village to Srimangal is Ramnagar. Local tours will usually include a trip here, but you can also walk here yourself. Of all the ethnic groups of this region, the Manipuri are the most integrated into mainstream Bangladeshi society, making villages like this one relatively accessible. Villagers have even opened shops here so tourists can buy the beautiful fabrics that you'll see being woven on handlooms in back yards.

Those not involved in weaving tend to work in agriculture, so you'll also see fruit trees galore (mango, lemon, jackfruit, banana) as well as rice paddies on the edge of the village. Most Manipuri are Hindu, and small temples and shrines dot the village. You may also notice the flame-like Hindu-from Spiderman-sized webs between trees and are supposedly completely harmless.

There are three walking trails (30 minutes, one hour and three hours), with maps on wooden signboards marking the way. A guide will be able to take you off-track without getting lost. These days, an armed guard will also likely accompany you into the forest ostensibly for your security.

Mind the railway line that runs right through the jungle; trains have a tendency to creep up on unsuspecting humans while they're immersed in photo-ops. There's a tea-and-snack stall by the visitor centre.

You can get here from Srimangal by bus (Tk 20) or CNG (Tk 100). Note there are two gates to the park. The first one, as you come from Srimangal, is on the right-hand side of the road and is mostly unmanned and unused. The main gate is about 2km beyond this (on the left-hand side of the road).

Satchari National Park   WILDLIFE RESERVE
(local/foreigner Tk 20/400; ☺ 9am-5pm) About 60km southwest of Srimangal, this out-of-the-way sanctuary is overseen by the Nishorgo Network (p133) and has a similar set-up to Lowacherra National Park with walking trails, but is much less visited. A superb slab of tropical forest, Satchari is home to a small population of hoolock gibbons as well as fishing cats, the gremlin-faced Phayre's langur, jungle fowl, pygmy woodpeckers and oriental pied hornbills. To get here, it's best to hire a taxi from Srimangal for the day (Tk 3000).

Alternatively, you could take a bus from Srimangal to the crossroads junction known as Shaista Ganj (Tk 50, 40 minutes, hourly from 9am). Then take a bus to Sunarghat (Tk 15, 20 minutes), from where you can pick up a shared jeep to Satchari (Tk 20, 30 minutes). Don't leave it too late coming back. Buses in Sunarghat start to thin out at around 5pm, although buses pass through Shaista Ganj all evening.

🏃 Activities

The area around Srimangal is one of the best in Bangladesh for cycling. Despite the rolling terrain, the roads are reasonably level and well maintained. And the scenery, of course, is beautiful.

There's an intricate network of lanes connecting all the tea estates and villages to the main roads. Only the major routes are tarred or bricked, but the dirt roads tend to be in decent condition, too.

It can be difficult to determine where one estate stops and another starts. Bear in mind that you might inadvertently pedal onto private property. Though you will find that most people are more likely to treat you like a guest than a trespasser, it is polite to seek advance permission if and where you can.

BANGLADESH TEA: FAST FACTS

➡ Bangladesh makes just over 60 million kilograms of tea each year, making it the world's 10th-largest tea producer.

➡ Commercial tea production in Bangladesh dates from 1857, when Malnichara Tea Estate, just north of Sylhet, was set up by the British.

➡ 166 tea estates are still in operation in Bangladesh, 133 of which are in Sylhet division. Only 27 are still British-owned.

➡ Most tea-estate workers are descendents of Indian labourers brought in by the British from the regions of Bihar, Orissa and West Bengal. As such, you will sometimes see Hindu shrines among the tea bushes.

➡ The working and social conditions of workers has often been called into question by nonprofit organisations.

➡ It is usually only women who pick tea leaves, apparently because they have smaller and more delicate hands.

➡ At just 75m above sea level, Srimangal is one of the world's lowest tea-growing areas. This gives the tea grown here a distinct flavour.

➡ The picking season here spans the spring, summer, monsoon and autumn months, from early March to late November. This is also when the factories are in full operation. Tea estates are eerily quiet during winter.

SEVEN LAYER TEA

Tea-maker extraordinaire Romesh Ram Gour, the man behind the legendary **Nilkantha Tea Cabin** (www.nilkantha.blog.com; Border Guard Canteen; teas Tk 10-75; ⊘10am-5.30pm), is the creator of one of the most famous types of tea in Bangladesh. His Willy Wonka-esque **seven-colour tea** (Tk 75) is known throughout the country and has even appeared in some foreign press articles. Yes, it really does have seven distinct layers of colour and seven equally differing tastes. It's so popular that Gour has opened a second tea cabin about 1km further south. You can order any number of layers, from two up to seven. Each layer costs Tk 10, as do the other more orthodox tea flavours on offer.

The original tea stall is an easy 10-minute walk from town; cross the railway line at the train station and keep going until you reach the Bangladesh Border Guard barracks on your left. The newer tea cabin is another 10 minutes by foot along the same road, to the right of the thoroughfare.

Note that other multilayer tea pretenders have opened up in and around Srimangal, but their tea layers tend to merge into a cloudy mess. Nilkantha is the original and, for now at least, still the best.

Most hotels and local guides can help arrange bike hire for about Tk 300 per day.

In 2015, following a few politically or communally motivated incidents where resident foreigners were killed or shot at across Bangladesh, the government issued a series of security alerts and travel advisories for foreign visitors. As a result, cycling activities in the region were put on hold until further notice; local authorities felt it was risky for foreigners to pedal their way into the countryside without being escorted. By the time you visit, however, things will probably have eased up again, so ask your hotel's reception when you check in.

Anam Cycle Store　　BICYCLE RENTAL
(Railway Station Rd; ⊘10am-8pm) Anam Cycle Store nominally rents out bicycles for Tk 300 per day. If and when cycling is officially allowed by the local authorities once again, it would be possible to grab a well-serviced bike here against furnishing a copy of your passport.

⌖ Tours

A number of resident English-speaking local guides offer informal tours of Srimangal and its leafy surrounds. Meet a couple of them beforehand to decide who you might prefer, depending on language skills and overall professionalism. Prices tend to be about the same: Tk 1500 for a guide for the day, plus about the same again for a CNG to cart you round the sights. Prices are per group (you can squeeze as many as three people into a CNG) and are, of course, negotiable.

Below are some guides you may wish to contact. You could also make arrangements through the **Nishorgo Network** (p133), a government-managed conservation scheme, which also runs the excellent Nishorgo Ecoresort Cottages.

Tapas Dash　　TOUR
(☏01723-292994) Excellent English. Perhaps the best guide you'll find. Customises tours according to individual preferences.

Rashed Husain　　TOUR
(☏01711-078362) Contactable through Tea Town Rest House. Punctual and amiable.

Liton Deb　　TOUR
(☏01710-994099) Enthusiastic, friendly and cooperative. Can also arrange for taxis to nearby locations.

🛏 Sleeping

🛏 In Srimangal

Green View Rest House　　HOTEL $
(☏01719-896788; Sagardighi Rd; d Tk 800, with air-con from Tk 1500; ❄) For travellers on a budget, this good-value hotel offers ultra clean rooms with tiled floors and wooden furniture. The more expensive rooms come with large windows, sit-down toilets and hot showers, while the cheaper ones have squat loos and may lack windows altogether. Nonetheless, the place scores well in terms of housekeeping, and the staff are eager to please.

HUM HUM FALLS

For an off-the-beaten-track adventure, set aside a full day and try hiking from Srimangal to **Hum Hum Falls**.

Hidden in the depths of tropical forests, this tall waterfall is only a truly impressive sight during and just after the rainy season. During the rest of the year, it's dry but still makes an excellent hike through farmland and villages, the gardens of Champarai Tea Estate and finally through the beautiful jungles of **Rajkandi Forest Reserve**. Like Lowacherra National Park, the forests here are home to macaques and a few hoolock gibbons, although felling of trees and bamboo is sadly quite common. The walk is steep at times, and part of it involves wading through a river. Take plenty of water and packed lunch.

You'll never find the falls on your own, so pick up a local guide (Tk 300) in **Kulmaghat**, the last stop on the bus before your hike begins. None of the guides speak English, but they will understand where you want to go if you just say 'Hum Hum'. You can buy provisions in Kulmaghat and even have lunch there.

The walk from Kulmaghat to the falls takes around three hours one way. There are two routes to the falls, so don't be alarmed if your guide walks back along a different track.

At the time of research, hiking along the trail was being discouraged by local authorities due to prevailing travel advisories for foreigners, so check with your hotel in Srimangal in advance to see if the route is once again safe.

To get to Kulmaghat, take a bus from the Lowacherra bus stand in Srimangal to **Upazilla** (Tk 25, 45 minutes, 8am to 4pm) then change for Kulmaghat (Tk 30, 45 minutes). The last bus back to Upazilla is at 4.30pm. The last bus from there to Srimangal is at 6pm. If you get stranded, a shared CNG from Upazilla to Srimangal will cost Tk 50 per person.

A private CNG from Srimangal to Kulmaghat and back will cost at least Tk 1000 including waiting charges. You may be able to get your CNG driver to drive all the way to Kolabagan village, saving you about an hour of walking time each way.

Tea Town Rest House HOTEL **$**
(☑08626-71065; Dhaka–Sylhet Rd; s/d/t Tk 600/800/1200, d/t with air-con Tk 2000/3000; ✳@) A long-time favourite for budget travellers, this central place has friendly staff and clean rooms, although bathrooms (a mix of squats and sit-downs) are somewhat cramped. The large triple room is lovely and bright, but others lack natural light, despite being good value. There's a computer terminal in the reception with a stuttering internet connection (per hour Tk 50).

🏠 Around Srimangal

★**Nishorgo Nirob Ecoresort** COTTAGE **$$**
(☑01715-041207, 01716-939540; www.nishorgo cottage.com; Radhanagar Village; cottages incl breakfast from Tk 1500) This community-based project developed by Nishorgo Network (p133) offers the perfect mix of rustic experiences and modern lodging amenities, all set in a beautiful garden-hemmed plot on the banks of a trickling stream. Once you settle into one of its three delightfully clean and airy bamboo cottages opening out to lush greenery, you may never want to leave!

Rustic as they are, the cottages here come with comfortable beds, power back-up, modern toilets, hot water upon request and a choice of local and western food (meals Tk 250). Do make it a point to book early, as the cottages don't seem to free up within short notice, especially during the high tourist season.

Nishorgo Litchibari Ecoresort COTTAGE **$$**
(☑01716-939540, 01715-041207; www.nishorgo cottage.com; Radhanagar Village; concrete huts incl breakfast Tk 2500, bamboo huts incl breakfast Tk 4000) Developed by Nishorgo Network (p133) as part of a community development project, this complex has a mix of concrete and bamboo cottages that are impeccably maintained and offer a reasonable level of comfort while being in perfect unison with the surrounding forests. Sumptuous lunch and dinner platters (Tk 250) are available in the dining hall in the main concrete block.

Hermitage Guest House HOMESTAY **$$**
(☑01711-595265; www.hermitageguesthouse.com; Radhanagar Village; r Tk 2000, with air-con from Tk 3000; ✳🛜) Run by the affable Dhaka-based

advocate Sultana, this excellent guesthouse on the far end of Radhanagar village has a handful of comfortable rooms with modern, hot-water bathrooms and lots of thoughtful homey touches. A garden terrace overlooks a gurgling forest stream to the rear. Hot and yummy meals are available on request at the dining room. Laundry is free!

With rising demand, Sultana has recently acquired an annexe-like second property five minutes down a village track across the road, which boasts vividly coloured family rooms, some with thatched roofing. Rates are seasonal, and while it's possible to get fat discounts during quieter months, booking ahead is recommended during the high tourist season.

★ **Grand Sultan Tea Resort**　　　RESORT $$$
(☑ 08626-73000;　www.grandsultanresort.com; Srimangal–Bhanugach Rd; d incl breakfast from Tk 11,500; ❄ @ ☎ ☲) Don't be thwarted by its gigantic size. Step in and you'll see that this fantastic resort has been designed to blend seamlessly with the lush surroundings, and resembles an oasis amid the greenery. Rooms are super-plush affairs; those in the upper floors have sweeping plantation views. The outdoor pool is a delight, and the in-house multicuisine food is simply delicious.

For an added fee, you can use the Thai spa within the property, or tee off at the manicured nine-hole golf course – some of the staff double as caddies for a tip. Depending on demand, room tariffs can go up by 10 per cent during weekends or through the peak season, but discounts are also usually available in one form or another.

✕ Eating

In Srimangal

★ **Kutum Bari**　　　BANGLADESHI $
(Railway Station Rd; mains Tk 90-160; ⊙ 11.30am-11pm) Split-level brick-walled seating with high windows and chic bamboo furnishings make this the coolest place to eat in town. It also serves up Srimangal's best local food – the *bhorta* preparations explode in the mouth with flavour, while the fish curries come in hearty portions and are finished in a diverse range of yummy gravies tempered with local spices.

Agra　　　CHINESE $$
(Guho Rd; mains Tk 120-240; ⊙ 11am-10pm) Popular with local diners with a taste for quasi Chinese and Thai fare, this clean and air-conditioned restaurant in the plusher, tree-shaded end of town serves up noodle and chicken dishes that seem to have a loyal following among patrons.

Around Srimangal

Sath Rong Restaurant　　　BENGALI $
(Srimangal–Bhanugach Rd; mains Tk 80-160, tea per layer Tk 10; ⊙ 6am-9pm) Opposite Grand Sultan Tea Resort, within walking distance of Radhanagar Village, Sath Rong (seven colours) is a cute roadside cafe-restaurant that serves its own version of the seven-layer tea made famous by Romesh at Nilkantha Tea Cabin (p135). It also does a few Chinese and Indian dishes, and a delicious quail curry (Tk 150) for lunch and dinner.

SYLHET DIVISION SRIMANGAL & AROUND

SELECTED TRAINS FROM SRIMANGAL

DESTINATION	TRAIN NAME	DEPARTS	ARRIVES	FARE *	OFF DAY
Chittagong	Parharika Ex	12.58pm	8.05pm	Tk 545/365/275	Sat
Chittagong	Udayan Ex	11.24pm	6.35am	Tk 545/365/275	Sun
Dhaka	Jayantika Ex	10.50am	4.20pm	Tk 445/295/225	Thu
Dhaka	Parabat Ex	5.14pm	10.35pm	Tk 445/295/225	Tue
Dhaka	Surma Mail	11.55pm	9.45am	Tk 445/295/225	none
Dhaka	Upaban Ex	12.23am	5.25am	Tk 445/295/225	none
Sylhet	Surma Mail	7.22am	12.20pm	Tk 250/170/125	none
Sylhet	Parabat Ex	11.10am	1.40pm	Tk 250/170/125	Tue
Sylhet	Parharika Ex	3.20pm	6pm	Tk 250/170/125	Mon
Sylhet	Jayantika Ex	5.13pm	7.45pm	Tk 250/170/125	none

*1st berth/1st seat/shuvon

Shopping

M/S Ahmed Tea House   TEA
(Railway Station Rd; tea per kg Tk 200-2000;
⊘11am-8pm) Ahmed, like many other shops
dotting the approach to the train station,
sells tea from the surrounding tea estates.
It's mostly Ispahani tea from the Zareen Tea
Estate (p132), although you'll also see Finlays (p132) teas. You can buy tea bags as
well as loose tea; remember that the quality
of loose tea is always superior.

ⓘ Information

AB Bank ATM (Railway Station Rd) This is a
foreign card–friendly ATM.

E-Zone Cyber Café (College Rd; internet per
hour Tk 50; ⊘11am-8pm) Has the fastest
connections in town.

ⓘ Getting There & Away

BUS

Hanif (p170) has regular coach services to
Dhaka (Tk 390, four hours) between 6am and
midnight.

Departures from **Habiganj bus stand** (Dhaka-
Sylhet Rd) include Sylhet (Tk 130, two hours,
7am to 8pm) and Shaista Ganj (for Satchari
National Park; Tk 50, 35 minutes, 9am to 4pm).

From **Lowacherra bus stand** (Kamalganj Rd)
buses go to Lowacherra National Park (Tk 25,
20 minutes, 8am to 6pm) and Upazilla (for Hum
Hum Falls; Tk 35, 45 minutes, 8am to 4pm).

TRAIN

Departing from the **Srimangal train station**
(Railway Station Rd), all Dhaka and Chittagong
trains stop at Akhaura (1st seat/shuvon Tk
130/100, three hours), for the Indian border. All
Chittagong trains also stop at Comilla (1st seat/
shuvon Tk 160/120, five hours).

Understand
Bangladesh

Bangladesh Today

As Bangladesh steps further into the 21st century, its leaders find their plates increasingly full of new challenges. The country's geography puts it at the sharp edge of countries affected by climate change. Meanwhile, with an ever-growing and increasingly young population, the balance must be struck between the politics of the electoral cycle and the street, secularism and Islamism, and the calls for justice left over from the country's bloody birth.

Best Nonfiction

A History of Bangladesh (Willem van Schendel, 2009)
Banker to the Poor (Dr Mohammad Yunus, 2003)
Rise of Islam and the Bengal Frontier (Richard Eaton, 1996)
The Sacred and the Secular: Bengal Muslim Discourses (Tazeen Murshid, 1996)
Pakistan: Failure in National Integration (Rounaq Jahan, 1996)

Best Novels

Lajja (Shame) (Taslima Nasrin, 1993)
Sultana's Dream (Rokeya Sakhawat Hussain, 1905)
The Good Muslim (Tahmima Anam, 2011)
A Golden Age (Tahmima Anam, 2007)
Like a Diamond in the Sky (Shazia Omar, 2009)

Best News Sources

BD News 24 (www.bdnews24.com) The country's first online newspaper.
Daily Star (www.thedailystar.net) Bangladesh's best English-language daily.
Thorn Tree (www.lonelyplanet.com/thorntree) The Bangladesh branch of Lonely Planet's Thorn Tree forum is easily the best place for up-to-date travel-related news on the region.

Elections & Aftermath

Politics in Bangladesh can frequently look to the outside as something of a zero-sum game, with the rival leaders Sheikh Hasina of the Awami League (AL) and Khaleda Zia of the Bangladesh Nationalist Party (BNP) carrying on the struggles led by their fathers – both prime ministers in their time – in a winner takes all contest.

This battle was seen most clearly in the 2014 election, which was fought on the street as much at the ballot box. The poll was the most violent in the country's history, with many left dead and the BNP choosing to boycott the election altogether. Sheikh Hasina was duly returned to power, but with a mandate in which only half the parliamentary seats were contested. The BNP called rolling protests to demand fresh elections and a caretaker government, but has found itself both increasingly marginalised on the street through its violent acts, and under pressure from a government that has seemed intent on clamping down on legitimate political opposition.

War Crimes Tribunals

In 2010, Sheikh Hasina sanctioned the establishment of a special tribunal to try a handful of key suspects charged with crimes against humanity, allegedly committed during the 1971 Liberation War by collaborators of the Pakistani regime. Several leading establishment figures had been granted immunity by previous administrations, for the sake of political stability, but calls to both tackle the political culture of impunity and heal the still-open wounds of 1971 had grown ever louder.

Leading figures of the Jamaat-e-Islami party, Bangladesh's largest Islamist party, were put on trial and convicted, with several subsequently executed. In 2015, the highest-profile convictions were of Jamaat's Ali Ahsan Mohammad Mujahid, and Salahuddin Quader Chowdhury, a leading light in the BNP. Although the judicial process was much criticised by Amnesty International, both were swiftly hanged after leave to appeal their convictions was refused. Although mostly popular with the country at large, the focus on certain parties has led some observers to worry that the hoped-for reconciliation brought about by the tribunals may unwittingly sow the seeds for future division.

Attacks on Secularism

Many secular writers had led the calls for the war crimes tribunals, but in seeking justice they have found themselves increasingly under attack. So-called 'free thinkers' have been repeatedly targeted for violent attacks by Islamists, and in 2015 five writers and one publisher were murdered in Dhaka, with others attacked with machetes. The focus on the internet as an outlet for secular writing has led to the popular perception of the term 'blogger' being equated with 'atheism'.

Despite secularism being officially enshrined in the Bangladeshi constitution, writers have faced as much official criticism for public stances on subjects like atheism as they have benefited from protection from further attacks. At the same time, the murder in late 2015 of two foreigners living and working in Dhaka raised the political temperature even higher, when the killings were claimed by a Bangladeshi offshoot of Islamic State.

Economy & Environment

While its recent political scene has been as troubled as ever, Bangladesh's economy continues to grow at between 5% and 6%. Some major development projects are in the pipeline, including big investments in transport infrastructure, particularly in Dhaka. The garment assembly business remains a key part of the economy, with moves to clean up industrial practices and workers' conditions after the 2013 Rana Plaza factory collapse that killed over 1100 people.

The economy may be growing at an impressive rate, but in a country that is the most densely populated of any large nation, millions still face harsh challenges. Bangladesh is particularly prone to climate change – melting glaciers in the Himalayas bring increased flooding, while increasingly unpredictable storms in the Bay of Bengal hit the low-lying coast hard. Salination of land and drinking water is causing many farmers to abandon their land and move to Dhaka, a city whose over-burdened infrastructure is already prone to both seasonal floods and drinking water shortages.

POPULATION: **168,958,000**

LITERACY RATE: **61.5% (MALE 64.6%, FEMALE 58.5%)**

LIFE EXPECTANCY: **71 YEARS**

POPULATION BELOW POVERTY LINE: **31.5%**

GDP PER CAPITA: **US$3400**

if Bangladesh were 100 people

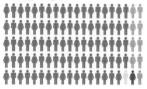

89 would be Muslim
9 would be Hindu
1 would be Buddhist
1 would be Other

age distribution
(% of population)

51 — 0–24 years
38 — 25–54 years
6 — 55–64 years
5 — 65 years and over

population per sq km

BANGLADESH   INDIA   USA

≈ 35 people

History

For much of history, the state that today we call Bangladesh was known only as Bengal; what happened elsewhere on the Indian subcontinent affected this region, too. Dominated at different periods of history by Buddists, Hindus, the Mughals and the East India Company, modern Bangladesh is a product of imperial Britain's Partition of India – a majority-Muslim nation initially joined to Pakistan, and finally born as an independent nation in 1971 after a bloody liberation war.

Willem van Schendel's *A History of Bangladesh* (2009) is the go-to single volume history of the country.

Buddhist Foundations

Strange though it may now seem in such an overwhelmingly Muslim country, Buddhism has been no small player in the nation's history and culture. Nationwide, less than 1% of people are Buddhists, but in certain areas, such as Chittagong Division, Buddhists make up 12% of the population.

The distance from Bodhgaya (in present-day India, where the Buddha reached enlightenment) to Bengal is not far, and the region has played a huge part in the development of the faith, including the creation of Tantric Buddhism.

By the reign of the great Indian Buddhist emperor Ashoka (304–232 BC), Buddhism was firmly entrenched as the number one religion of Bengal and, aside from a few minor skirmishes, it continued to thrive in the region until the 12th century AD, making Bengal the last stronghold of Buddhism in an increasingly Hindu- and Muslim-dominated subcontinent.

Gopala, a Kshatriya tribal chief from Varendra, became the founding figure of the Buddhist Pala dynasty (8th to 11th centuries). He was succeeded by his son Dharmapala, who established the gigantic Somapuri Vihara in Varendra, known today as Paharpur.

In the 12th century, Hindu *senas* (armies) came to rule Bengal, and crushed Buddhism. Surviving Buddhists retreated to the Chittagong area. In less than a century, though, the *senas* were swamped by the tide of Islam.

TIMELINE	Back in Time	262 BC	4th century AD
	The earliest mention of the region is in the 9th century BC Hindu epic Mahabharata, which tells of Prince Bhima's conquest of eastern India, including Varendra, an ancient kingdom in what is now Bangladesh.	Chandragupta Maurya creates an empire, then known as Pundravardhana Bhukti. It spreads across northern India under his grandson, Emperor Ashoka, whose conversion to Buddhism has a lasting effect.	In the 4th century AD, northern India comes under the imperial rule of the Guptas; during their reign Buddhism reaches its zenith.

Though somewhat beaten, Buddhism never totally died out in Bangladesh, and in the Chittagong Hill Tracts there are several monasteries that look to Myanmar (Burma) for religious inspiration, plus a number of schools in which children learn to read Burmese and Pali (an ancient Buddhist language). As in neighbouring Myanmar, many Buddhist men in this region spend a part of their lives as monks.

The exact origin of the word 'Bangla' is unclear, but is thought to derive from the Dravidian-speaking Bang tribe that lived in the region around 1000 BC.

The Muslim Period

They took some time to arrive, but when they did they left a legacy that continues to define the country to this very day. The arrival of the Muslims began with the trickle of a few Sufi (Muslim mystic) missionaries in the 12th century and the construction of the odd mosque on the fringes of Bengal. Then came Mohammed bin Bakhtiar (a Khilji from Turkistan) who, with only 20 men under his command, made short work of capturing Bengal and bringing the area under the rule of the sultanate of Delhi, the centre of Muslim power in India.

Under the Muslims, Bengal entered a new era. Cities developed; palaces, forts, mosques, mausoleums and gardens sprang up; roads and bridges were constructed; and new trade routes brought prosperity and a new cultural life. In 1576, Bengal became a province of the mighty Mughal Empire, which ushered in another golden age in India. Mughal power extended over most of Bengal except the far southeast around Chittagong, and it was during this period that a small town named Dhaka emerged from obscurity to become the Mughal capital of Bengal.

British Rule

It was during the reign of Mughal emperor Aurangzeb (1618–1707) that a Bengali nawab (Muslim prince) sold three local villages to the British East India Company. Today one of those villages goes by the name of Kolkata (Calcutta). From here the British gradually extended their influence to take in all of Bengal and finally all of the subcontinent, but the going was far from easy.

It has been said that the British Raj ushered Bengal into a period of growth and development, but historians hotly dispute this. The British brought infrastructure, law and government, but they also introduced dictatorial agricultural policies and the establishment of the zamindar (feudal landowner) system, which many people consider responsible for draining Bengal of its wealth, along with the devastation wreaked upon Bengal's economically important fabric industry by cheap British factory imports.

Most Hindus cooperated with the British, entering British educational institutions and studying the English language. The majority of Muslims, on the other hand, refused to cooperate, preferring to remain landlords

Originally a mere clerk for the British East India Company, Robert Clive rose to become local head of the company and, eventually, the effective ruler of Bengal.

1202	1342–1487	1575	1707
Muslims storm into Bengal and convert the region. The Mameluk sultanate is established, until the Tughlaq dynasty overthrows it in 1320. The Tughlaqs are defeated by a wave of Muslim invaders in 1398.	Under the Ilyas Shahi dynasty, a distinct Bengali identity begins to form. The city of Gaud emerges as a cosmopolitan metropolis, remaining the centre of power until the capital is moved to Dhaka in 1608.	Under the command of Akbar, the Mughals defeat Bengali sultan Daud Karrani at the Battle of Tukaroi. His defeat announces the beginning of the Mughal adventure in Bengal.	The last great Mughal ruler Aurangzeb dies and the Mughal empire is thrown into disarray. Bengal has long had autonomy, and now breaks away completely from the rest of the empire.

and farmers. This religious dichotomy formed a significant basis for future conflict, not least when in 1905 the British split the region into majority-Hindu West Bengal (centred on Calcutta) and Muslim-majority East Bengal (centred on Dhaka).

Partition & East Pakistan

At the close of WWII it was clear that European colonialism had run its course. The Indian National Congress continued to press for Indian self-rule and the British began to map out a path to independence.

With the Muslim population of India worried about living in an overwhelmingly Hindu-governed nation, the Muslim League was formed. It pushed for two separate Muslim states in south Asia. Lord Mountbatten, viceroy of British India, realising the impossibility of the situation and, quite possibly, looking for a quick British escape, decided to act on these desires and partition the subcontinent. West Bengal remained with India, while East Bengal became a physically isolated part of Pakistan.

Though support for the creation of Pakistan was based on Islamic solidarity, the two halves of the new state (East and West Pakistan) had little else in common. Bengali (Bangla) was denied status as an official language of the new country, immediately alienating its Bengali-speaking population. Furthermore, the country was administered from West Pakistan, which tended to favour its own citizens in the distribution of revenues.

The Awami League, led by Sheikh Mujibur Rahman, emerged as the national political party in East Pakistan, with the Language Movement as its ideological underpinning. The 1971 national elections saw the Awami League win with a clear majority; in East Pakistan it won all seats but one. Constitutionally, the Awami League should have formed the government of Pakistan, but faced with this unacceptable result, President Khan postponed the opening of the National Assembly.

The *Bangladesh Newsletter* is a compilation of American newspaper cuttings from the coverage of the Bangladesh Liberation War. Dhaka's Liberation War Museum has copies available for sale.

The War of Liberation

At the racecourse rally of 7 March 1971 in Dhaka (at what is now Ramna Park), Sheikh Mujibur (Mujib) stopped short of declaring East Pakistan independent. In reality, however, Bangladesh (land of the Bangla speakers) was born that day. Sheikh Mujib was jailed in West Pakistan, igniting smouldering rebellion in East Pakistan.

When the Mukti Bahini (Bangladesh Freedom Fighters) captured the Chittagong radio station on 26 March 1971, Ziaur Rahman, the leader of the Mukti Bahini, announced the birth of the new country and called upon its people to resist the Pakistani army. President Khan sent more troops to quell the rebellion.

1758–1857	1885–1905	1947	1952
The British East India Company controls Bengal, but their policies do not endear them to the Bengalis. The Sepoy Rebellion inflames local passions. In 1857 the British government takes control of India.	Supported by Hindus and Muslims, the Indian National Congress is founded in 1885. But the division of Bengal in 1905 by Lord Curzon, seen as a religious partition, prompts the formation of the All India Muslim League.	Pakistan and India come to life. Pakistan is divided into two regions, the Punjab and Bengal (West and East Pakistan, respectively). A bloody exodus occurs as Hindus move to India and Muslims to East or West Pakistan.	The Pakistani government declares Urdu will be the national language. Riots break out in Dhaka, and on 21 February, 12 students are killed by the Pakistani army. Pakistan's democracy gives way to military government.

THE SLAUGHTER OF THE INTELLECTUALS

Immediately following Sheikh Mujib's arrest on 26 March 1971, all hell broke out. Blaming the Hindu intellectuals for fomenting the rebellion, the generals immediately sent their tanks to Dhaka University and began firing into the halls, killing students. This was followed by the shelling of Hindu neighbourhoods and a selective search for intellectuals, business people and other alleged subversive elements. One by one they were captured, hauled outside the city and shot in cold blood. Over the ensuing months, the Pakistani soldiers took their search for 'subversives' to every village. By then, if there had ever been a distinction made between intellectuals and Hindus, it was gone. When captured, men were forced to lift their lungis (sarongs) to reveal if they were circumcised; if not, they were slaughtered.

General Tikka Khan, known to Bangladeshis as the 'Butcher of Balochistan', began the systematic slaughter of Sheikh Mujib's supporters. Tanks began firing into the halls of Dhaka University. Hindu neighbourhoods were shelled and intellectuals, business people and other 'subversives' were hauled outside the city and shot.

By June the struggle had become a guerrilla war. More and more civilians joined the Mukti Bahini as the Pakistani army's tactics became more brutal. Bangladeshi authorities say that napalm was used against villages, and that rape was both widespread and systematic.

By November 1971 the whole country was suffering the burden of the occupying army. During the nine months from the end of March 1971, 10 million people fled to refugee camps in India.

With border clashes between Pakistan and India becoming more frequent, the Pakistani air force made a pre-emptive attack on Indian forces on 3 December 1971, precipitating a quick end. Indian troops crossed the border, liberated Jessore on 7 December and prepared to take Dhaka. The Pakistani army was attacked from the west by the Indian army, from the north and east by the Mukti Bahini, and from all quarters by the civilian population.

By 14 December the Indian victory was complete and West Pakistan had been defeated. The cost was enormous – according to Bangladeshi authorities, around three million people were killed in the nine-month war, 200,000 women were raped and 10 million people were forced from their homes.

Forty years later, the country would open an internal war-crimes trial, which would see several contemporary political leaders face accusations of crimes against humanity.

My Story of 1971 (2001) by university professor Muhammad Anisur Rahman is a personal account of the horrors of the Liberation War. You can buy it at Dhaka's Liberation War Museum.

1970	1971	1974–6	1981
A catastrophic cyclone kills around 500,000 people in East Pakistan. The Pakistani government is criticised for doing little. War between East and West Pakistan looms large on the horizon.	War between East and West Pakistan. After nine months, the Indian army intervenes. Pakistan's General Niazi surrenders, and on 16 December Sheikh Mujib takes the reins of an independent Bangladesh.	A state of emergency is declared in 1974 and Sheikh Mujib proclaims himself president. He is killed in a military coup on 15 August 1975. His surviving daughter Sheikh Hasina becomes prime minister in 1996.	During an attempted military coup in May, President Zia is assassinated. Justice Abdul Sattar is appointed as acting president and, as candidate for the BNP, wins 66% of the vote in the ensuing general election.

TENSIONS IN THE HILL TRACTS

Since the Liberation War, more and more Bengalis have been migrating into the Chittagong Hill Tracts, a geographically remote part of Bangladesh and traditionally an Adivasi (tribal) stronghold. In 1973, the Adivasi rebel group Shanti Bahini initiated an insurgency over demands for autonomy of the region. To counter it, the national government, in 1979, started issuing permits to landless Bengalis to settle there, with titles to Adivasi land. This practice continued for six years and resulted in a mass migration of approximately 400,000 people into the area – almost as many as all the Adivasi groups combined. Countless human-rights abuses occurred as the army tried to put down the Adivasi revolt.

From 1973 until 1997, the Hill Tracts area was the scene of a guerrilla war between the Bangladeshi army and the Shanti Bahini rebels.

Sheikh Hasina's first government cemented an internationally acclaimed peace accord in December 1997 with Adivasi leader Jyotirindriyo Bodhipriya (Shantu) Larma, but the struggle to have the accord fully honoured continues today.

The Early Years of Independence

The People's Republic of Bangladesh was born into chaos – it was shattered by war, and had a ruined economy and a totally disrupted communications system. Henry Kissinger once described the newly independent Bangladesh as an 'international basket case'. As if to reinforce this point, famine struck between 1973 and 1974 and set the war-ravaged country back even further.

After a couple of years of tumultuous power struggles, General Ziaur Rahman, now the head of the army, took over as martial-law administrator and assumed the presidency in late 1976.

The overwhelming victory of President Zia (as Ziaur Rahman was popularly known) in the 1978 presidential poll was consolidated when his party, the newly formed Bangladesh Nationalist Party (BNP), won two-thirds of the seats in the parliamentary elections of 1979. Martial law was lifted and democracy returned to Bangladesh. Zia proved to be a competent politician and statesman. Assistance began pouring in, and over the next five years the economy went from strength to strength.

Though the country progressed economically during the late 1980s, in early 1990 the economy began to unravel and massive rallies and hartals (strikes) were held. During this period Zia's wife, Begum Khaleda Zia, who had no political experience, became head of the BNP. In the ensuing election, the Awami League won a majority 33% of the vote. But with more seats to its name, the BNP still won the election and Begum Khaleda Zia became prime minister in 1991.

1988	1998	2007	2009
Islam becomes the state religion. In the same year, cyclones cause floods that cover three-quarters of the country, leaving millions homeless.	A Dhaka court sentences 15 former army officers to death for their involvement in the 1975 assassination of President Mujib.	Fakhruddin Ahmed's caretaker government declares emergency rule and arrests former prime ministers Begum Khaleda Zia and Sheikh Hasina Wajed, before rescheduling elections for late 2008. Cyclone Sidr leaves 3500 dead.	Having won the elections with a landslide victory, the Awami League's Sheikh Hasina becomes prime minister for the second time.

Never fully accepting the election result, the Awami League, headed by Sheikh Hasina, began to agitate against the BNP. A long and economically ruinous period of hartals eventually brought down the BNP government in June 1996, and the Awami League took power.

A Brighter Future

Since the 1990s, the BNP and Awami League seemed to swap power with almost metronomic regularity, with boycotts becoming an increasingly important card to play at election time. Khaleda Zia's Nationalist Party and its three coalition partners won the 2001 elections. Arguing that the elections were rigged, the Awami League began parliamentary boycotts. When two Awami League politicians were murdered, it triggered a spate of hartals (strikes), and in 2004 a series of general strikes attempted to force the government from power.

In 2007, a state of emergency resulted in a military-backed caretaker government taking control. Elections were held in late 2008 that saw Sheikh Hasina return to power in a landslide. A year later, an attempted army mutiny resulted in the massacre of over 70 people. Although Bangladesh's economic forecast improved, the collapse of the Rana Plaza garment factory in 2013, which killed more than 1100, shone light on the troubled path to development for the world's eighth-most populous nation.

In *Bangladesh: From a Nation to a State* (1997), Craig Baxter discusses the development of national identity. It's a comprehensive and ambitious work that contextualises the nationalistic pride evident in Bangladesh today.

HISTORY A BRIGHTER FUTURE

February 2009	2012–13	2014	2015
Soldiers from paramilitary group Bangladesh Rifles (BDR) stage a bloody yet unsuccessful mutiny at their Dhaka headquarters, slaughtering 74 people, including 57 of their own officers.	Bangladesh's cheap garment industry comes under scrutiny after the Tazreen Factory fire kills 117, and the Rana Plaza building collapse results in 1129 deaths and 2500 injuries.	Sheikh Hasina's Awami League return to power after elections widely boycotted by the opposition parties.	Salahuddin Quader Chowdhury and Ali Ahsan Mohammad Mujahid, senior figures respectively in the BNP and Jamaat-e-Islami Party, are hanged for war crimes committed during the 1971 liberation war.

Environment

Bangladesh is predominantly tropical. The country is home to vast stretches of ever-green forests as well as patches of deciduous mountain vegetation. The abundance of river water also means that the country's expansive floodplains are extremely fertile. Conservation, however, is still a nascent concept here, and the environment is thus vulnerable to degradation in many ways.

The Land

In all of Bangladesh, the only place that has any stone is a quarry in the far northwestern corner of Sylhet division. It's one reason you'll see bricks being hammered into pieces all over the country: brick fragments are substituted for stones when making concrete.

Famous for being flat and wet, Bangladesh is, largely speaking, one massive piece of gorgeously green farmland crisscrossed by an unfeasibly large network of rivers. It's a rural wonderland, and beautiful to behold.

There are two exceptions to this flatter-than-flat vista, although neither is any less green than the rest of the country. First there's Sylhet, in the northeast, with its soft, rolling hills covered in tropical forests and dark-green, waist-high tea bushes. Then there's the Chittagong Hill Tracts, in the far southeast, a forested region punctuated by cliffs, ravines and some small mountain ranges. It's no Himalaya, but the peaks here are comparable in height to those found in the Scottish Highlands, and make for some good hiking.

The great news for travellers is that Bangladesh is very small. With a total area of just 143,998 sq km (roughly the same size as England and Wales combined), it's an easy country to explore, and you can visit much of it in a single trip.

It is surrounded on three sides by India, but also shares a short southeastern border with Myanmar (Burma) for 255km. To the south is the Bay of Bengal, into which flow all the rivers after merging with each other and meandering through the dense Sundarbans, heritage-listed by Unesco for being the world's largest mangrove forest.

The two great Himalayan rivers, the Ganges – here known as the Padma – and Brahmaputra, help divide the land into seven major regions, which correspond to the seven governmental divisions: northwest (Rangpur), west (Rajshahi), southwest (Khulna), south-central (Barisal), central (Dhaka), northeast (Sylhet) and southeast (Chittagong).

Almost all of Bangladesh's coastline forms the so-called Mouths of the Ganges, the final destination of the Ganges (Padma) River, and the largest estuarine delta in the world. The coastal strip from the Sundarbans, in the west, to Chittagong, in the east, is one great patchwork of shifting river courses and silt islands. Across the whole delta, which extends into India, rivers make up 6.5% of the total area.

Animals

Endangered Species

The Royal Bengal tiger is endangered and, although the government has set aside three areas within the Sundarbans as tiger reserves, numbers are low.

Other rare or threatened species include the Indian elephant, the hoolock gibbon, the black bear and the Ganges River dolphin. Reptiles under threat include the Indian python, the crocodile and various turtles.

Many of the diverse bird species are prolific, but some are vulnerable, including Pallas' fishing eagle and Baer's pochard.

Birds

Sitting like a cushion between the plains of India and the hills of Myanmar (Burma), the waterways of Bangladesh are a bird-watcher's dream. The country contains more than 650 species of birds – almost half of those found on the entire subcontinent.

The country's positioning means that Bangladesh attracts both Indian species in the west and north of the country, and Malayan species in the east and southeast. It is also conveniently located for migrants heading south towards Malaysia and Indonesia, and those moving southwest to India and Sri Lanka. In addition, a number of Himalayan and Burmese hill species move into the lowlands during the winter.

Madhupur National Park, in Dhaka division, is an important habitat for a variety of owls, including the rare brown wood owl, wintering thrushes and a number of raptors, although sadly it also the victim of ongoing logging. The Jamuna River floods regularly, and from December to February provides winter habitats for waterfowl, waders and the occasional black stork.

The low-lying basin of Sylhet division has extensive natural *haors* (wetlands), and during winter it is home to huge flocks of wild fowl, including Baer's pochard and Pallas' fishing eagle, along with a great number of ducks and skulkers. The remaining fragments of evergreen and teak forests are also important habitats, especially along the Indian border near the Srimangal area, where the blue-bearded bee-eater, red-breasted trogon and a variety of forest birds are regularly seen.

One of two important coastal zones is the Noakhali region, particularly the islands near Hatiya, where migratory species and a variety of wintering waders (including large numbers of the rare spoon-billed sandpiper, Nordman's greenshank and flocks of Indian skimmers) find suitable refuge.

Birdwatchers will enjoy *A Photographic Guide to the Birds of India & the Indian Subcontinent* by Bikram Grewal and Bill Harvey. It has useful maps and pictures, and is compact enough to take with you in a day pack.

ENVIRONMENT ANIMALS

THE CYCLONE ZONE

Every few years, Bangladesh is hit by natural disasters. While periodic floods and droughts are common annual affairs, the most catastrophic disasters in terms of human loss are cyclones.

Bangladesh is in the world's worst area for cyclones, averaging one major storm every three years. The worst months are May, June, October and November, and the area where damage tends to most frequently occur is in the east around Chittagong and Cox's Bazar.

People still talk about the 1970 cyclone, which claimed between 300,000 and 500,000 lives. The 1991 cyclone, which occurred during big spring tides, was stronger; it affected more than twice as many people and destroyed four times as many houses. However, the death toll (between 140,000 and 200,000) was less than half that of the 1970 disaster.

Most recently, in 2007, Cyclone Sidr became the strongest storm to hit the country in 15 years. It struck the southwest coast and left 3500 people dead, but it's generally acknowledged that the death toll would have been far higher were it not for the early warning system that was installed after the 1991 storm. Since then, the warning system has again been of great use: as recently as in 2015, it helped alert and evacuate people in the wake of Cyclone Komen.

WATER WORLD

Floods are almost the first thing that people think of when talk turns to Bangladesh, but even so, if you arrive by air during the monsoon season you'll be astounded at how much of the country appears to be under water. Many first-time visitors to Bangladesh assume that the flooding is due to heavy rainfall during that time of year. In fact, local rainfall is only partly responsible – most of the water comes pouring down the Padma (known as the Ganges upstream in India), the Meghna and the Jamuna (Brahmaputra) Rivers.

For Bangladeshis, annual flooding is a fact of life and one that, with an ever-increasing population, bad land management and global climate change, is only likely to get worse. However, much of the flooding (which affects about a third of the country) is regarded by farmers as beneficial, as worn soils are replenished with nutrients. It's when the rivers rise above their normal limits that problems emerge.

Major flooding struck northwest Bangladesh and Chittagong in 2007, but in 2004 really heavy flooding over much of the country resulted in the deaths of around 800 people, while in 1998 all three of the country's major rivers reached flood levels at the same time and 16 million people were left homeless. In Dhaka, even houses on fairly high ground were inundated, and the airport was covered with water and had to be shut down.

The Sundarbans, with its miles of marshy shorelines and brackish creeks, supports a number of wetland and forest species, along with large populations of gulls and terns along the south coast. Eight varieties of kingfisher have been recorded here, including the brown-winged, the white-collared, the black-capped and the rare ruddy kingfisher.

The most exciting time of year for birdwatching is during winter, from November to March.

Plants

About 10% of Bangladesh is still forested. Half of the forest is in the Chittagong Hill Tracts and a quarter in the Sundarbans, with the rest scattered in small pockets throughout the country.

The forests fall into three distinct regional varieties: the tidal zones along the coast (often mangrove but sometimes hardwood) in much of the Sundarbans; the sal trees around Dhaka, Tangail and Mymensingh; and the upland forests of tropical and subtropical evergreens in the Chittagong Hill Tracts and parts of Sylhet.

Away from the forests, Bangladesh is still a land of trees. Lining the old trunk road in the west are huge rain trees, and every village is an arboreal oasis, often with spectacular banyan trees, known as *bawt* or *oshoth*. The red silk-cotton (*shimul*) tree is easily spotted throughout the countryside in February and March, when it loses its leaves and sprouts myriad red blossoms. Teak was introduced into the Hill Tracts in the 19th century and its quality approaches that of Burma (Myanmar).

Flowering plants are an integral part of the beauty of Bangladesh. Each season produces its special variety of flowers. Among them is the prolific water hyacinth, its carpet of thick green leaves and blue flowers giving the impression that solid ground lies beneath. Other decorative plants that are frequently seen are jasmine, water lily, rose, hibiscus, bougainvillea, magnolia and an incredible diversity of wild orchids in the forested areas.

A rare specimen of *Corypha taliera*, a wild palm tree on the brink of extinction, was discovered growing on the Dhaka University campus during the East Pakistan era. It has since died, but saplings were reportedly harvested from the tree for culture in later years.

Environmental Issues

Bangladesh faces huge environmental problems, many of which boil down to overpopulation. Farmland soils are being damaged by overuse, rivers are being polluted by chemical pesticides and forests are being chopped down at an alarming rate. The water table is under threat as deep tube-wells extract clean water for drinking.

Annual flooding during the monsoon season is part of life in Bangladesh. Some experts are questioning whether the flooding is getting worse and, if so, whether deforestation in India and especially Nepal (which causes increased run off) is the reason. Another theory holds that the river beds have become choked with silt from once-forested land, making flooding more severe. Regardless, there has been increased pressure to 'do something' and find a 'permanent solution'. Part of the problem of doing anything, however, is that the country depends on regular flooding for its soil fertility. Building dykes along river banks could be disastrous for agricultural output and, in the past, has contributed to increased erosion by altering the course and flow of water.

With the continuance of global warming, Bangladesh, as one of the 10 countries most vulnerable to a rise in sea level, will be drastically affected. If predictions are correct, a 1m rise in the Bay of Bengal would result in a loss of 12% to 18% of the country's land.

Loss of land is just one consequence – severe flooding and reduced agricultural potential are almost inevitable. This is indeed a cruel twist of fate, since Bangladesh, as a poor, agricultural society, has contributed very little to global warming. Even with assistance from the Dutch, who are helping to devise a strategy to cope with rising water levels, the question remains whether Bangladesh will have the capacity to develop and apply the appropriate technologies.

However, there is some good news. Bangladesh is now taking environmental issues very seriously and has implemented some highly commendable policies.

Responding to the high levels of litter, much of which was plastic, Bangladesh became one of the first countries to almost completely ban plastic bags. In many places, especially Dhaka, goods you buy are now packaged in cloth bags. Although you will still see plastic bags being used and discarded, especially in smaller towns, the amount is noticeably less than in other parts of south Asia.

Given its notorious reputation as one of the most air-polluted cities in the world, the government has also taken steps to improve the horrendous air quality in Dhaka by banning petrol/gasoline and diesel vehicles and replacing them with cleaner, greener (and cheaper to run) CNG (compressed natural gas) vehicles. Almost all auto-rickshaws in Bangladesh now are CNG-run. In fact, they are now known colloquially as 'CNGs'.

The government's recent work at improving and protecting national parks should also be lauded, as it attempts to step up environmental education for the public. Although poaching of animals and illegal logging of tress still occur in forest areas such as the Sundarbans, the government has made efforts to contain such cartel-run practices in recent times.

The government-endorsed conservation agency Wild Team (www.wild-team.org) tells you all you ever wanted to know about tigers, the Sundarbans and the ongoing conservation projects taking place there.

ENVIRONMENT ENVIRONMENTAL ISSUES

Bangladesh's rivers contain unusually high levels of arsenic. When you buy bottled water, always check that it reads 'arsenic free' and that the seal is unbroken.

Arts & Literature

The art, music and literature of Bengal is among the richest in the Indian subcontinent. The people of the Bengal region, whether they're from Bangladesh or India, share a similarity of language, dress, music and literature that crosses national boundaries.

For current news on the arts scene in Bangladesh, as well as what's-on listings in Dhaka, go to the Arts & Entertainment section of the *Daily Star* website (www.thedaily star.net).

From the poetry of Nobel Laureate Rabindranath Tagore to the unmistakeable sound of the folk music of the Bauls (mystic minstrels) and Fakirs (mendicant musicians), Bengali culture is steeped in tradition and loved by millions.

Literature

Best known in the literature of Bangladesh are the works of the great Bengali poets Rabindranath Tagore (1861-1941) and Kazi Nazrul Islam (1899-1976), who was later proclaimed Bangladesh's national bard and whose photos are displayed in establishments countrywide.

Tagore received international acclaim in 1913, when he was awarded the Nobel Prize for Literature for his book *Gitanjali* (Song Offerings). Despite his Hindu upbringing, Tagore wrote from a strong cosmopolitan and multicultural perspective that transcended any particular religion. He celebrated 'humble lives and their miseries' and supported the concept of Hindu–Muslim unity. His love for the land and people of Bengal is reflected in many of his works, and one of his songs, *Amar Shonar Bangla,* has been adopted as Bangladesh's national anthem (interestingly, Tagore also wrote and composed *Jana Gana Mana,* India's national anthem). Travellers can soak up inspiration from the great man by visiting his former home in a small village just outside Kushtia.

Unlike Tagore, who spent much of his later life in India, the 'rebel poet' and composer Kazi Nazrul Islam spent his last years in Bangladesh. When undivided India was suffering under colonial rule, Islam employed poetry to challenge intellectual complacency and spark feelings of nationalism among those involved in the freedom movement.

Of Bangladesh's modern writers, the most famous is the exiled feminist writer Taslima Nasrin, whose controversial book *Lajja* (Shame; 1993) was not only banned in Bangladesh but also earned her a *fatwa* (death sentence for blasphemy), and forced her to flee the country. It recounts the history surrounding the contentious destruction of the Babri Mosque in Ayodhya (in India), but depicts it through the eyes of a Hindu family in Bangladesh.

Tahmina Anam's acclaimed debut novel, *A Golden Age* (2007), is a story of love, betrayal and family loyalties, set against the backdrop of the Liberation War. The second of her planned trilogy, *The Good Muslim* (2011), follows a war-scarred family as it faces the challenges of peace.

One of the world's first examples of feminist science fiction, *Sultana's Dream* (Rokeya Sakhawat Hussain, 1905) is a ground-breaking novel that depicts a feminist utopia in which women run everything and men are secluded – a mirror image of the traditional Islamic practice of purdah.

Like a Diamond in the Sky (Shazia Omar, 2009) is a brave attempt to raise awareness of drug addiction among Dhaka's young middle class.

Non-Bangladeshi authors who have written about the country include Katy Gardner, whose *Songs at the Rivers Edge* (1991) is a wonderful memoir of her year spent living in a small village in Sylhet; and James Novak, whose *Reflections on the Water* (1993) is a passionate account of the birth of Bangladesh by a journalist who worked there in the mid-1980s.

Music

The distinctive folk music of the Bauls (mystic minstrels) and the closely related Fakirs (mendicant musicians) can be heard across Bengal, as well as in some films about the region. Bauls most commonly play the one-stringed plucked instrument known as the *ektara,* accompanied by other musicians playing lutes, flutes, the four-stringed *dotara* and cymbals. You can sit in at plenty of folk music renditions if you travel to Kushtia, the resting place of the legendary Fakir musician Lalon Shah, and the location of a biannual folk-music festival.

The poet Rabindranath Tagore was also a prolific songwriter, and undoubtedly influenced much of the Bengali music that's composed today. His anthology of songs known as Rabindra Sangeet (notations for which were set by Tagore himself) are popularly performed by artistes in both Bengals.

Western influence helped spawn the new phenomenon of Bangla Bands, the generic name given to any band that plays modern music – ranging from pop and rock to grunge and heavy metal – performed in Bengali. Over the past two decades, this contemporary musical tradition has evolved considerably, and present-day bands often attract stadium-sized crowds at sell-out concerts, as well as getting plenty of airplay on local FM stations.

You can train your ears to the sound of Bangla music before you leave home these days, by tuning in to BBC Radio's Asian Network (www.bbc.co.uk/asiannetwork), which has a regular Bengali slot.

Cinema

The 1984 short film *Agami,* directed by Morshedul Islam, is widely regarded as the catalyst for the birth of the Alternative Film Movement, the name given to Bangladesh's independent film industry. It provides an alternative to the largely musical-based blockbusters that are churned out each year by Dhaka's mainstream film industry, 'Dhallywood', and has spawned creative talents such as the late Tareque Masud, whose award-winning 2002 film *The Clay Bird* is arguably the best independent film to have come out of Bangladesh.

Folk Art

Weaving has always held a special place in the artistic expression of the country. In the 7th century, the textiles of Dhaka weavers found their way to Europe, where they were regarded as *textiles ventalis* (fabrics woven of air).

The most artistic and expensive ornamental fabric – worn as a sari – is the *jamdani* (loom-embroidered muslin or silk), which was exclusively woven for the imperial household centuries ago and evolved as an art form under the influence of Persian design. The other sought-after hand-woven fabric is *tangail* silk, which takes its name from the production centre of Tangail, about 80km northwest of Dhaka.

Needlework is yet another formidable cottage industry in Bangladesh. Best known are elaborate pieces called *nakshi kantha,* embroidered and quilted patchwork cloths that hold an important place in village life, with motifs often recording local history, culture or myth.

From popular music and latest movies to trending topics and events around town, www.dhakatribune.com provides news, commentary and listings from Bangladesh's entertainment and lifestyle industry.

RICKSHAW ART

One of your first, and perhaps strongest, impressions of Bangladesh is likely to be the rainbow colours of a cycle-rickshaw. More than just a cheap and environmentally sound form of transport, the humble rickshaw is a work of art in Bangladesh, and a fleet of rickshaws is the finest art gallery any country could conjure up. Art passing by on wheels needs to be bold and eye-catching, and able to be taken in quickly. Rickshaw artists aim to decorate the vehicles with as much drama and colour as possible, and paint images that are both simple and memorable. This is street art for the ordinary man or woman, and it is unashamedly commercial.

Maliks, the owners of rickshaw fleets, commission *mistris* (rickshaw makers) to build and decorate the machines to their specification. The artists working in the *mistris'* workshops learn on the job, sometimes starting out as young as 10, when they work on decorating the upholstery and smaller sections of the vehicle.

The main 'canvas' is recycled tin, which forms the backboard of the rickshaw. Enamel paints are used; the artist may also decorate the seat, handlebars, the curved back of the seat, the chassis, the hood and just about every other surface.

All the dreams of the working man appear on rickshaws. Common themes include idealised rural scenes, wealthy cities crammed with cars, aeroplanes and high-rise buildings, and unsullied natural environments. Images of Bangladeshi and Indian film and pop stars are by far the most popular designs. Images of women with heart-stopping stares are clearly a figment of the male artists' imaginations, and are a great contrast to the real women on the street.

These days, however, many rickshaw *maliks* choose to skimp on the cost of paint and go for less elaborate designs, mostly in the newer boroughs of town. To see some of the best specimens still plying the roads, head into the lanes of Old Dhaka.

The Art of Kantha Embroidery, by Naiz Zaman, uses drawings and photographs to explain the technique of nakshi kantha (elaborately embroidered and quilted patchwork cloths) and give a face to the women involved in its production.

Once found only among a woman's private possessions, *nakshi kanthas* can now be seen hanging on the walls of upmarket hotels, offices and in museums. It's an artistic symbol not just of Bangladeshi women but the nation as well.

Traditionally, *nakshi kanthas* were mostly made in the central and western divisions of Bangladesh. They are made from worn-out clothing, particularly saris, and six or so layers of material are stitched together in a way that leaves a rippled surface. They are often given as wedding gifts to a daughter leaving home, or to a grown son as a reminder of his mother. Besides the usefulness of recycling old material, there is also a folk belief that a *nakshi kantha* made from old material brings good luck. The jealous gods won't harm someone dressed in rags – infants are often dressed in *nakshi kantha* nappies for this reason.

There are women's cooperatives that produce *nakshi kantha* commercially; one good place to look is Aarong (p51) in Dhaka.

Modern Art

Without a shade of doubt, the most pervasive form of popular culture in Bangladesh is the genre of paintings found on rickshaws. The turbulence of life in Bangladesh has given local artists much to express, which they do with wondrous diversity. On the other end of the intellectual spectrum, a number of contemporary Bangladeshi visual artistes have also taken their brand of new-age fine art to galleries around the world, in forms such as paintings, graphic art, sculpture, video art and installations.

Photography is also one of Bangladesh's favourite art practices. Pioneered by documentary photographer Shahidul Alam, the photography movement has now attracted countless enthusiasts at both amateur and professional levels. The biennial Dhaka Chhobi Mela (literally 'photo fair') is a good place to catch some of the best frames shot by local photographers.

Bangladeshi Cuisine

Drawing on centuries of cooking traditions inspired by Islamic, Hindu and tribal cultures, Bangladesh's kitchens churn out a diverse range of mouth-watering dishes, most of which are made from indigenous local produce. Bengalis (both in Bangladesh and India's West Bengal) consider their food to be the most refined in the subcontinent, and while this causes considerable debate in culinary circles, everyone is in agreement that Bengali sweets truly are the finest you can dip your sticky fingers into.

Main Meals

A typical Bangladeshi meal includes an assortment of *bhorta* (mash) and *bhaji* (fried vegetables) preparations, dhal (yellow lentil soup), and a few curries made with vegetables *(shobji)*, beef, mutton, chicken, fish or egg. The *bhorta* and *bhaji* dishes can potentially incorporate everything from seasonal vegetables to dried fish or shrimps, tempered with diverse spices and condiments. Almost everything is cooked in a mustard-oil base, which lends its signature sharpness to go with fiery gravies. Rice (the chief local produce) is considered a higher-status food than bread.

Popular sweet treats include *mishti doi* (sweetened yoghurt), *rosh malai* (miniature fried cottage cheese balls dipped in a creamy base), *chom chom* (a syrup-coated cake made from paneer) and *monda* (sweetened yoghurt cake).

Curries

Many curry menus in Bangladesh refer to *bhuna* (or *bhoona*), which is the process of stage-cooking meat or fish in spices and hot oil reduced to a dense gravy. A timeless local favourite is the *bhuna khichuri*, which comprises rice, yellow lentils and occasionally chunks of meat slow-cooked together in the same spicy base. Another common non-vegetarian curry is *dopiaza* (literally 'double onions') which, as the name suggests, contains large amounts of onion added to the curry in two separate stages.

Rice

The four main forms of rice dishes are biryani, *pulao* or *polao* (similar to biryani but without the meat), *bhuna khichuri* and *bhat* (plain rice). The biryani is almost always of the *kachchi* variety, where the meat and the rice are slow-cooked together from start to finish in the same cauldron. Bangladesh is home to several strains of aromatic rice grains, which are widely used and lend distinct flavours to all these items.

Fish

Fish is every Bangladeshi's favourite meal. The fish you are most likely to eat – curried, smoked or fried – are *ilish* (hilsa) and *bhetki* (sea bass). These are virtually the national dishes of Bangladesh, and it's said they can both be prepared in around 30 different ways. If you have a more adventurous palate, there are numerous shrimp, lobster, pomfret (locally called *rupchanda*), crab, eel and sardine dishes available, too.

Kebabs

Kebabs in Bangladesh are similar to their Indian counterparts and are widely available. They come in many delicious avatars, including the flat, patty-like *shami kebab,* made with fried minced meat, and the long, skewered *sheekh kebab,* which is prepared with less spice and usually with mutton or beef. You'll also find tandoori chicken grilled on spit rods.

HABITS & CUSTOMS

Traditionally, Bengali meals were served on the floor and eaten with fingers rather than cutlery. Each person sat on a *pati* (a small piece of straw carpet). In front of the *pati* was a large eating platter or banana leaf, around which bowls would be placed. These days, however, it's mostly a table-and-chair affair, with food served in metal or plastic plates and containers.

Eating with one's fingers, however, still remains *de rigueur*. For the uninitiated, it's a strangely liberating experience and we recommend you try it. Bangladeshis say that it allows for an appreciation of textures before the morsels are enjoyed by the tongue.

Dos & Don'ts

➡ It is courteous to use only the right hand to eat. The left hand is considered unclean, given its use in the bathroom for ablutions. However, considering that the fingers of your right hand will be coated in gravy while you eat, you should use the left hand to pass things around the table.

➡ You may break bread with both hands, but never put food into your mouth with the left.

➡ Water may be drunk from a glass with the left hand as it is not being directly touched.

➡ Always wash your hands before you eat – for the sake of courtesy as well as hygiene.

As in India, *cha* (tea) is sold on practically every street corner in Bangladesh. Unlike in India, though, each cup is made individually (rather than stewing all day), which means you can order it without sugar (*chini sara*) or without milk (*lal cha*; literally 'red tea').

Chicken tikka is also common, and is usually served with Indian-style naan (slightly puffed wholewheat bread cooked in a tandoori oven).

Breakfast

The standard pan-Bangladeshi breakfast usually comprises *shobji* and dhal with a few roti (flat bread), sometimes eaten with a spicy omelette or fried egg, and nearly always washed down with a cup of *cha* (tea). It's fresh, filling and delicious. Meat-lovers often ask for a side-order of the subtle *nihari* (beef trotter stew), which makes a great dip for the roti.

Vegetarians & Vegans

Finding purely vegetarian dishes can be quite challenging in Bangladesh. The key phrase to learn here is '*ami mangsho khai na*' (I don't eat meat), followed closely by '*ami maach khai na*' (I don't eat fish). While Bengali cuisine makes abundant use of vegetables, getting restaurants to grasp the fact that you really do only survive on them can be tough.

In suburban and rural Bangladesh, your best option is to ask for rice and dhal with a few servings of vegetable *bhaji*, *bhorta* and *shobji*. You'll also find a good range of freshly baked flat breads – naan and roti being the most common. Eggs, often in the form of delicious spicy omelettes, are also widely available. A recent explosion of Chinese restaurants has introduced other vegetarian options, such as noodles and paneer in sauce.

Your on-the-road saviour will be Bangladesh's wonderful array of fresh fruit. Oranges, apples and bananas are everywhere, while the mango orchards in western Rajshahi grow some of the world's best mangoes. Mango season is May to June.

In metropolitan Dhaka, however, your choice of restaurants with good vegetarian food will be pretty decent. Don't forget to try the Western-style cafes as well.

Drinks

Officially a teetotalling nation, Bangladesh quenches its thirst with juices, traditional beverages and soft drinks. While *cha* (tea) is the nation's favourite beverage, other popular drinks include sugar-cane juice, local and imported soft drinks, and yoghurt-based *burhani* and *labaan* (both similar to buttermilk, but with a spicy and sweet aftertaste respectively).

People & Culture

Bangladesh has a population just north of 160 million, which currently makes it the eighth most populous nation in the world. Needless to say, the large number of people also means that Bangladesh has a rich culture that comes out of the intermingling of its different religions, traditions and communities.

Religion

Islam is the predominant religion of Bangladesh, with nearly 90% of its citizens being Muslims. Constitutionally, however, it remains a secular state, and there is no official religion. Hindus, at about 9% of the population, form Bangladesh's second largest religious community. The remainder (less than 2%) are made up of minorities such as Christians and Buddhists.

Given the predominant Islamic population, much of Bangladesh's culture derives from Islamic traditions, but there's a distinct overlap of regional Bengali customs as well, which are common to the Hindu-majority state of West Bengal on the Indian side.

In areas adjoining Burma (Myanmar) and the tribal Indian states of Assam, Meghalaya and Tripura, you will come across a fair number of Adivasis (indigenous tribal people), who are either animists or have converted to Christianity in recent times.

Religious skirmishes and communally tinged acts of rioting and violence have occurred in Bangladesh from time to time, but the society is largely tolerant in terms of mutual respect, and harmony prevails at most times.

Cricket is the most popular sport in Bangladesh. You'll see men of every age play the game in all parts of the country, when they're not glued to live matches on TV sets. The domestic T20 league is extremely popular.

Language

Bengali is the official language, although English remains widely spoken (or at least understood) across Bangladesh's bigger cities and towns. In Dhaka, Chittagong and Sylhet, you will have few problems striking up a conversation with locals, or at least getting your point across. Many of Bangladesh's upper-class citizens go to school or university abroad, and are fluent in English.

In rural areas, however, Bengali rules. Signs are largely in Bengali, as are addresses, paperwork (which includes, forms, tickets and receipts), bus numbers, and menu cards in restaurants. Bangladeshis are a friendly folk, though, and will gladly and enthusiastically come to your rescue whenever you are in a spot.

The colloquial language in Bangladesh is peppered with Urdu words, which is the result of the erstwhile Pakistan government introducing Urdu as the official language during the East Pakistan era. While Bengali was reinstated as the official language post-1971, a number of common Urdu words and phrases have remained in everyday speech.

Family

Bangladeshi society is largely patriarchal. In rural areas, it is still common to see women in the family being relegated to duties in the household and kitchen, while the men go out and earn a living. In the urban sphere,

THE ADIVASIS

Adivasis (indigenous tribal people) constitute a tiny proportion of Bangladesh's masses, but bring a substantial amount of diversity into the country's cultural matrix. Numbering around 1% of the total population, the Adivasis are found mostly in the Chittagong Hill Tracts, along areas adjoining Burma (Myanmar) and northeast India, though they also live in parts of Sylhet, Mymensingh and Dinajpur that are contiguous with Indian tribal regions. These days, a number of them can also be seen in big cities such as Dhaka, where they migrate for work.

The largest tribes are the Chakmas, the Marmas, the Khasis, the Garos, the Jaintias and the Santals, although smaller tribes such as the Tripuris and the Manipuris also exist. Each tribe is distinctly different from the other in terms of customs, cuisines and dialects, although to an outsider's perception, the differences may not entirely manifest themselves.

In everyday life, tribes are well integrated with the greater Bangladeshi population. Almost everyone speaks Bengali and many Adivasis have converted to Christianity over the years and adhere to local orders and churches. You can sample tribal culture in its most authentic form in the Chittagong Hill Tracts, where many centuries-old traditions are still at their purest.

men and women are more on par with each other, although that said, Bangladeshi women still fight for their rights at home and work every day.

With modernity making greater inroads into Bangladeshi society, families have become more nuclear in the urban areas, but the traditional practice of living with the extended family still continues. In the traditional family set-up, children live with their parents and other siblings under the same roof. After a wedding, the bride usually moves into the house of her in-laws, instead of the newly wed couple moving out to find a home of their own.

Within a traditional household, the patriarch of the family usually makes executive decisions, while the children simply obey. At social occasions such as religious festivals, births, weddings or deaths, extended families usually assemble and participate in proceedings together, and these are occasions when bonds with far-flung relatives are strengthened.

Customs

In Bangladeshi society, elders are treated with utmost respect. It is considered offensive to smoke, drink or generally play the fool in front of older people.

Anyone, irrespective of age, gender or religion, is greeted with the Islamic salutation 'Assalamualaikum' ('May peace be upon you') which elicits the response 'Walaikumassalam' ('And peace to you too'). Bangladeshis are extremely polite and deferential when it comes to interacting with foreigners. You are unlikely to be subjected to rude or smug behaviour during your stay here.

Standard honorifics used to address strangers include *Bhaiya* (Elder Brother) for a man and *Apa* (Elder Sister) for a woman – and are used regardless of age. Hindus will sometimes use *Dada* and *Didi* (which have similar meanings to *Bhaiya* and *Apa*) instead. It is considered impolite to address people only by their names; the right way to do it is to say the name, followed by *Bhaiya* or *Apa*.

Despite keeping up with modernity, the society is still plagued by certain regressive practices. Child marriage remains a sensitive issue: two out of three Bangladeshi girls are married off before they turn 18. While timely interventions by NGOs as well as global organisations such as the UN have contributed to tackling the practice, it is still far from over.

Survival Guide

Directory A–Z

Accessible Travel

Outside Dhaka's five-star hotels, facilities for travellers with disabilities are almost non-existent in Bangladesh, and conditions in general make travelling extremely challenging. Some footpaths are difficult for even the able-bodied to traverse. In fact, with its squat toilets, overcrowded buses and absence of elevators in all but the finest buildings in Dhaka, the country is largely hostile in its conditions for all but the most fit and able.

On the other hand, hiring private transport and guides, and enlisting the services of a tour company to help you get around, is much cheaper than in other countries. Remember, however, that there are no Bangladesh-based travel companies that specialise in travel for travellers with disabilities.

SLEEPING PRICE RANGES

The following price ranges refer to a double room with bathroom and do not include breakfast, unless otherwise stated.

$ less than Tk 1000

$$ Tk 1000–Tk 3000

$$$ more than Tk 3000

For more information about accessible travel, download Lonely Planet's free Accessible Travel guide from http://lptravel.to/AccessibleTravel.

Accommodation

The best accommodation options in Bangladesh are concentrated in popular destinations such as Dhaka, Cox's Bazar, Sylhet and Srimangal. A few outlying places, such as **RDRS Guesthouse** (p96) in Rangpur, can also provide a truly unique experience.

Hotels Bangladesh's hotels range from lavish resorts to threadbare pigeonholes, depending on budget. Barring the better midrange and top-end addresses, standards usually range from average to poor.

Guesthouses These smaller boutique places can often provide better attention to detail, catering to a more niche clientele.

Ecoresorts In places like tea-draped Srimangal, these addresses provide a nature-oriented experience.

Budget

Places we list as budget really are no-frills. If you're used to roughing it as a budget backpacker around places like India, then they will be clean enough, although they are often far from spotless. In the very cheap places you may want to use your own sleeping sheet or sleeping bag rather than the sometimes grubby bed sheets provided. Budget rooms will come with a small attached bathroom (unless stated otherwise), although budget hotel showers are often cold-water only and the toilets are often squat jobs.

Note that budget hotels are sometimes reluctant to accept foreigners because of the red tape required by the government. Places listed were accepting foreign guests at the time of writing, but be aware that this can change.

Midrange

Midrange hotels will be clean, and will come with air-con, TV and an attached bathroom that will usually have a hot-water shower. Rooms in this bracket tend to be rather spartan, though.

Top End

There are a few international-standard top-end hotels in Dhaka, but apart from these, the top-end hotels we list in this guide are, generally speaking, comfortable business-class hotels, rather than luxurious places to stay.

Hotel Facilities

Pretty much every hotel room in every price bracket in Bangladesh comes with a TV, and the good news for sports and movie fans is that TV is almost always multi-channel cable TV, with plenty of English-language options.

Very few hotels outside Dhaka have wi-fi, or an internet connection of any sort, but we've indicated those that do.

Almost all midrange and top-end hotels have their own restaurant. Many budget ones do, too.

Budget hotels without hot-water showers will provide a bucket of hot water if you ask.

In tourist hotspots such as Srimangal and Cox's Bazar, getting a hotel room in the peak season (from October to March) can be a challenge, especially over weekends. The same applies to festive windows in certain places, such as the twice-yearly folk music festivals in Kushtia. Advance bookings are recommended during these periods.

Activities

Some of Bangladesh's most memorable experiences lie in the lap of unspoilt nature. Whether it's a boat trip down a mighty tropical river, a lazy bicycle ride through the lush countryside or a vigorous hike through dense forests, travellers will find enough reason to step out of urban limits and come face-to-face with the pristine beauty of the country.

With the changeable security situation, some activities are periodically restricted by the authorities. At the time of writing, officials were reluctant to allow foreigners to trek in the Chittagong Hill Tracts and cycle in the hills around Srimangal, but this could change at any time – seek local advice before you travel.

Children

Travelling with young children in Bangladesh is tough because of low levels of hygiene and general health and safety issues, but that doesn't mean it can't be done. Bangladeshis, who are among the most welcoming people you'll ever meet, are fascinated by foreign children and will go out of their way to help you if you have kids in tow.

➡ Dishes of boiled rice and unspiced dhal (yellow lentils), scrambled or boiled eggs, oatmeal and the huge variety of fruits and vegetables should be enough to keep kids happy.

➡ Snacks like biscuits and crisps are also widely available.

➡ Lonely Planet's *Travel with Children* offers more advice.

Electricity

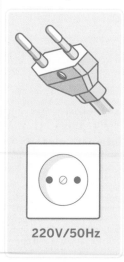

220V/50Hz

220V/50Hz

Customs Regulations

The usual '200 cigarettes, 1L of alcohol' rule applies, though a relatively casual approach is employed at border crossings. Foreigners are permitted to bring in US$5000 without declaring it and Bangladeshis can bring in US$2500.

On departure, tourists are allowed to reconvert 25% of the total foreign currency encashed in the country. This is only possible at the airport in Dhaka, and you will need to have your encashment slips with you as proof.

Embassies & Consulates

The following selected embassies and consulates are all in Dhaka.

Australian High Commission (Map p44; ☎02-881 3101-5; www.bangladesh.embassy.gov.au; 184 Gulshan Ave, Gulshan II)

Canadian High Commission (Map p44; ☎02-988 7091-7; www.canadainternational.

gc.ca/bangladesh; Madani Ave, Baridhara)

French Embassy (Map p44; ☑02-881 3811-4; www.amba france-bd.org; House 18, Rd 108, Gulshan)

German Embassy (Map p44; ☑02-985 3521; www.dhaka. diplo.de; 178 Gulshan Ave, Gulshan II)

Indian High Commission (Map p44; ☑02-988 9339; www. hcidhaka.org; House 2, Rd 142, Gulshan I)

Italian Embassy (Map p44; ☑02-882 2781-3; www.amb dhaka.esteri.it; Plot 2/3, cnr Rds 74 & 79, Gulshan II)

Myanmar Embassy (Map p44; ☑02-988 8903; www.mofa. gov.mm/myanmar missions/ bangladesh.html; House 3, Rd 84, Gulshan II)

Netherlands Embassy (Map p44; ☑02-984 2715-18; http:// bangladesh.nlembassy.org; House 49, Road 90, Gulshan II)

Thai Embassy (Map p44; ☑02-881 2795-6; www.thaidac.com; 18-20 Madani Ave, Baridhara)

UK High Commission (Map p44; ☑02-882 2705-9; ukin bangladesh.fco.gov.uk; cnr 13 United Nations Rd & Dutabash Rd, Baridhara)

US Embassy (Map p44; ☑02-885 5500; dhaka.usembassy. gov; Madani Ave, Baridhara)

LGBT Travellers

Homosexuality is illegal in Bangladesh, and homosexual acts are punishable under Bangladesh law with deportation, fines and/or prison. Such harsh laws are rarely enforced, but nevertheless, gay travellers would be wise to be discreet in Bangladesh.

Boys of Bangladesh (www. boysofbangladesh.org) is the oldest and largest organisation of self-identified Bangladeshi gay men.

Sakhiyani (groups.yahoo.com/ group/sakhiyani) is Bangladesh's first online group for lesbian and bisexual women.

Dhaka is home to **Roopban** (www.facebook.com/Roop baanBD), Bangladesh's only LGBT magazine, although it is only published in Bengali. In 2014, Dhaka also saw its first ever Pride parade, led by the city's *hijra* (transgender) community. *Hijras* are both legally recognised as a third gender and socially excluded.

Insurance

Any policy you get should cover medical expenses and an emergency flight home. Always check the fine print. Some policies exclude coverage of 'dangerous activities', which can include motorcycling and trekking.

For theft and loss, you will require documentation from the Bangladeshi police. Getting it can be a hassle and often requires a 'fee'.

Worldwide travel insurance is available at www. lonelyplanet.com/bookings. You can buy, extend and claim online any time – even if you're already on the road.

Internet Access

Wi-fi

Wi-fi services are widespread in Bangladesh. In Dhaka, it's hard to spend a day without coming across hotspots in cafes, restaurants and private homes. All top-end and most midrange hotels in big cities provide free wi-fi and/or internet connections through a cable for laptop users. In smaller towns, the better hotels all have free wi-fi access, although speed may be an issue.

Internet Cafes

Internet cafes are found in every town and city, although their numbers are gradually diminishing given the rapid spread of 3G enabled smartphones. Connections are generally good, but don't quite stand up to 3G speeds, both for browsing and downloading. Note that internet

cafes, like most business, are always closed on Fridays.

Remote Modems

If you're staying for a few weeks or more, it's worth considering buying a remote modem (called an 'internet dongle') for your laptop, so you can connect to the internet anywhere you have phone reception. They come in the form of a USB stick and can be bought from any of Bangladesh's major mobile telephone providers. We recommend **Grameenphone** (Map p44; ☑02-988 5261; www.grameenphone.com; cnr of Gulshan Ave & Rd 113, Dhaka; ◷9am-7pm), which has reliable coverage and well-run retail outlets. One month's unlimited use costs around Tk 1400.

Legal Matters

Drug offences are taken seriously in Bangladesh and can result in the death penalty if considerable quantities are seized. Anyone, including foreigners, caught smuggling virtually any amount of drugs can end up with a prison sentence for life. As a matter of practice, courts permit those charged to have access to a lawyer. There are also severe penalties for smuggling gold, which is regularly transported into Bangladesh and on to India to bypass high government taxes.

Under the Vienna Convention on Consular Relations, to which Bangladesh is a signatory, any foreign national under detention has a right to request that their embassy be notified of their situation.

Maps

The best map publisher, **Mappa** (www.mappa.com.bd), produces English-language maps for Bangladesh, Dhaka, Chittagong, Sylhet and Cox's Bazar. You can find them in some bookshops and the better handicrafts shops in Dhaka.

Money

The local currency of Bangladesh is the taka (Tk), which is (notionally) further divided into 100 paisas. The largest note is Tk 1000. The smallest coin is Tk 1.

Bangladesh is unbelievably tolerant when it comes to accepting (and handing out) torn or soiled banknotes, although mint-fresh notes also do the rounds.

ATMs

A growing number of ATMs accept foreign bank cards, particularly Visa and MasterCard. The most reliable ATMs are AB Bank, Dutch Bangla Bank, Brac Bank, Standard Chartered Bank and HSBC, all of which have branches in Dhaka, Chittagong and Sylhet.

It's worth stocking up on taka when you can, though, because there are still a lot of places, particularly in more remote areas, where you can't change or withdraw money.

Cash

It's always a good idea to bring a small amount of cash, preferably in American dollars, for emergencies. In smaller towns, hotels may not accept payment by card; restaurants most certainly will not.

Credit Cards

Visa, MasterCard and American Express are usually accepted by major hotels and restaurants in Dhaka and Chittagong.

Cash advances on credit cards can be made at Standard Chartered and HSBC banks.

Moneychangers

You will find official moneychangers upon arriving at Dhaka airport. Most top-end hotels as well as banks in big cities will also change foreign currency for a small surcharge. Only the bigger border crossings such as Benapole and Akhaura have private moneychangers; at smaller crossings, you'll be at the mercy of random people offering random rates.

Tipping

Hotels Attendants are happy with a tip of Tk 50 or Tk 100.

Standard restaurants In most basic restaurants, it's not necessary to tip, although a Tk 20 note can light up a waiter's face.

Top-end restaurants In expensive restaurants in Dhaka that are mostly frequented by foreigners, waiters often expect a small tip, typically about 5% (on top of the service charge and VAT).

Taxis & CNGs Drivers don't expect tips in Bangladesh.

Travellers Cheques

Put simply, don't bother! Only the biggest international banks are likely to accept them and even then it will be with great reluctance. Rely on cash and cards instead.

Opening Hours

Opening hours vary throughout the year. We've provided high-season opening hours; hours will generally decrease in the shoulder and low seasons. Note that Friday is the official weekly holiday in Bangladesh. Depending on the type of office or business, Saturday may either be a holiday (in full or part) or a full working day.

Banks 10am to 4pm Sunday to Thursday

Government offices 10am to 4pm Sunday to Thursday (sometimes 12pm to 4pm Saturday)

Corporate offices 9am to 5pm Saturday to Thursday

Restaurants 7am to 11pm (sometimes noon to 3pm and 7pm to 11pm)

Shops & markets 10am to 8pm Sunday to Thursday

Post

Bangladesh's postal system is slow and unreliable, although you should be fine if you use Dhaka's main post office, which is also the poste restante.

BAKSHEESH

Baksheesh (*bok*-sheesh), in the sense of a tip or gift rather than a bribe (an admittedly fine line), is part of life in Bangladesh. It's not really seen as begging here; it's part of accepted local morality that rich people give some of their income to those less fortunate. There are some peculiarities to this system, though; if you're going to be repeatedly using a service, an initial tip ensures that decent standards will be kept up.

Don't feel persecuted – well-to-do locals also pay baksheesh on a regular basis. Always be conscious of the expectations that will be placed on the next foreigner in light of the amount you give and don't feel embarrassed about not giving baksheesh to someone who rendered absolutely no service at all.

If you want to be certain that the item you are sending will actually reach its destination, we suggest you use a courier company. DHL and FedEx both have branches in Dhaka.

Public Holidays

International Mother Language Day 21 February

Sheikh Mujibur Rehman's Birthday 17 March

Independence Day 26 March

Pohela Boishakh (Bengali New Year) 14 April

May Day 1 May

Buddha Purnima Full moon phase usually in May

Eid ul-Fitr Dates vary according to lunar and Islamic calendar

National Mourning Day (death anniversary of Sheikh Mujibur Rehman) 15 August

Eid ul-Adha Dates vary according to lunar and Islamic calendar

Durga Puja September/October. Dates vary according to lunar calendar

Victory Day 16 December

Christmas 25 December

Safe Travel

Bangladesh is far from being a volatile or dangerous country, and Bangladeshi citizens are some of the most hospitable and friendly people you'll ever meet. But that said, nasty incidents do happen, sometimes without warning or anticipation. Always keep your ears to the ground and your wits about you, and avoid getting into a sticky situation if you ever sense one coming your way.

Road Safety

The most real danger when travelling around Bangladesh is road safety, which is extremely poor, especially on intercity highways. Bus travel is, quite frankly, scary, and road deaths are all too common. Travel by train when you can, or take domestic flights if your budget allows.

Within larger towns and cities, take extra care when walking as a pedestrian because city-centre roads – and pathways – can best be described as hectic, and are often downright dangerous. Many roadside pavements are laid directly over sewer culverts so be wary of broken slabs.

Crime

Bangladesh is generally safe and few tourists experience serious crime. Pickpocketing and snatching on crowded buses and at busy markets is not as endemic as in some other Asian countries, but it does happen.

Some foreigners have been mugged, some at gunpoint, in upmarket areas of Dhaka, such as Gulshan – be careful after dark.

There have also been reports of theft committed by both touts and officials at Dhaka and Sylhet airports. Keep a very close eye on your passport and other papers and make sure luggage zips are secured, preferably with a lock.

Rickshaws present theft and mugging opportunities (keep your handbags out of sight). Women especially should be extremely careful of any taxi containing a driver and his 'friend'.

We have had some rare reports of harassment of foreigners in the form of pushing, stone throwing and spitting, but such incidents are very uncommon.

Pollution & Illness

Pollution levels are very high in Dhaka and Chittagong and may affect people prone to allergies.

Stomach upsets are common for visitors to Bangladesh, and malaria is a serious risk in the Chittagong Hill Tracts region.

For more information, see p177.

Scams

Tourism has not really established itself in Bangladesh, and neither have tourist-related scams. Generally speaking, people are incredibly honest. The most common problem is that of being over-charged, but in a non-fixed price market, this can hardly be called a scam.

There are the usual hassles with rickshaw, CNG (auto-rickshaw) and taxi drivers, though even here the level of harassment is minimal compared to some nearby countries, and in many towns it's possible to just hop on a rickshaw without pre-negotiating a price and not suffer the consequences.

Political Violence

Bangladesh has a history of terrorist activity, targeted assassinations, politically motivated attacks and, sometimes, violent religious rivalry. The most recent significant attacks were in 2015, when resident foreigners were killed or shot at in places such as Dhaka and Rangpur, and bombs targeting Hindu and Shia Muslim religious events in Dhaka, Bogra and Dinajpur. Travel advisories issued by the government following

GOVERNMENT TRAVEL ADVICE

The following government websites offer travel advisories and information on current hot spots.

Australian Department of Foreign Affairs & Trade (www.smarttraveller.gov.au)

British Foreign & Commonwealth Office (www.fco.gov.uk/countryadvice)

US State Department (http://travel.state.gov)

these incidents have warned foreign nationals to stay away from large gatherings as well as to avoid travelling unescorted in rural areas.

When in Bangladesh, you're quite likely to get tangled up in a hartal (strike). These can turn violent and it's not unusual for locals who are involved in them to be killed or seriously injured as a result. In the event of a hartal, stay away from the action, ideally inside your hotel.

The Chittagong Hill Tracts is the only part of the country where there is a continuous security concern, because of an ongoing insurgency against government control of lands belonging to Jumma, Chakma and other tribal people. The problem areas here are usually out of bounds to foreign tourists, so check the situation locally before travelling to the Hill Tracts.

Telephone

Mobile Phones

You can easily obtain a local 3G SIM from carriers such as **Grameenphone** (p162) and **Banglalink** (www.banglalink.com.bd) as long as your phone is 'unlocked'.

Landlines

Only top-end hotels, and small business centres, which are dotted around the country, will have international lines, but using them will be much more expensive than using your mobile phone with a local SIM. The numbers for long-distance information are ☑103 (domestic) and ☑162 (international). International operators speak English; others usually don't.

Phonecodes

To call a number in Bangladesh from outside the country, dial the country code ☑880, followed by the city code without the leading zero, and then the number. To call a different city from within Bangladesh, dial

---

---

the city code including the leading zero, followed by the number.

Mobile phone numbers come prefixed with a zero, which you must dial even if you're calling a local phone within the country. To call a local mobile phone from outside Bangladesh, dial ☑880 and then the mobile number excluding the leading zero.

To call another country from Bangladesh, dial ☑00 followed by the country code and city code.

Time

Bangladesh is six hours ahead of GMT.

Apart from the Gregorian calendar, Bangladeshi society also follows the Islamic calendar, as well as the lunar calendar that is dictated by moon phases. Certain religious festivals (Islamic, Hindu or even Buddhist) that are aligned with the lunar calendar can thus fall on varying dates between years.

Toilets

In midrange and top-end establishments, you'll find sit-down toilets. Otherwise it's squat loos the whole way.

The ablution ritual in Bangladeshi toilets involves the use of your left hand and

---

water, rather than toilet paper. A strategically placed tap and jug are usually at hand. If you can't master the local method or don't even want to try, toilet paper is widely available to buy, although not available in public bathrooms themselves. Sometimes a basket is provided where paper and tampons can be discarded.

There are very few facilities at bus stations and other public places, and whatever facilities exist are pretty horrific. It pays to do your thing back at your hotel. Hotel rooms usually have a roll of toilet paper in the bathroom.

By and large you will find that Bangladeshi hospitality extends to letting you use a toilet, if you ask nicely enough.

In rural areas, it can be difficult to find both toilets and privacy. For women in a desperate situation, a long skirt will make this awkward position a little less so.

Tourist Information

The national tourist office is the **Bangladesh Parjatan Corporation** (Map p40; ☑02-811 7855-9, 02-914 0790; www.bangladeshtourism.gov. bd; 233 Airport Rd, Dhaka), although it has more of a presence simply in terms of nationwide hotels than useful information or infrastructure. Its hotels are overpriced, but they do offer reliable levels of comfort and cleanliness, and in smaller towns they are often the best place to sleep in terms of quality as well as safety.

In general, though, for anything other than the most basic tourist-related questions, it's better to consult a private tour company. Run by the enthusiastic Mahmud Hasan Khan, **Trip 2 Bangladesh** (☑01714-044498; www. trip2bangladesh.com) is a good source of local information.

Visas

With some obscure exceptions, visas are required for citizens of all countries, but note that Israeli passport-holders are forbidden from entering Bangladesh. Maximum stay is usually two months, but can be extended. Travellers from several Western nations can obtain a one-month 'visa on arrival' upon arriving at Dhaka airport.

Visa validity and the granted length of stay seems to vary from embassy to embassy, but typically you will be issued with a visa, which is valid for three months from the date of issue, and good for stays of one to two months. Visa fees vary according to nationality, whether you are seeking single or multiple entry, and which embassy you are applying through.

Visa Extensions

To apply for visa extensions, you will need to visit the **Immigration & Passport Office** (Map p40; ☑02-815 9525; www.dip.gov.bd; Passport Bhaban, E-7 Agargaon, Sher-e-Bangla Nagar; ☉Sun-Thu 10am-1pm) in Dhaka. This is also the office where long-term visitors are required to register.

Extending a tourist visa is relatively painless: fill in the relevant form, pay the fee (this should be the same as the fee for a one-month visa), and pick up a receipt, which will tell you when to return (usually three or four days later – you can keep hold of your passport during this time).

If you just want an extension of a few days, it may be simpler to pay the penalty fee at the airport for overstaying your visa, although that's not something we recommend. It's Tk 200 per day, for up to 15 days. After 15 days, though, it's Tk 500 per day, from day one.

Change of Route Permits

Officially, if you exit Bangladesh by means other than that by which you entered (ie, you flew in, but are leaving by land), you will need a change of route permit, also sometimes referred to as a road permit. Change of route permits can be acquired at the **Immigration & Passport Office** in Dhaka. They are free and shouldn't take more than 24 hours to process. You will need a couple of passport photos.

However, it's worth noting that in recent years, very few travellers have been asked to show this permit, so in practice, you may be able to get by without it. To be absolutely sure, though, check the Thorn Tree forum (www.lonelyplanet.com/thorntree) to see what other travellers have had to do recently.

Volunteering

NGOs and other charitable organisations have a big presence in Bangladesh and many welcome help from foreign visitors. The following organisations may be able to provide information on volunteer opportunities, but Lonely Planet does not endorse any organisations that we do not work with directly, and you should carry out your own research to make sure that organisations are operating according to accepted best practice.

Banchte Shekha (☑0421-68885; www.banchteshekha.com; off Airport Rd) Fights to improve the quality of life for poor women and children in and around the Jessore region.

BRAC (Bangladesh Rural Advancement Committee; ☑02-988 1265; www.brac.net) One of

VISA ON ARRIVAL

If you are coming from USA, Canada, Australia or Europe and just want an ordinary one-month, single-entry tourist visa, you may get them on arrival at the airport (although not at land borders).

You'll see a visa payment counter just before you reach the immigration desks. You can only get a one-month visa on arrival, and you have to pay for one full month even if you plan to stay for less time. It costs the same as a one-month visa would have cost you at the Bangladesh embassy in your home country. You can pay in any major currency, or in taka, but you get the best rate if you pay in American dollars.

The whole process takes five minutes. There's no need for any photos, photocopies or application forms. You just need your passport and some cash.

Note that visas on arrival were only reintroduced in 2011, and immigration rules in Bangladesh are changeable. Before you leave, double-check your visa status with the Bangladeshi embassy or consulate in your country.

the world's largest NGOs; has a range of internship programs.

BRIF (Bangladesh Rural Improvement Foundation; ☏01713- 200717; www.brif.org; Goaldihi village) Works to raise the socio-economic conditions of poor people across the area. May have volunteer opportunities for skilled workers in fields such as agriculture, business, IT, teaching and childcare.

CRP (Centre for the Rehabilitation of the Paralysed; ☏02-774 5464; www.crp-bangladesh. org; Savar, Dhaka Division) The only organisation of its kind in Bangladesh; focuses on a holistic approach to rehabilitation. May offer short-term volunteer opportunities as well as longer-term positions for medically trained professionals such as physiotherapists.

RDRS (Rangpur-Dinajpur Rural Service; Map p95; ☏0521-66490; www.rdrsbangla.net; Jail Rd) Works on health, education and agricultural projects in Bangladesh's far northwest. Has a formal internship program.

Women Travellers

By and large the default response to the unusual sight of a Western woman travelling in Bangladesh is respect; try not to do anything that would make you less than worthy of it. Bangladesh is safer than a lot of other countries around the world, but it's wise to be careful. How you carry yourself subtly determines how you are treated. A woman who is politely assertive can ask for space and usually gets it. The other side of the harassment coin, and almost as much of a nuisance, is that people are constantly making elaborate arrangements to protect you from harassment.

Keep in mind that in this society women are not touched by men when in public, but because you're a foreigner, it might happen. A clear yet tactful objection should end the matter.

What to Wear

Dressing like a local is not obligatory, or even expected, but it will certainly impact on the way you are treated. You will still get attention, but people will be more respectful and appreciative of the fact that you have made the effort to blend in. Many foreigners invest in a *salwar kameez* (a long dress-like tunic worn over baggy trousers). A dupatta (long scarf) to cover your head also increases the appearance of modesty and is a handy accessory in the Bangladesh heat. You can get away with wearing baggy trousers and a long loose-fitting shirt in most parts of the country. Long, loose skirts are also acceptable and provide the added advantage of a modicum of privacy in the absence of a public toilet. Make sure you wear a headscarf at places of worship. Most mosques don't allow women inside, although some have a special women's gallery. If in doubt, ask.

Getting Around

On buses, unaccompanied women are expected to sit at the front. If you are travelling with your 'husband' you are expected to sit on the window side, away from the aisle. Avoid travelling alone at night; Bangladeshi women avoid going out alone at night as much as possible.

Accommodation

Women, with or without men, are sometimes unwelcome in budget hotels, usually because the manager thinks the hotel is not suitable. This knee-jerk reaction can sometimes be overcome if you hang around long enough. On the other hand, staying in one of these cheaper establishments, especially if you are going solo, can be more trouble than it is worth. Mid-range hotels that are accustomed to foreigners are the best bet. Unmarried couples are better off simply saying they're married.

Eating

In a Bangladeshi middle-class home, you would most likely be expected to eat first with the men while the women of the household dutifully serve the meal. In rural areas, you might not eat with either; instead, you would be served first and separately, as a gesture of respect. Accept either graciously. Protest would cause great embarrassment on the part of your host.

In restaurants, you may be shown to the curtained women's rooms (if there are any) to one side of the dining area. This is a courteous offer that you can decline, though you may find that the curtain provides something of a respite from the eyes that will be on you if you sit elsewhere.

Work

Most foreign workers in Bangladesh are involved in aid and development. To work in Bangladesh, a Bangladeshi company must apply for a work permit on your behalf.

Transport

GETTING THERE & AWAY

Entering the Country

To enter Bangladesh, you will need a passport that's valid for at least six months beyond the duration of your stay. An onward/return ticket is preferred, although not always essential.

Rules and procedures for entering and exiting Bangladesh seem to be in a constant state of flux. Since 2011, Bangladesh has offered visas on arrival to citizens of USA, Canada, Australia and the bigger European countries, but check if you are still on that list before arriving.

Air

Airports & Airlines

There are three international airports in Bangladesh:

Dhaka Hazrat Shahjalal International Airport (DAC; www.shahjalalairport.com)

Chittagong Shah Amanat International Airport (CGP)

Sylhet Osmani International Airport (ZYL)

In practice, the vast majority of foreign visitors arrive at Dhaka's Hazrat Shahjalal International Airport. It's pretty basic for a capital-city airport but it has money-changing facilities, including ATMs that accept foreign cards, some duty-free shops and a couple of restaurants.

There's an official taxi rank, although it's cheaper to try your luck with taxis and CNGs (auto-rickshaws) outside. The 30-minute haul to Banani, the first prominent residential neighbourhood on your way into the city, will cost you Tk 750 by taxi or Tk 300 by CNG. If you ask your hotel for an airport pick-up, expect to pay around Tk 1000.

The unofficial airport website (www.shahjalalairport.com) has a flight-status feed.

Biman (www.bimanairlines.com) is the national carrier of Bangladesh. It's a scruffy and curiously disorganised operation, but the fleet is fairly well maintained and the airline has a good safety record.

Land

Bangladesh shares several border checkposts with its neighbour India, and many of these allow civilian transit between the two nations. Crossings such as Benapole, Tamabil and Akhaura remain popular with tourists, and have fairly good road transport networks on both sides.

For all the details on how to travel overland in and out of Bangladesh, see Border Crossings (p24).

GETTING AROUND

Travelling around Bangladesh is extremely cheap, although in some cases it can be quite

---

CLIMATE CHANGE & TRAVEL

Every form of transport that relies on carbon-based fuel generates CO_2, the main cause of human-induced climate change. Modern travel is dependent on aeroplanes, which might use less fuel per kilometre per person than most cars but travel much greater distances. The altitude at which aircraft emit gases (including CO_2) and particles also contributes to their climate change impact. Many websites offer 'carbon calculators' that allow people to estimate the carbon emissions generated by their journey and, for those who wish to do so, to offset the impact of the greenhouse gases emitted with contributions to portfolios of climate-friendly initiatives throughout the world. Lonely Planet offsets the carbon footprint of all staff and author travel.

uncomfortable. Road safety is a real issue in Bangladesh. The country has some of the worst road-accident figures in the world, and the Dhaka–Chittagong Hwy is notoriously bad.

Buses Dirt cheap if you don't mind squashing into the local ones; more comfortable, more expensive coaches are usually available, too.

Trains Safer option than road travel, although the network and tickets are limited.

Rickshaws (cycle-rickshaws) or **CNGs** (auto-rickshaws) Best way to get between sights in cities and between villages.

Boat In Barisal and Khulna divisions, the riverboat is the king of travel. Joining locals on a long ferry ride is one of the undisputed highlights of your Bangladesh trip.

Plane Domestic flights to divisional towns from Dhaka are worth considering if your time is limited.

Air

Airlines in Bangladesh

Bangladesh has several prominent domestic airlines. Most travellers say Novoair and US Bangla Airlines – both private companies – are better than Biman, the state-owned carrier.

Domestic routes connect Dhaka to Chittagong, Sylhet and Jessore on a daily basis. Barisal, Rajshahi and Saidpur (in Rangpur) are also connected by twice- or thrice-weekly flights, mostly by Biman.

Biman (www.biman-airlines.com)

Novoair (www.flynovoair.com)

US Bangla Airlines (www.us-banglaairlines.com)

Bicycle

If you base yourself in Dhaka or Chittagong, the surrounds of both these cities can be wonderful for cycling, and a self-guided bicycle ride could easily be one of the highlights of your trip here. Neither city is particularly easy or safe to ride, given manic traffic and pollution, although if you leave early, say 5.30am, you should be able to get out of the city and hit the countryside without incident. Srimangal (p131) is another good location for scenic bike rides within easy cycling distance of the town.

The trick to cycling in Bangladesh is to avoid major highways as much as possible; look instead for quieter back-roads that will get you to the same destination. Android and Apple maps of Bangladesh are pretty accurate and if you get lost, you can always ask around.

Most rural paths are bricked and in good condition, and even if it's just a dirt path, bikes will be able to pass during the dry season. A river or a canal won't hinder your travel, since there's invariably a boat to take you and your bike across. The ideal time to go cycling is in the dry season from mid-October to late March; during the monsoon many tracks become impassable.

Note that prevailing security concerns and travel advisories issued in late 2015 pertaining to the safety of foreigners in Bangladesh mean that tourists can not embark on extended self-guided bicycle tours, though daytrips in the Dhaka and Chittagong areas are permitted. At the time of writing, cycling was not allowed in Sylhet due to safety issues, but check to see if this has changed.

Be aware that snatches from saddlebags are not unheard of.

Boat

Bangladesh is made for boat travel. For more information, see Boat Trips (p28).

Bus

Local bus travel is cheap and extremely convenient. Buses to main towns leave frequently, and tickets don't need to be booked in advance, so you can just turn up at a bus station and wait for the next one.

The downside, though, is the often extreme lack of comfort and worryingly poor safety. For something more comfortable (but no safer) try a private coach instead, although these are less frequent and more expensive.

It's illegal to ride on top of a bus, like many locals do, but the police won't stop you. If you do ride on top, though, remember that low trees do kill people each year.

GETTING A BIKE IN DHAKA

It's best to bring your own bicycle and all other safety and technical gear with you, though a couple of decent-quality bicycle shops exist in Dhaka. Head to **Bangshal Rd** (Map p38; Bicycle St; ⊙Sat-Thu), an area of Old Dhaka that specialises in making and repairing bikes and rickshaws. Most places sell ordinary, single-gear town bicycles, but a couple of places sell decent-quality bikes and equipment. Try **Lion Cycle Store** (☏01947-431260; www.facebook.com/LionCycle; 28/1 Bangshal Rd, Old Dhaka). You may also find decent bike shops in Chittagong.

Bike repair shops, catering to all those cycle-rickshaws, are two-a-penny almost everywhere in Bangladesh, so finding basic spare parts shouldn't be a problem unless your bike is unusual.

POPULAR COACH COMPANIES

Green Line (☑02-833 1302; www.greenlinebd.com)

Soudia (☑031-9701 5610)

Hanif (☑01711-922415, 02-913 5018)

Shohagh Paribahan (www.shohagh.biz)

Many bus stations are located on the outskirts of towns, often with different stations for different destinations. If you're unsure of which bus station to use, just hop in a rickshaw and utter the name of your destination followed by the words 'bus stand'. The rickshaw rider will know where to take you. Note, however, that bus stations are nearly always called bus stands, while some larger ones are known as bus terminals.

Coach companies often have their ticket offices in the town centre rather than at the bus stands, and you sometimes need to book tickets in advance, especially if you want to ride the pricey and comfortable air-con vehicles, which are fewer in number.

Coaches

The most comfortable bus options are private coaches, which have adjustable seats and extra leg room. Some also have air-con.

Departure hours are fixed and less frequent than local buses, especially for long journeys. Seats should be reserved in advance, although turning up at the ticket office half an hour before the coach leaves sometimes suffices.

Some coach services travelling between Dhaka and cities on the western side of the country operate at night, typically departing sometime between 5pm and 9pm and arriving in Dhaka at or before dawn. While you'll save on a night's accommodation, you probably won't get a decent night's sleep as there are no proper sleeper buses; you'll just be in a reclinable seat.

Prices vary from company to company, but there are basically two types of coach –

those with air-con and those without. Those with air-con cost about twice as much as those without. Unlike local buses, coaches will often make a lunch stop at a roadside restaurant if you're travelling through the middle of the day.

Local buses

Among the ordinary buses there are express buses and local ones, which stop en route. The latter charge about 25% less but can be very slow. In more remote areas local buses may be your only option. Most buses are large, but there are a few minivans (coasters).

The buses run by private companies tend to be in better condition than those of the state-run BRTC.

If you're tall, you're in for a shock; leg room hardly allows for short people to sit with their knees forward, let alone 6ft-tall Westerners. On long trips this can be exceedingly uncomfortable, so try to get an aisle seat if you can.

Women travelling alone sit together up the front, separate from the men. If there is an accident, this is the most dangerous part of the bus to be on. Women travelling with their husbands sometimes sit in the main section, usually on the window side. On long-distance bus trips *cha* (tea) stops can be agonisingly infrequent and a real hassle for women travellers – toilet facilities are rare indeed and sometimes hard to find when they do exist.

One of the most under-appreciated professions would have to be the bus-wallah. These are the men who hang out the door helping people on and off,

load oversized luggage onto the roof, bang on the side of the bus telling the driver to stop and go, and uncannily keep track of who needs how much change. They are usually extremely helpful – they often rearrange things so you are comfortably seated and rarely fail to let you know when the bus has arrived at your destination.

Car & Motorcycle

Travelling by private car has some obvious advantages and disadvantages. On the plus side, it gives you the freedom to quickly and easily go where you please, when you please, and allows for all manner of unexpected pit stops and adventures. On the minus side, it does insulate you somewhat from Bangladesh and it is far more expensive than public transport. Self-drive rental is not available in Bangladesh, so car hire really means hiring a car with a driver.

Motorcycles can be hired on self-ride basis only in a few places, such as Kuakata in Barisal. Touring the country on a motorcycle isn't a popular activity as yet.

Hire

Self-drive rental cars are not available in Bangladesh, and that's probably a good thing. However, renting cars with drivers is easy, at least in the big towns.

In Dhaka there are innumerable companies in the rental business. For the best cars and the safest drivers, try one of the more reputable tour operators. Expect to pay at least Tk 4000 a day for a car, plus fuel and driver expenses. When you stay out of town overnight, you must pay for the driver's food and lodging, but this won't cost much. Make sure you determine beforehand what all those extra rates will be, to avoid any misunderstandings. Insurance isn't required because you aren't the driver.

Outside Dhaka, the cost of renting vehicles is often marginally less, but actually finding an available car and driver is much harder. Asking at the town's top hotels normally produces results.

Hitching

Hitching is never entirely safe in any country, and we don't recommend it. Travellers who decide to hitch should understand that they are taking a small but potentially serious risk. Those who hitch will be safer if they travel in pairs, and let someone know where they are planning to go. Solo women would be particularly unwise to hitchhike. Generally speaking, you will be expected to pay for any ride, as the locals do.

Local Transport

Bangladesh has an amazing range of vehicles – on any highway you can see buses, cars, rickshaws, CNGs, tempos (shared auto-rickshaws), tractors with trays laden with people, motorbikes, scooters, bicycles carrying four people, bullock and water-buffalo carts, and bizarre homemade vehicles all competing for space. One local favourite in Rajshahi and Khulna divisions is a sort of minitractor, known as a *nazaman,* which is powered by incredibly noisy irrigation-pump motors.

In Dhaka and Chittagong, motorised transport has increased greatly over the past decade, and traffic jams in Central Dhaka are a nightmare. In Old Dhaka it's not unusual to get caught up in an hour-long traffic jam consisting just of cycle-rickshaws; in Old Dhaka, it's almost always quicker to walk.

What freaks out new arrivals the most is the total chaos that seems to pervade the streets, with drivers doing anything they please and pedestrians being the least of anybody's worries. Accidents do happen and

sometimes people are killed, but the odds of you being involved are still fairly slim.

Boat

Given that there are over 8000km of navigable inland waterways, boats are a common means of getting around. Even if you're not on a long-distance trip, you may find yourself having to cross rivers by boat. Usually you pay a couple of taka for a place on a small wooden ferry. You can also hire private boats, known as reserve boats, to get from one town to another. Public ferries, known as a launch, are worth inquiring about if you're at a town with a river ghat. They may be slow, but they're cheap and are the most pleasant way to get from A to B.

Bus

If you thought long-distance buses were crowded, wait till you try a local city-centre bus. Just getting on one is a challenge in itself. Firstly, assess whether the bus will get you to your destination by screaming the name of the destination to the man hanging out the door (he's the conductor). If he responds in the affirmative, run towards him, grab firmly onto a handle, if there is one, or him if there isn't, and jump aboard, remembering to check for oncoming traffic. Chances are you won't be able to squeeze any further inside than the doorway, so just hang on.

CNG

In Bangladesh, three-wheeled auto-rickshaws are called CNGs because these days, most of them run on Compressed Natural Gas. As with the pedal-driven rickshaw-wallahs, CNG drivers almost never own their vehicles. They're owned by powerful fleet-owners called *mohajons,* who rent them out on an eight-hour basis. Also like rickshaws, they're designed to take two or three people, but entire families can and do fit.

CNGs are ubiquitous across Bangladesh – most people use them instead of regular taxis. Faster and more comfortable than rickshaws, CNGs cost about twice as much. Thanks to the wire-mesh doors that secure the passenger seat on both sides of the vehicle, they are also somewhat safer to travel in, especially at night.

Rickshaw

In Bangladesh, all rickshaws are pedal-driven. Many vehicles come fitted with battery kits these days, which boost speed while saving the rickshaw-wallahs (drivers) from pedalling all the time. Rickshaw-wallahs usually do not speak English, although you may find some English-speaking ones hanging around outside top-end hotels; this is certainly the case in Dhaka.

Fares vary a lot, and you must bargain if you care about paying twice as much as locals, although even that still won't be very expensive. In any case, it is probably unrealistic to expect to pay exactly what Bangladeshis do. As a very rough guide, Tk 10 per kilometre is about right.

Taxi

Taxis are less abundant than you'd think. Even in Dhaka, most people use CNGs. You might be able to hail one from the side of the road if they are on their way to their usual hangout, but if they're all occupied you are better off heading straight to an intersection or top-end hotel, where you will find a fleet of them waiting. Taxis are usually not metered, so you should negotiate the fare before boarding. Dhaka now has a radio taxi service called **Toma Taxi** (☏01866-667070; www.tomataxi.com.bd), which has about 200-odd cabs plying the greater Dhaka area.

Outside Dhaka, there are precious few taxis. In Chittagong, you'll find a few at the airport or at large hotels and around GEC Circle. In

Sylhet, Khulna, Saidpur and possibly Rajshahi you'll see no taxis except for a few at the airport. They are not marked, so you'll have to ask someone to point them out.

Tempo

This is a larger, shared auto-rickshaw, with a cabin in the back. Tempos run set routes, like buses, and while they cost far less than CNGs, they're more uncomfortable because of the small space into which the dozen or so passengers are squeezed. On the other hand, they're a lot faster than rickshaws and as cheap as local buses. You will find tempos in most towns, even relatively small ones.

Train

Trains are a lot easier on the nerves than buses. Those plying the major routes aren't too bad, and if you travel in 1st class, they are positively luxurious. However, travel is sometimes slowed down by circuitous routing and different gauges, which means that a train ride usually takes longer than a bus ride.

For a full list of routes, times, journey durations and prices of tickets of all the trains in Bangladesh, go to the official website of **Bangladesh Railway** (www.railway.gov.bd). You can't book tickets here, but it's very useful for planning your journey.

Classes

Intercity (IC) trains are frequent, relatively fast, clean and reasonably punctual, especially in the eastern zone. Fares in 1st class are fairly high (about a third more than an air-con coach), but in shuvon chair (2nd class with reserved seating, and better carriages than ordinary shuvon) the fare is comparable to that in a non-air-con coach, and the trip is a lot more pleasant and safe.

The carriages in 1st class, which have three seats across, facing each other and separated by a small table, initially seem similar to those in shuvon, which have four seats across without tables. The difference is that there's always room for just one more passenger in shuvon, whereas in 1st class what you see is what you get. Some IC trains also have an air-con 1st class, which is well worth the extra money. Seats here are of the soft and comfortable variety. This class is always popular but seats are limited. It's a good idea to reserve as far in advance as you can to get a seat or berth in air-con 1st class, though a quiet word to the station master can sometimes work wonders.

There are generally no buffet cars, but sandwiches, snacks and drinks are available from attendants.

Second-class cars with unreserved seating are always an overcrowded mess, and on mail trains (which

allow for some passenger cargo), your trip will be even slower than on an IC train.

The only sleeper berths are on night trains or those with more than eight hours of running time, and the fare is about 40% more than a 1st-class seat.

Fares

There are 11 possible classes of train tickets, although it's rare that they're all available on one train. We've generally listed fares for shuvon (ordinary 2nd class), 1st-class seat and 1st-class berth, but to show you what the other options are, here is a broader sample list of train fares. This shows seven possible train classes, and their respective fares, for the five-hour journey from Dhaka to Srimangal:

Air-con berth Tk 765

Air-con seat Tk 512

1st-class berth Tk 445

1st-class seat Tk 295

Snigdha (air-con) Tk 426

Shuvon chair Tk 225

Shuvon Tk 185

Reservations

A recently launched fully automated e-ticketing system, called **Bangladesh Railway Esheba** (www.esheba.cnsbd.com) allows you to buy tickets online; you can pay by either Visa or MasterCard.

Note that the ticket-reservation system only allows passengers to buy tickets five days in advance of their journey. Check that this is still the case when you arrive, as it's wise to book your tickets as soon as they become available to buy.

Ticket clerks will often assume that you want the most expensive seats, unless you make it clear otherwise. Buying tickets on local short-distance trains is a drag because they don't go on sale until the train is about to arrive, which means that while you're battling the ticket queue all the seats are being filled by locals.

TICKETS BY TEXT

It has recently become possible to book train tickets through a few local mobile-phone networks. You'll need a local SIM card with enough credit on it to cover the cost of the ticket. You must pick up the paper ticket at the train station you're departing from at least an hour in advance (or from select retail outlets of the phone company), but the procedure can save you some time.

Tickets are booked through a series of prompted text messages, and can be booked up to five days in advance. **Grameenphone** (www.grameenphone.com) and **Banglalink** (www.banglalink.com.bd) have all the details on their websites.

Health

Travellers tend to worry about contracting infectious tropical diseases in this part of the world, but infections are a rare cause of serious illness or death in travellers. Pre-existing medical conditions such as heart disease, and accidental injury (especially traffic accidents), account for most life-threatening problems.

Broadly speaking, Bangladesh has decent medical facilities (more in big cities than in small towns) to treat everyday ailments, infections and injuries. That said, falling ill is very much a possibility. Environmental issues such as heat and pollution can cause health problems. Hygiene is generally poor throughout the region, so food- and water-borne illnesses are common. Many insect-borne diseases are present too, particularly in tropical forested areas. Fortunately, most illnesses can either be prevented with basic common sense, or be treated easily with a well-stocked traveller's medical kit.

The following advice is a general guide only and does not replace the advice of a doctor trained in travel medicine.

BEFORE YOU GO

Pack medications in their original, clearly labelled, containers. A signed and dated letter from your physician describing your medical conditions and prescription drugs, including generic names, is very useful. If carrying syringes or needles, be sure to have a physician's letter documenting their medical necessity. If you have a heart condition, bring a copy of your ECG taken just prior to travelling.

If you take any regular medication, bring double your needs (you may not find the exact combination drug in local pharmacies). In most south Asian countries, including Bangladesh, you can buy many medications – such as antibiotics – over the counter without a doctor's prescription, but it can be difficult to find some of the newer drugs, particularly the latest antidepressant drugs, blood-pressure medications and contraceptive pills.

Insurance

Even if you are fit and healthy, don't travel without health insurance – accidents do happen. Declare any existing medical conditions you have – the insurance company *will* check if your problem is pre-existing and will not cover you if it is undeclared. If your health insurance doesn't cover you for medical expenses abroad, consider getting extra insurance. If you're uninsured, emergency evacuation can cost you dearly.

Find out in advance if your insurance plan will make payments directly to providers, or whether the company will reimburse you later for your overseas health expenditures. In Bangladesh, doctors expect to be paid in cash, although some hospitals accept payments on a credit card.

Vaccinations

Specialised travel-medicine clinics are your best source of information; they stock all available vaccines and will be able to give specific recommendations for you and your trip.

Most vaccines don't produce immunity until at least two weeks after they're given, so visit a doctor four to eight weeks before your planned departure. Ask your doctor for an International Certificate of Vaccination (otherwise known as 'the yellow booklet'), which will list all the vaccinations you've received. Note that common vaccination side effects are fever, sore arm and/or headache.

The World Health Organization (WHO) recommends the following vaccinations for travellers to south Asia:

Adult diphtheria and tetanus Single booster recommended if none in the past 10 years.

Hepatitis A Provides almost 100% protection for up to a year; a booster after 12 months provides at least another 20 years' protection.

Hepatitis B Now considered routine for most travellers. Given as three shots over six months. A rapid schedule is also available, as is a combined vaccination with Hepatitis A. In 95% of people, lifetime protection results.

Measles, mumps and rubella Two doses of MMR are required unless you've had the diseases. Occasionally a rash and flulike illness can develop a week after receiving the vaccine. Many young adults require a booster.

Polio In 2003 polio was still present in Nepal, India and Pakistan, but it has been eradicated in Bangladesh. Only one booster is required for an adult for lifetime protection. Inactivated polio vaccine is safe during pregnancy.

Typhoid Recommended for all travellers to Bangladesh, even if you only visit urban areas. The vaccine offers around 70% protection, lasts for two to three years and comes as a single shot. Tablets are also available, however the injection is usually recommended as it has fewer side effects.

Varicella If you haven't had chickenpox, discuss this vaccination with your doctor.

These are recommended for long-term travellers (more than one month) or those at special risk:

Japanese B Encephalitis Three injections in all. Booster recommended after two years. Rarely, an allergic reaction comprising hives and swelling can occur up to 10 days after any of the three doses.

Meningitis Single injection. There are two types of vaccination: the quadravalent vaccine gives two to three years' protection; meningitis group C vaccine gives around 10 years' protection. Recommended for long-term backpackers aged under 25.

Rabies Three injections in all. A booster after one year will then provide 10 years' protection.

Tuberculosis A complex issue. Long-term adult travellers are usually recommended to have a TB skin test before and after travel, rather than vaccination. Only one vaccine given in a lifetime.

Required Vaccinations

The only vaccine required by international regulations is yellow fever. Proof of vaccination will only be required if you have visited a country in the yellow-fever zone within six days prior to entering Bangladesh. If you are travelling to Bangladesh from Africa or South America, you should check to see if you will require proof of vaccination.

Websites

World Health Organization (www.who.int/ith) Publishes the superb *International Travel and Health*, which is revised annually and available for free online.

MD Travel Health (www.mdtravelhealth.com) Provides complete travel-health recommendations for every country and is updated daily.

Centers for Disease Control and Prevention (www.cdc.gov) Good general information.

Further Reading

Travelling Well (Dr Deborah Mills) Also has its own website (www.travellingwell.com.au) and smartphone app.

Traveller's Health (Dr Richard Dawood)

IN BANGLADESH

Availability & Cost of Health Care

Medical facilities in Bangladesh are not quite up to international standards, especially for critical and serious cases (for which evacuation may be the only

option). Facilities are limited outside Dhaka and bigger cities such as Sylhet and Chittagong, and it can be very difficult to find reliable medical care in rural areas. Your embassy and insurance company can be good contacts. Note that doctors expect up-front payment for medical treatments, usually in cash.

Self-treatment may be appropriate if your problem is minor (eg traveller's diarrhoea or common cold), if you are carrying the relevant medication and if you cannot attend a recommended clinic. If you think you may have a serious disease, such as dengue or malaria, do not waste time – travel to the nearest quality facility to receive attention.

Buying medication over the counter is easy, but not generally recommended, as fake medications and drugs that have been poorly stored or are out of date are common.

Infectious Diseases

Dengue Fever

This mosquito-borne disease (locally pronounced 'dengoo') is becoming increasingly problematic in the tropical world, especially in the cities. As there is no vaccine available it can only be prevented by avoiding mosquito bites. The mosquito that carries dengue bites day and night, so use insect avoidance measures at all times. Symptoms include high fever, severe headache and body ache (dengue was previously known as 'breakbone fever'). Some people develop a rash and experience diarrhoea. There is no specific treatment, just rest and take paracetamol – do *not* take aspirin as it increases the likelihood of haemorrhaging. See a doctor to be diagnosed and monitored.

Hepatitis A

A problem throughout the region, this food- and water-borne virus infects the liver, causing jaundice (yellow skin and eyes), nausea and lethargy. There is no specific treatment for hepatitis A; you just need to allow time for the liver to heal. All travellers heading to south Asia should be vaccinated against hepatitis A.

Hepatitis B

The only sexually transmitted disease that can be prevented by vaccination, hepatitis B is spread by body fluids, including sexual contact. In some parts of south Asia, up to 20% of the population are carriers of hepatitis B, and usually are unaware of this. In Bangladesh the number of carriers is just below 10%.

The long-term consequences can include liver cancer and cirrhosis.

Hepatitis E

Transmitted through contaminated food and water, hepatitis E has similar symptoms to hepatitis A, but is far less common. It is a severe problem in pregnant women and can result in the death of both mother and baby. There is currently no vaccine, and prevention is by following safe eating and drinking guidelines.

HIV & AIDS

HIV is spread via contaminated body fluids. Avoid unsafe sex, unsterile needles (including those in medical facilities) and procedures such as tattoos. The rate of HIV infection in south Asia is growing rapidly, although

Bangladesh itself is a low HIV-prevalence country, with less than 0.1% of the population estimated to be HIV-positive.

Influenza

Present year-round in the tropics, influenza (flu) symptoms include high fever, muscle aches, runny nose, cough and sore throat. It can be very severe in people over the age of 65 or in those with underlying medical conditions such as heart disease or diabetes – vaccination is recommended for these individuals. There is no specific treatment, just rest and take paracetamol to control the fever.

Avian influenza has been confirmed in Bangladesh; short-term travellers are not considered to be at high risk.

MEDICAL TRAVEL KIT

The following items could be considered for your personal medical kit:

☐ antibacterial cream eg Mupirocin

☐ antibiotics for skin infections eg Amoxicillin/Clavulanate or Cephalexin

☐ antibiotics for diarrhoea eg Norfloxacin or Ciprofloxacin; for bacterial diarrhoea, Azithromycin; for giardia or amoebic dysentery, Tinidazole

☐ antifungal cream eg Clotrimazole

☐ antihistamine, eg Cetrizine for daytime and Promethazine for night

☐ antiseptic eg Betadine

☐ antispasmodic for stomach cramps, eg Buscopan

☐ contraceptive method

☐ decongestant eg Pseudoephedrine

☐ DEET-based insect repellent

☐ diarrhoea treatment: consider an oral rehydration solution (eg Gastrolyte), diarrhoea 'stopper' (eg Loperamide) and antinausea medication (eg Prochlorperazine)

☐ first-aid items such as scissors, elastoplasts, bandages, gauze, thermometer (but not mercury), sterile needles and syringes, safety pins and tweezers

☐ Ibuprofen or another anti-inflammatory

☐ iodine tablets to purify water (unless you are pregnant or have a thyroid problem)

☐ laxative eg Coloxyl

☐ paracetamol

☐ permethrin to impregnate clothing and mosquito nets

☐ steroid cream for allergic/itchy rashes, eg 1% to 2% hydrocortisone

☐ sunscreen and hat

☐ thrush (vaginal yeast infection) treatment eg Clotrimazole pessaries or Diflucan tablet

☐ Ural or equivalent, if you're prone to urine infections.

Japanese B Encephalitis

This viral disease is transmitted by mosquitoes and is rare in travellers. Like most mosquito-borne diseases, it is becoming a more common problem in tropical countries. Most cases occur in rural areas and vaccination is recommended for travellers spending more than one month outside of cities. There is no treatment, and a third of infected people will die, while another third will suffer permanent brain damage.

Malaria

For such a serious and potentially deadly disease, there is an enormous amount of misinformation concerning malaria. You must get expert advice as to whether your trip puts you at risk. In the Chittagong Hill Tracts region in particular, the risk of contracting malaria far outweighs the risk of any tablet side effects. Remember that malaria can be fatal. Before you travel, seek medical advice on the right medication and dosage for you. Malaria in south Asia, including Bangladesh, is chloroquine resistant.

Malaria is caused by a parasite, transmitted through the bite of an infected mosquito. The most important symptom of malaria is fever, but general symptoms such as headache, diarrhoea, cough or chills may also occur. A diagnosis can only be made by taking a blood sample.

Two strategies should be combined to prevent malaria: mosquito avoidance and antimalarial medications. Most people who catch malaria are taking inadequate or no antimalarial medication.

There is a variety of antimalarial medications:

Doxycycline This daily tablet is a broad-spectrum antibiotic that has the added benefit of helping to prevent a variety of tropical diseases including leptospirosis, tick-borne diseases and typhus. The potential side effects include photosensitivity (a tendency to sunburn), thrush in women, indigestion, heartburn, nausea and interference with the contraceptive pill. More serious side effects include ulceration of the oesophagus – you can help prevent this by taking your tablet with a meal and a large glass of water, and never lying down within half an hour of taking it. It must be taken for four weeks after leaving the risk area. Note: while we advise you bring any antimalarial medication with you from home, Doxycycline is available to buy at Lazz Pharma, a 24-hour pharmacy in Dhaka.

Lariam (Mefloquine) Lariam has received much bad press, some of it justified, some not.

This weekly tablet suits many people. Serious side effects are rare but include depression, anxiety, psychosis and having fits. Anyone with a history of depression, anxiety, other psychological disorders or epilepsy should not take Lariam. It is considered safe in the second and third trimesters of pregnancy. Tablets must be taken for four weeks after leaving the risk area.

Malarone This drug is a combination of Atovaquone and Proguanil. Side effects are uncommon and mild, most commonly nausea and headache. It is the best tablet for scuba divers and for those on short trips to high-risk areas. It must be taken for one week after leaving the risk area.

A final option is to take no preventive medication but to have a supply of emergency medication should you develop the symptoms of malaria. This is less than ideal, and you'll need to get to a good medical facility within 24 hours of developing a fever. If you choose this option, the most effective and safest treatment is Malarone (four tablets once daily for three days). Other options include Mefloquine and Quinine but the side effects of these drugs at treatment doses make them less desirable. Fansidar is no longer recommended.

Measles

Measles remains a significant problem in Bangladesh. This highly contagious bacterial infection is spread via coughing and sneezing. Most people born before 1966 are immune as they had the disease in childhood. Measles starts with a high fever and rash, and can be complicated by pneumonia and brain disease. There is no specific treatment.

Rabies

This is a common problem in south Asia. Around 30,000 people die from rabies in India alone each year, and there are more than 2000 deaths annually in Bangladesh. This uniformly fatal disease is

---

HELP PREVENT MOSQUITO BITES

➡ Use a DEET-containing insect repellent on exposed skin. Wash this off at night, as long as you are sleeping under a mosquito net. Natural repellents such as citronella can be effective, but must be applied more frequently than products containing DEET.

➡ Sleep under a mosquito net impregnated with permethrin.

➡ Choose accommodation with screens and fans (if not air-conditioned).

➡ Impregnate clothing with permethrin in high-risk areas.

➡ Wear long sleeves and trousers in light colours.

➡ Use mosquito coils.

➡ Spray your room with insect repellent before going out for your evening meal.

spread by the bite or lick of an infected animal – most commonly a dog or monkey. You should seek medical advice immediately after any animal bite and commence post-exposure treatment. Having pre-travel vaccination means the post-bite treatment is greatly simplified. If an animal bites you, gently wash the wound with soap and water, and apply an iodine-based antiseptic. If you are not pre-vaccinated, you will need to receive rabies immunoglobulin as soon as possible. This is very difficult to obtain outside of Dhaka.

Respiratory Infections

Respiratory infections are common in Bangladesh. This usually starts as a virus and is exacerbated by environmental conditions such as pollution in the cities. Commonly a secondary bacterial infection will intervene – marked by fever, chest pain and coughing up discoloured or blood-tinged sputum. If you have these symptoms, seek medical advice or commence a general antibiotic.

Tuberculosis

While TB is rare in travellers, those who have significant contact with the local population, such as medical and aid workers, and long-term travellers, should take precautions. Vaccination is usually only given to children under the age of five, but adults at risk are recommended to have pre- and post-travel TB testing. The main symptoms are fever, cough, weight loss, night sweats and tiredness.

Typhoid

This serious bacterial infection is spread via food and water. It gives a high and slowly progressive fever and headache, and may be accompanied by a dry cough and stomach pain. It is diagnosed by blood tests and treated with antibiotics. Vaccination is recommended for all travellers spending more than a week in south Asia. In Bangladesh the risk is medium level but the infection is also antibiotic resistant. Be aware that vaccination is not 100% effective, so you must still be careful with what you eat and drink.

Traveller's Diarrhoea

Traveller's diarrhoea is by far the most common problem affecting travellers; between 30% and 70% of people will suffer from it within two weeks of starting their trip. In over 80% of cases, traveller's diarrhoea is caused by bacteria, and therefore responds promptly to treatment with antibiotics. Treatment with antibiotics will depend on your situation – how sick you are, how quickly you need to get better, where you are etc.

Traveller's diarrhoea is defined as the passage of more than three watery bowel actions within 24 hours, plus at least one other symptom such as fever, cramps, nausea, vomiting or generally feeling unwell.

Treatment consists of staying well hydrated; rehydration solutions such as Gastrolyte are the best for this. Antibiotics such as Norfloxacin, Ciprofloxacin or Azithromycin will kill the bacteria quickly.

Loperamide is just a 'stopper' and doesn't get to the root of the problem. It can be helpful, for example, if you have to go on a long bus ride. Don't take Loperamide if you have a fever, or blood in your stools. Seek medical attention quickly if you do not respond to an appropriate antibiotic.

Amoebic Dysentery

Amoebic dysentery is rare in travellers but is often misdiagnosed by poor-quality labs in south Asia. Symptoms are similar to bacterial diarrhoea: fever, bloody diarrhoea and generally feeling unwell. You should always seek reliable medical care if you have blood in your diarrhoea. Treatment involves two drugs: Tinidazole or Metronidazole to kill the parasite in your gut, and then a second drug to kill the cysts. If left untreated, complications such as liver or gut abscesses can occur. Bacterial dysentery is more common.

Giardiasis

Giardia is a water-borne parasite that is relatively common in travellers. Symptoms include nausea, bloating, excess gas, fatigue and intermittent diarrhoea. 'Eggy' burps are often attributed solely to giardia, but work in Nepal has shown that they are not specific to giardia. The parasite will eventually go away if left untreated, but this can take months. The treatment of choice is Tinidazole, with Metronidazole being a second-line option.

Environmental Hazards

Air Pollution

If you have severe respiratory problems, speak with your doctor before travelling to any heavily polluted urban centres. Dhaka and Chittagong are among the most polluted cities in the world. This pollution also causes minor respiratory problems such as sinusitis, dry throat and irritated eyes. If troubled by the pollution, leave the city for a few days and get some fresh air. There's plenty of it in Bangladesh!

Food

Eating in unhygienic restaurants can cause traveller's diarrhoea. Ways to avoid it include eating only freshly cooked food, and avoiding shellfish and food that has been sitting around in buffets. There have also been reports of vegetables and fruits being sprayed with formaldehyde by some unscrupulous vendors in the country, with the objective of increasing their shelf life. Peel all fruit, cook vegetables, and soak salads in iodine water for at least 20 minutes. If you order salads or fresh fruit for meals, make sure you do it only at a restaurant which has a steady local patronage and a high turnover of customers. Even so, insist that they are washed well before being served.

TAP WATER

➡ Never drink tap water, and avoid ice.

➡ Bottled water is generally safe – check that the seal is intact, and that it is labelled 'arsenic free'.

➡ Avoid fresh juices, especially in smaller eateries. They may have been watered down.

➡ Boiling water for 10 minutes is the most efficient method of purifying it.

➡ The best chemical purifier is iodine. It should not be used by pregnant women or those with thyroid problems.

➡ Water filters should also filter out viruses. Ensure your filter has a chemical barrier such as iodine and a small pore size, eg less than four microns.

Heat

Parts of Bangladesh are hot and humid throughout the year. For most people it takes at least two weeks to adapt to the hot climate. Swelling of the feet and ankles is common, as are muscle cramps caused by excessive sweating. Prevent these by avoiding dehydration and excessive activity in the heat. Take it easy when you first arrive. Don't eat salt tablets (they aggravate the gut); drinking rehydration solution or eating salty food helps. Treat cramps by stopping activity, resting, rehydrating with double-strength rehydration solution, and gently stretching.

HEAT EXHAUSTION

Dehydration is the main contributor to heat exhaustion. Symptoms include feeling weak, headache, irritability, nausea or vomiting, sweaty skin, a fast, weak pulse and a slightly elevated body temperature. Treatment involves getting out of the heat and/or sun, fanning the victim and applying cool, wet cloths to the skin, laying the victim flat with their legs raised, and rehydrating with water containing one-quarter of a teaspoon of salt per litre. Recovery is usually rapid, but it is common to feel weak for some days afterwards.

HEATSTROKE

Heatstroke is a serious medical emergency. Symptoms come on suddenly and include weakness, nausea, a hot, dry body with a temperature of over 41°C, dizziness, confusion, loss of coordination, fits and eventually collapse and loss of consciousness. Seek medical help and commence cooling by getting the person out of the heat, removing their clothes, fanning them, and applying cool, wet cloths or ice to their body, especially to the groin and armpits.

PRICKLY HEAT

Prickly heat is a common rash in the tropics, caused by sweat being trapped under the skin. The result is an itchy rash of tiny lumps. Treat by moving out of the heat and into an air-conditioned area for a few hours and by having cool showers. Creams and ointments clog the skin, so they should be avoided. Locally bought prickly-heat powder can be helpful.

Bites & Stings

BEDBUGS

Bedbugs don't carry disease, but their bites are very itchy. They live in the cracks of furniture and walls, and then migrate to the bed at night to feed on you. You can treat the itch with an antihistamine.

TICKS

Ticks are contracted after walking in rural areas. They are commonly found behind the ears, on the belly and in the armpits. If you have had a tick bite and experience symptoms such as a rash at the site of the bite or elsewhere, fever or muscle aches, you should see a doctor. Doxycycline prevents tickborne diseases.

LEECHES

Leeches are found in humid rainforest areas. They do not transmit disease, but their bites are often intensely itchy for weeks afterwards and can easily become infected. Apply an iodine-based antiseptic to leech bites to help prevent infection.

Skin Problems

Fungal rashes are common in humid climates. There are two common fungal rashes that affect travellers. The first occurs in moist areas that get less air, such as the groin, armpits and between the toes. It starts as a red patch that slowly spreads and is usually itchy. Treatment involves keeping the skin dry, avoiding chafing and using an antifungal cream such as Clotrimazole or Lamisil. *Tinea versicolor* is also common; this fungus causes small, light-coloured patches, usually on the back, chest and shoulders. Consult a doctor.

Cuts and scratches become easily infected in humid climates. Take meticulous care of any cuts and scratches to prevent complications such as abscesses. Immediately wash all wounds in clean water and apply antiseptic. If you develop signs of infection (increasing pain and redness), see a doctor.

Sunburn

Even on a cloudy day sunburn can occur rapidly. Always use a strong sunscreen (at least factor 30) and always wear a wide-brimmed hat and sunglasses outdoors.

Language

Bengali (বাংলা *bang*·la) is the national language of Bangladesh and the official language of the Indian states of Tripura and West Bengal. It belongs to the Indic group of the Indo-Aryan family of Indo-European languages (with Hindi, Assamese and Oriya among its close relatives), and is spoken by approximately 220 million people. Today's Bengali has two literary forms – *sha*·d'u·b'a·sha সাধুভাষা (lit: elegant language), the traditional literary style of 16th-century Middle Bengali, and *chohl*·ţi·b'a·sha চলতি ভাষা (lit: running language), a more colloquial form based on the Bengali spoken in Kolkata.

Bengali is written in the Brahmi script. Just read our coloured pronunciation guides as if they were English, and you'll be understood. Most Bengali vowel sounds are very similar to English ones. The length of vowels (like the difference between the sounds a and aa) is important. Note that a is pronounced as in 'run', a̧ as in 'tap', aa as in 'rather', ai as in 'aisle', ay as in 'day', e as in 'red', ee as in 'bee', i as in 'bit', o as in 'shot', oh as in 'both', oy as in 'boy', u as in 'put', and ui as in 'quick'. Bengali has 'aspirated' consonants (produced with a puff of air, ie a slight 'h' sound). In this language guide we've used the apostrophe to indicate aspirated consonants (eg b'). Another feature of Bengali is the 'retroflex' consonant (pronounced with the tongue bent backwards). In this language guide the retroflex variants of d, r and t are represented by ḍ, ṛ and ţ respectively. Stress normally falls on the first syllable; in our pronunciation guides the stressed syllable is indicated in italics.

WANT MORE?

For in-depth language information and handy phrases, check out Lonely Planet's *Hindi, Urdu & Bengali Phrasebook*. You'll find it at **shop.lonelyplanet.com**, or you can buy Lonely Planet's iPhone phrasebooks at the Apple App Store.

BASICS

'Please' and 'thank you' are rarely used in Bengali. Their absence shouldn't be misread as rudeness – instead, these sentiments are expressed indirectly in polite conversation.

Hello. (Muslim greeting)
আস্সালাম ওয়ালাইকুম।   as·*sa*·lam wa·*lai*·kum

Hello. (Muslim response)
ওয়ালাইকুম আস্সালাম।   wa·*lai*·kum as·*sa*·lam

Hello. (Hindu greeting and response)
নমস্কার।   *no*·mohsh·kar

Goodbye. (Muslim)
আল্লাহ হাফেজ।   *al*·laa *ha*·fez

Goodbye. (Hindu)
নমস্কার।   *no*·mosh·kar

Yes./No.
হ্যাঁ।/না।   ha̧ng/naa

Please.
প্রিজ।   pleez

Thank you (very much).
(অনেক) ধন্যবাদ।   (*o*·nek) *d'oh*·noh·baad

Excuse me. (before a request)
শুনুন।   *shu*·nun

Excuse me. (to get past)
একটু দেখি।   ek·tu *de*·k'i

Sorry.
সরি।   *so*·ri

How are you?
কেমন আছেন?   *ka̧*·mohn aa·ch'en

Fine, and you?
ভাল, আপনি?   *b'a*·loh *aap*·ni

What's your name?
আপনার নাম কি?   *aap*·nar naam ki

My name is ...
আমার নাম ...   *aa*·mar naam ...

Do you speak English?
আপনি কি ইংরেজি   *aap*·ni ki ing·*re*·ji
বলতে পারেন?   bohl·ţe *paa*·ren

I don't understand.
আমি বুঝতে পারছি না।   *aa*·mi *buj'*·ţe *paar*·ch'i na

ACCOMMODATION

Where's a ...?	... কোথায়?	... koh·ṭ'a·e
guesthouse	গেষ্ট হাউস	gest ha·us
hotel	হোটেল	hoh·tel
tourist bungalow	টুরিষ্ট বাংলো	tu·rist baang·loh
youth hostel	ইউথ হস্টেল	ee·uṭ' hos·tel

Do you have a ... room?	আপনার কি ... রুম আছে?	aap·nar ki ... rum aa·ch'e
double	ডবল	do·bohl
single	সিঙ্গেল	sin·gel

Can I see it?		
আমি কি এটা দেখতে পারি?		aa·mi ki e·ta dek'·ṭe paa·ri

How much is it per ...?	প্রতি ... কত?	proh·ṭi ... ko·ṭoh
night	রাতে	raa·ṭe
person	জনে	jo·ne
week	সপ্তাহে	shop·ṭa·he

heating	হিটার	hi·tar
hot water	গরম পানি	go·rohm pa·ni
running water	কলের পানি	ko·ler pa·ni

The ... doesn't work.	... কাজ করে না।	... kaaj koh·re na
air con	এয়ারকন্ডিশনার	e·aar·kon·di·shoh·nar
fan	ফ্যান	fan
toilet	টয়লেট	toy·let

DIRECTIONS

Where's the (station)?		
(ট্রেশন) কোথায়?		(ste·shohn) koh·ṭ'ai

What's the address?		
ঠিকানা কি?		ṭ'i·kaa·na ki

How far is it?		
এটা কত দূর?		e·ta ko·ṭoh dur

How do I get there?		
ওখানে কি ভাবে যাব?		oh·k'a·ne ki b'a·be ja·boh

Can you show me (on the map)?		
আমাকে (ম্যাপে) দেখতে পারেন?		aa·ma·ke (ma·pe) da·k'a·ṭe paa·ren

Turn ...	... টার্ন করবেন	... taarn kohr·ben
at the corner	কর্নারে	koṛ·na·re
at the traffic lights	ট্রাফিক লাইটে	tra·fik lai·te
left	বামে	baa·me
right	ডানে	daa·ne

SIGNS

General

ভিতর	Enter
বাহির	Exit
ধুমপান নিষেদ	No Smoking
হোটেল	Hotel
বাস	Bus
শৌচাগার	Toilets
মহিলা	Women (also for reserved bus seats)
পুরুষ	Men
পুলিশ স্টেশন	Police Station
হাসপাতাল	Hospital

Cities

ঢাকা	Dhaka
খুলনা	Khulna
রাজশাহি	Rajshahi
সিলেট	Sylhet
চট্টগ্রাম	Chittagong
বরিশাল	Barisal

near ...	...-এর কাছে	...·er ka·ch'e
on the corner	কর্নারে	koṛ·na·re
straight ahead	সোজা	shoh·ja

EATING & DRINKING

Can you recommend a ...?	একটা ভাল ... কোথায় হবে বলেন তো?	ak·ta b'a·lo ... koh·ṭ'a·e ho·be boh·len ṭoh
cafe	ক্যাফেটেরিয়া	ka·fe·te·ri·a
restaurant	রেস্তোরা	res·ṭoh·ra

Where would you go for (a) ... ?	... জন্য কোথায় যাবো?	... john·no koh·ṭ'a·e ja·boh
cheap meal	সস্তা খাবারের	shos·ṭa·e k'a·ba·rer
local specialities	এখানকার বিশেষ খাবার	e·k'an·kar bi·shesh k'a·bar

I'd like to reserve a table for ...	আমি ... একটা টেবিল রিজার্ভ করতে চাই।	aa·mi ... ak·ta te·bil ri·zarv kohr·ṭe chai
(eight) o'clock	(আটার) সময়	(aat·tar) sho·moy
(two) people	(দুই) জনের জন্য	(dui) jo·ner john·no

What would you recommend?
আপনি কি খেতে বলেন? *aap*·ni ki *k'e*·ṭe *boh*·len

What's in that dish?
এই খাবারে কি কি আছে? ei *k'a*·ba·re ki ki *aa*·ch'e

I'll have that.
আমি ওটা নিব। *aa*·mi *oh*·ta *ni*·boh

I'm vegan.
আমি মাছ মাংস ডিম *aa*·mi maach *mang*·shoh
দুধ খাই না। dim dud' k'ai na

I'm vegetarian.
আমি ভেজিটেরিয়ান। *aa*·mi ve·ji·te·ri·an

I don't eat (meat/chicken/fish/eggs).
আমি (মাংস/মুরগী/মাছ/ডিম) *aa*·mi (mang·shoh/*mur*·gi/
খাই না। mach/dim) k'ai na

Not too spicy, please.
মশলা কম, প্লিজ। *mosh*·la kom pleez

Is this bottled water?
এটা কি বোতলের পানি? e·ta ki *boh*·ṭoh·ler *pa*·ni

No more, thank you.
আর না, ধন্যবাদ। aar naa d'oh·noh·baad

That was delicious.
খুব মজা ছিল। k'ub *mo*·ja ch'i·loh

I'm allergic আমার ...-এ *aa*·mar ...·e
to ... এ্যালার্জি আছে। *a*·lar·ji *aa*·ch'e

   nuts বাদাম *baa*·dam
   shellfish চিংড়ি মাছ *ching*·ṛi maach'

Please bring ... ... আনেন প্লিজ। ... *aa*·nen pleez
   a fork একটা কাটা *ạk*·ta *ka*·ta
   a glass একটা গ্লাস *ạk*·ta glash
   a knife একটা ছুরি *ạk*·ta ch'u·ri
   a menu মেনু *me*·nu
   a spoon একটা চামুচ *ạk*·ta cha·much
   an ashtray একটা এ্যাসট্রে *ạk*·ta *ạsh*·tre
   the bill বিলটা *bil*·ta

Key Words

beer	বিয়ার	*bi*·ar
bread	রুটি	*ru*·ti
breakfast	নাস্তা	*nash*·ṭa
chilli	মরিচ	*moh*·rich
coffee	কফি	*ko*·fi
dinner	রাতের খাবার	ra·ṭer *k'a*·bar
egg	ডিম	dim
fish	মাছ	maach'
fruit	ফল	p'ol
lentils	ডাল	ḍaal
lunch	দুপুরের খাওয়া	du·pu·rer *k'a*·wa
meat	মাংস	*mang*·shoh
milk	দুধ	dud'

rice	ভাত	b'aaṭ
tea	চা	cha
vegetable	সবজি	*shohb*·ji
water	পানি	*pa*·ni
wine	মদ	mod

EMERGENCIES

Call ...! ... ডাকেন! ... *da*·ken
   a doctor ডাক্তার *dak*·ṭar
   the police পুলিশ *pu*·lish

Help!
বাচান! *ba*·chan

Go away!
চলে যান! *choh*·le jan

I'm lost.
আমি হারিয়ে গেছি। *aa*·mi ha·ri·ye *gạ*·ch'i

Where are the toilets?
টয়লেট কোথায়? *toy*·let *koh*·ṭ'a·e

I'm sick.
আমি অসুস্থ। *aa*·mi o·shush·ṭ'oh

It hurts here.
এখানে ব্যাথা করছে। e·*k'a*·ne *bạ*·ṭ'a *kohr*·ch'e

I'm allergic to (antibiotics).
আমার (এ্যান্টিবায়োটিক)এ *aa*·mar (*ạn*·ti·bai·o·tik)·e
এ্যালার্জি আছে। *ạ*·lar·ji *aa*·ch'e

SHOPPING

Where's ... কোথায়? ... *koh*·ṭ'a·e
a/the ...?
   bank ব্যাংক bạnk
   department ডিপার্টমেন্ট di·*part*·ment
   store স্টোর stohr
   market বাজার *baa*·jar
   tourist পর্যটন pohr·joh·tohn
   office কেন্দ্র ken·droh

I'd like to buy (an adaptor plug).
একটা (এ্যাড্যাপটার প্লাগ) *ạk*·ta (*ạ*·ḍap·tar plag)
কিনতে চাই। *kin*·ṭe chai

I'm just looking.
আমি দেখছি। *aa*·mi *dek*·ch'i

Can I look at it?
এটা দেখতে পারি? e·ta *dek'*·ṭe *paa*·ri

How much is it?
এটার দাম কত? e·tar dam *ko*·ṭoh

Can you write down the price?
দামটা কি লিখে দিতে *dam*·ta ki *li*·k'e *di*·ṭe
পারেন? *paa*·ren

That's too expensive.
বেশী দাম। be·shi dam

Can you lower the price?
দাম কমান। dam *ko*·man

TIME & DATES

Bengalis use the 12-hour clock. There's no such concept as 'am' or 'pm' – the time of day is indicated by adding *sho*·kaal (morning), *du*·pur (afternoon) or raat (night) before the time. To tell the time, add the suffix ·ta to the ordinal number which indicates the hour.

What time is it?
কয়টা বাজে? *koy*·ta *baa*·je

It's (10) o'clock.
(দশটা) বাজে। (*dosh*·ta) *baa*·je

Quarter past ...
সোয়া ... *shoh*·aa ...

Half past ...
সাড়ে ... *shaa*·ṛe ...

Quarter to ...
পৌনে ... *poh*·ne ...

At what time ...?
কটার সময় ...? *ko*·tar *sho*·moy ...

At (10) in the morning.
সকাল (দশটা)। *sho*·kaal (*dosh*·ta)

today
আজকে *aaj*·ke

yesterday ...	গতকাল ...	*go*·ṭoh·kaal ...
tomorrow ...	আগামিকাল ...	*aa*·ga·mi·kaal ...
morning	সকাল	*sho*·kaal
afternoon	দুপুর	*du*·pur
evening	বিকাল	*bee*·kaal

Monday	সোমবার	*shohm*·baar
Tuesday	মঙ্গলবার	*mohng*·gohl·baar
Wednesday	বুধবার	*bud'*·baar
Thursday	বৃহস্পতিবার	*bri*·hosh·poh·ṭi·baar
Friday	শুক্রবার	*shuk*·roh·baar
Saturday	শনিবার	*shoh*·ni·baar
Sunday	রবিবার	*roh*·bi·baar

January	জানুয়ারি	*jaa*·nu·aa·ri
February	ফেব্রুয়ারি	*feb*·ru·aa·ri
March	মার্চ	maarch
April	এপ্রিল	*ep*·reel
May	মে	me
June	জুন	jun
July	জুলাই	*ju*·lai
August	আগস্ট	*aa*·gohst
September	সেপ্টেম্বর	*sep*·tem·baar
October	অক্টোবার	*ok*·toh·baar
November	নভেম্বর	*no*·b'em·baar
December	ডিসেম্বর	*di*·sem·baar

TRANSPORT

Public Transport

Which ... goes to (Comilla)?	কোন ... (কুমিল্লা) যায়?	kohn ... (ku·*mil*·laa) *ja*·e
bus	বাস	bas
train	ট্রেন	tren
tram	ট্রাম	ṭṛam

When's the ... (bus)?	... (বাস) কখন?	... (bas) *ko*·k'ohn
first	প্রথম	*proh*·t'ohm
last	শেষ	shesh
next	পরের	*po*·rer

... bus	... বাস	... bas
city	শহর	*sho*·hohr
express	এক্সপ্রেস	*eks*·pres
intercity	ইন্টারসিটি	*in*·tar·see·ti
local	লোকাল	*loh*·kaal
ordinary	অর্ডিনারি	*o*·ḍi·naa·ri

NUMBERS

1	১	aͅk
2	২	dui
3	৩	ṭeen
4	৪	chaar
5	৫	paach
6	৬	ch'oy
7	৭	shaaṭ
8	৮	aat
9	৯	noy
10	১০	dosh
20	২০	beesh
30	৩০	*ṭi*·rish
40	৪০	*chohl*·lish
50	৫০	*pon*·chaash
60	৬০	shaat
70	৭০	*shohṭ*·ṭur
80	৮০	*aa*·shi
90	৯০	*nohb*·boh·i
100	১০০	aͅk shoh
200	২০০	dui shoh
1000	১০০০	aͅk *haa*·jaar
100,000	১০০০০০	aͅk laak'
one million	১০০০০০০	dosh laak'

QUESTION WORDS

how many	কয়টা	koy·ta
how much	কত	ko·toh
when	কখন	ko·k'ohn
where	কোথায়	koh·t'ai
who	কে	ke
why	কেন	kạ·noh

A ... ticket (to Dhaka).	(ঢাকার) জন্য একটা ... টিকেট।	(d'aa·kaar) john·noh ạk·ta ... ti·ket
1st-class	ফার্স্ট ক্লাস	farst klaas
2nd-class	সেকেন্ড ক্লাস	se·kend klaas
one-way	ওয়ানওয়ে	wan·way
return	রিটার্ন	ri·tarn
student	ছাত্র	ch'aṭ·roh

Where's the booking office for foreigners?
বিদেশিদের জন্য বুকিং অফিস কোথায়?
bi·de·shi·der john·noh bu·king o·feesh koh·t'a·e

Where do I buy a ticket?
কোথায় টিকেট কিনবো?
koh·t'a·e ti·ket kin·boh

What time does it leave?
কখন ছাড়বে?
ko·k'ohn ch'aaṛ·be

How long will it be delayed?
কত দেরি হবে?
ko·toh de·ri ho·be

How long does the trip take?
যেতে কতক্ষণ লাগবে?
je·ṭe ko·tohk·k'ohn laa·ge

Do I need to change trains?
আমাকে কি চেঞ্জ করতে হবে ট্রেন?
aa·maa·ke ki chenj kohr·ṭe ho·be tren

Is this seat available?
এই সিট কি খালি?
ay seet ki k'aa·lee

What's the next stop?
পরের স্টপ কি?
po·rer stop ki

Please tell me when we get to (Sylhet).
(সিলেট) আসলে আমাকে বলবেন, প্লিজ।
(si·let) aash·le aa·maa·ke bohl·ben pleez

I'd like to get off at (Mongla).
আমি (মঙ্গলাতে) নামতে চাই।
aa·mi (mong·laa·ṭe) naam·ṭe chai

Is this taxi available?
এই ট্যাক্সি খালি?
ay ṭạk·si k'aa·li

How much is it to ...?
... যেতে কত লাগবে?
... je·ṭe ko·toh laag·be

Please put the meter on.
প্লিজ মিটার লাগান।
pleez mee·tar laa·gan

Please take me to this address.
আমাকে এই ঠিকানায় নিয়ে যান।
aa·ma·ke ay t'i·kaa·nai ni·ye jaan

Driving & Cycling

I'd like to hire a/an ...	আমি একটা ... ভাড়া করতে চাই।	aa·mi ạk·ta ... b'a·ṛa kohr·te chai
4WD	ফোর হুয়িল ড্রাইভ	fohr weel draiv
bicycle	সাইকেল	sai·kel
car	গাড়ি	gaa·ṛi
motorbike	মটরসাইকেল	mo·tohr·sai·kel
diesel	ডিজেল	di·zel
regular	পেট্রোল	pet·rohl
unleaded	অকটেন	ok·ten (octane)

Is this the road to (Rangamati)?
এটা কি (রাঙ্গামাটির) রঙ্গ?
e·ta ki (raang·a·maa·tir) raas·ta

Where's a petrol station?
পেট্রোল স্টেশন কোথায়?
pet·rohl ste·shohn koh·t'a·e

Please fill it up.
ভর্তি করে দেন, প্লিজ।
b'ohr·ṭi koh·re dạn pleez

I'd like (20) litres.
আমার (বিশ) লিটার লাগবে।
aa·mar (beesh) li·tar laag·be

I need a mechanic.
আমার একজন মেকানিক লাগবে।
aa·mar ạk·john me·kaa·nik laag·be

The car/motorbike has broken down at (Sylhet).
গাড়ি/মটরসাইকেল (সিলেট) নষ্ট হয়ে গেছে।
gaa·ṛi/mo·tohr·sai·kel (si·let) nosh·toh hoh·e gạ·ch'e

I have a flat tyre.
আমার গাড়ির একটা চাকা পাংচার হয়ে গেছে।
aa·mar gaa·ṛir ạk·ta chaa·ka pank·char hoh·e gạ·ch'e

I've run out of petrol.
আমার পেট্রোল শেষ হয়ে গেছে।
aa·mar pet·rohl shesh hoh·e gạ·ch'e

GLOSSARY

Adivasis – tribal people

AL – Awami League; the mainstream centre-left, secular political party in Bangladesh

baby taxi – auto-rickshaw, usually called a CNG these days

baksheesh – donation, tip or bribe, depending on the context

Bangla – the national language of Bangladesh (see *Bengali*); also the new name for the Indian state of West Bengal

bangla – architectural style associated with the Pre-Mauryan and Mauryan period (312–232 BC); exemplified by a bamboo-thatched hut with a distinctively curved roof

Bengali – the national language of Bangladesh, where it is also known as *Bangla*, and the official language of the state of Bangla (formerly West Bengal) in India

BIWTC – Bangladesh Inland Waterway Transport Corporation

BNP – Bangladesh Nationalist Party; the mainstream centre-right political party in Bangladesh

BRAC – Bangladesh Rural Advancement Committee

BRTC – Bangladesh Road Transport Corporation

cha – tea, usually served with milk and sugar

char – a river or delta island made of silt; highly fertile but highly susceptible to flooding and erosion

CNG – auto-rickshaw run on compressed natural gas

DC – District Commissioner

Eid – Muslim holiday

ghat – steps or landing on a river

hammam – bathhouse

haors – wetlands

hartals – strikes, ranging from local to national

jamdani – ornamental loom-embroidered muslin or silk

kantha – traditional indigo-dyed muslin

khyang – Buddhist temple

kuthi – factory

launch – public ferry

maidan – open grassed area in a town or city, used as a parade ground during the Raj

mandir – temple

masjid – mosque

mazar – grave/tomb

mela – festival

mihrab – niche in a mosque positioned to face Mecca; Muslims face in this direction when they pray

mistris – rickshaw makers

mohajons – rickshaw- or taxi-fleet owners (also known as *maliks*)

Mughal – the Muslim dynasty of Indian emperors from Babur to Aurangzeb (16th to 18th century)

nakshi kantha – embroided quilt

nawab – Muslim prince

paisa – unit of currency; there are 100 paisa in a taka

Parjatan – the official Bangladesh-government tourist organisation

Raj – also called the British Raj; the period of British government in the Indian subcontinent, roughly from the mid-18th century to the mid-20th century

raj – rule or sovereignty

raja – ruler, landlord or king

rajbari – Raj-era palace or mansion built by a *zamindar*

Ramzan – Bengali name for Ramadan

reserve – privately hired vehicles, including boats

rest house – government-owned guesthouse

rickshaw – small, three-wheeled bicycle-driven passenger vehicle

rickshaw-wallah – rickshaw rider

Rocket – paddle steamer

sadhu – itinerant holy man

salwar kameez – a long, dress-like tunic (kameez) worn by women over a pair of baggy trousers (salwar)

shankhari – Hindu artisan

Shiva – Hindu god; the destroyer, the creator

shulov – lower-2nd class on a train

shuvon – upper-2nd class on a train

stupa – moundlike structure or spire containing Buddhist relics, typically the remains of the Buddha

Sufi – ascetic Muslim mystic

taka – currency of Bangladesh

tea estate – terraced hillside where tea is grown; also tea garden

tempo – shared auto-rickshaw

vihara – monastery

zamindar – landlord; also the name of the feudal-landowner system itself

Behind the Scenes

SEND US YOUR FEEDBACK

We love to hear from travellers – your comments keep us on our toes and help make our books better. Our well-travelled team reads every word on what you loved or loathed about this book. Although we cannot reply individually to your submissions, we always guarantee that your feedback goes straight to the appropriate authors, in time for the next edition. Each person who sends us information is thanked in the next edition – the most useful submissions are rewarded with a selection of digital PDF chapters.

Visit **lonelyplanet.com/contact** to submit your updates and suggestions or to ask for help. Our award-winning website also features inspirational travel stories, news and discussions.

Note: We may edit, reproduce and incorporate your comments in Lonely Planet products such as guidebooks, websites and digital products, so let us know if you don't want your comments reproduced or your name acknowledged. For a copy of our privacy policy visit lonelyplanet.com/privacy.

OUR READERS

Many thanks to the travellers who used the last edition and wrote to us with helpful hints, useful advice and interesting anecdotes: Aäron van der Sanden, Alex King, Ali Kingston, Barney Smith, Carlijn Simons, David Butler, David Martin, Edward Aitken, Frank Francis, George Hart, Jane Green, Jody Martin, Julie Clarkson, Kath Gardiner, Katherine Chiu, Laura Gispert, Loredana Ducco, Marcos Mendonca, Max Steinacher, Roberta Haas, Stefano Dalmonte, Steven Haas

WRITER THANKS
Paul Clammer

In Dhaka, thanks to Mostafizur Rahman Jewel for his assistance and friendship, and to my co-author Anirban Mahapatra for coffee-fuelled strategy meetings. In Chittagong, thanks to Didarul Islam Didar for his advice, and help with hill tribes permits. In Cox's Bazar, thank you to Jafar Alam for the insights into the Bangla surf scene. At my desk, long-time editor Joe Bindloss deserves thanks and patience for more than the usual number of questions as new systems were rolled out. Finally, thanks and love to Robyn, who wasn't a sidekick for this trip, but remains the best one everywhere else.

Anirban Mahapatra

A million thanks to fellow author Paul Clammer, destination editor Joe Bindloss and everyone at Lonely Planet for making this fantastic book come to life. To the wonderful people of Bangladesh, including Enayet, Murshed, Taufiq, Rafiq, Swapan, Jameel and Halim for their invaluable support along the way. To friends in Dhaka, including Farhan, Thomas, Roseanne, Keya, Arnob, Samir and Nadeem for sharing their own insights into Bangladesh. And most of all, to Roshni, for her unending encouragement, patience and support.

ACKNOWLEDGEMENTS

Climate map data adapted from Peel MC, Finlayson BL & McMahon TA (2007) 'Updated World Map of the Köppen-Geiger Climate Classification', Hydrology and Earth System Sciences, 11, 163344.

Cover photograph: Royal Bengal tiger, Sundarbans National Park, Neelsky/Shutterstock ©

THIS BOOK

This 8th edition of Lonely Planet's *Bangladesh* guidebook was researched and written by Paul Clammer and Anirban Mahapatra, with the Health chapter based on text written by Dr Trish Bachelor. The previous two editions were written by Daniel McCrohan

and Stuart Butler. This guidebook was produced by the following:

Destination Editor Joe Bindloss

Product Editor Luna Soo

Senior Cartographer David Kemp

Book Designer Michael Buick

Senior Editors Andi Jones, Claire Naylor, Karyn Noble

Assisting Editors Judith Bamber, Kate James, Jodie Martire, Rosie Nicholson

Cover Researcher Naomi Parker

Thanks to Shahara Ahmed, Liz Heynes, Catherine Naghten, Kirsten Rawlings, Angela Tinson, Lauren Wellicome, Tracy Whitmey, Amanda Williamson

Index

Map Legend

Sights

- Beach
- Bird Sanctuary
- Buddhist
- Castle/Palace
- Christian
- Confucian
- Hindu
- Islamic
- Jain
- Jewish
- Monument
- Museum/Gallery/Historic Building
- Ruin
- Shinto
- Sikh
- Taoist
- Winery/Vineyard
- Zoo/Wildlife Sanctuary
- Other Sight

Activities, Courses & Tours

- Bodysurfing
- Diving
- Canoeing/Kayaking
- Course/Tour
- Sento Hot Baths/Onsen
- Skiing
- Snorkelling
- Surfing
- Swimming/Pool
- Walking
- Windsurfing
- Other Activity

Sleeping

- Sleeping
- Camping

Eating

- Eating

Drinking & Nightlife

- Drinking & Nightlife
- Cafe

Entertainment

- Entertainment

Shopping

- Shopping

Information

- Bank
- Embassy/Consulate
- Hospital/Medical
- Internet
- Police
- Post Office
- Telephone
- Toilet
- Tourist Information
- Other Information

Geographic

- Beach
- Hut/Shelter
- Lighthouse
- Lookout
- Mountain/Volcano
- Oasis
- Park
- Pass
- Picnic Area
- Waterfall

Population

- Capital (National)
- Capital (State/Province)
- City/Large Town
- Town/Village

Transport

- Airport
- Border crossing
- Bus
- Cable car/Funicular
- Cycling
- Ferry
- Metro station
- Monorail
- Parking
- Petrol station
- Subway station
- Taxi
- Train station/Railway
- Tram
- Underground station
- Other Transport

Note: Not all symbols displayed above appear on the maps in this book

Routes

- Tollway
- Freeway
- Primary
- Secondary
- Tertiary
- Lane
- Unsealed road
- Road under construction
- Plaza/Mall
- Steps
- Tunnel
- Pedestrian overpass
- Walking Tour
- Walking Tour detour
- Path/Walking Trail

Boundaries

- International
- State/Province
- Disputed
- Regional/Suburb
- Marine Park
- Cliff
- Wall

Hydrography

- River, Creek
- Intermittent River
- Canal
- Water
- Dry/Salt/Intermittent Lake
- Reef

Areas

- Airport/Runway
- Beach/Desert
- Cemetery (Christian)
- Cemetery (Other)
- Glacier
- Mudflat
- Park/Forest
- Sight (Building)
- Sportsground
- Swamp/Mangrove

OUR STORY

A beat-up old car, a few dollars in the pocket and a sense of adventure. In 1972 that's all Tony and Maureen Wheeler needed for the trip of a lifetime – across Europe and Asia overland to Australia. It took several months, and at the end – broke but inspired – they sat at their kitchen table writing and stapling together their first travel guide, *Across Asia on the Cheap*. Within a week they'd sold 1500 copies. Lonely Planet was born.

Today, Lonely Planet has offices in Franklin, London, Melbourne, Oakland, Beijing, Dublin and Delhi, with more than 600 staff and writers. We share Tony's belief that 'a great guidebook should do three things: inform, educate and amuse'.

OUR WRITERS

Paul Clammer

Paul has contributed to over 25 Lonely Planet guidebooks, and worked as a tour guide in countries from Turkey to Morocco. In a previous life he may even have been a molecular biologist. For Lonely Planet he's covered swathes of the sub-continent from both sides of the Khyber Pass to Rajasthan and Kashmir, so was pleased to finally add Bangladesh to his tally. Follow @paulclammer on Twitter.

Anirban Mahapatra

A Bangla speaker by birth, a folk music aficionado by taste and a *kachchi* biryani lover by choice, Anirban has made repeated forays into the green landscape of Bangladesh. He has experienced its amazing variety, from riding a boat into tiger territory in the Sundarbans and socialising with wandering Bauls in Kushtia, to sipping aromatic tea in Sylhet and exploring ancient citadels in Rajshahi and Rangpur. Anirban has also written for multiple editions of Lonely Planet's *India* guidebook.

Published by Lonely Planet Global Limited
CRN 554153
8th edition – December 2016
ISBN 978 1 78657 213 4
© Lonely Planet 2016   Photographs © as indicated 2016
10 9 8 7 6 5 4 3 2 1
Printed in China

Although the authors and Lonely Planet have taken all reasonable care in preparing this book, we make no warranty about the accuracy or completeness of its content and, to the maximum extent permitted, disclaim all liability arising from its use.